ACT YOUR AGE

DADDY DEAREST, BOOK #1

EVE DANGERFIELD

~

For Him. And Her.

ACKNOWLEDGEMENT OF COUNTRY

This novel was written on the unceded ground of the indigenous people of Australia, specifically the Wurundjeri Woi-wurrung people of the Kulin Nation. I honour the traditional custodians of the lands and waterways and pay my respects to Elders, past, present and emerging.
Always was, always will be Aboriginal land.

PREFACE

Act Your Age contains kinky scenes enacted between two consenting adults. This includes age play, forced seduction, spanking and some light daddy-daughter stuff. If the idea of this grosses ye out, cease reading now or forever hold ye peace (I won't tell anyone.)

1

The pub was almost empty. Gone were the families, older couples, and tourists, all that remained were the degenerates who wanted to get off their heads on a Wednesday night: uni students, labourers, alcoholics, and him, Tyler Henderson, drunk, alone and watching Middleton peer into a rugby players' mouth. She touched a finger to the piercing embedded in the guy's tongue. "That's so cool! Did it hurt?"

She sounded as breathless as if the stud were already fiddling with her clit, but then she sounded like that all the time. It was one of the many things Ty loathed about her.

The rugby player, whom Ty had privately dubbed 'Buddy', pulled his idiot tongue back into his head. "Not much. I can do all kinds of things with it."

"Like get stuck on magnets?"

"Better."

Middleton dissolved into a fit of trademark giggles, and Buddy beamed like he was the king of the fucking world. Ty glowered into his bourbon. For the past hour he'd been forced to listen to Middleton flirt with this guy. Was it annoying? Sure. Did he wish she and her barely pubescent lover would fuck off and have young person sex already? Yes. Was it unprofessional of her to be picking up students at the local pub? Very much so. Especially since she and the rest of Golden Glaze Solar were in Bendigo on a work trip. That's what he couldn't understand about this situation. Unprofessional sexual conduct suited Middleton about as much as a bald head would have.

If he'd had to guess ahead of time what she'd get up to tonight, he'd have said 'brushing, flossing and climbing into bed with a stuffed animal,' but Middleton had apparently left her 'I'm so sweet it'll rot your fucking teeth' attitude back in Melbourne.

She was the youngest and only female engineer at GGS. Most female engineers Ty knew acted like the boys: drinking hard, swearing like sailors, wearing gender-neutral clothes as though baggy slacks might make men mistake them for one of their own. Others emphasised their femininity: high heels, tight tops, raunchy jokes. They took control of the flirting and perving before it was inflicted on them, or at least pretended to.

Middleton, on the other hand, never swore, she never drank, never said a mean word about anyone. She baked chocolate chip cookies and wore floaty pink blouses and headbands with ribbons on them. Once, while babysitting his nephews, Ty had watched a kids' TV show. The host was a curvy brunette who by all the laws of biology should have been smoking hot. Instead, she projected such brightly-coloured asexuality he felt guilty just trying to picture what her tits looked like. That was the frequency Middleton operated on. Ty wouldn't be surprised if she too was sewn into her outfits so she wouldn't accidentally show cleavage or stomach.

The week she started at GGS, Ty had run into her in a hallway. He was hungover and wearing a three-day-old suit. Middleton was in a pink dress and what looked like yellow tap shoes, her waist-length brown hair was pinned back by a silver clip shaped like a humming-bird. A fucking hummingbird.

"Hi, Mr Henderson!" She held up the huge pink cake tin she was carrying. "Would you like a lemon-curd meringue?"

Ty thought she was going to be eaten alive by the other engineers. He was wrong. Within six weeks all the guys were chatting to her in the break room, sponsoring her roller derby team, begging her to make them chocolate éclairs. They never said anything sleazy about her and admonished outsiders who did. Somehow this Shirley Temple caricature had gotten every bozo in their office to not only tolerate, but like her.

Just a few hours ago Johnno—the big boss—had slung his arm around Ty's neck. "Middleton's a proper little lady, isn't she?" he said. "Pretty as a picture, gets along with everyone. Just a great girl."

Ty didn't think Middleton was a great girl. He thought Middleton was a pain in the ass. Waltzing around with her shiny hair and long legs and her throaty voice, being cuter than a fistful of buttons. Where did she get off?

On Buddy, apparently. When he glanced back at the bar, he saw the younger man tickling Middleton's sides. She slapped his hands, giggling madly. "Stop it!"

"I can't!" Buddy told her. "It's your fault you have such a cute laugh."

Ty drained his glass. He was leaving. At least, he would be leaving if there was anywhere else in Bendigo where he could get a drink. The small inland town wasn't exactly known for its nightlife. He caught the eye of a passing bartender, a glum woman in her fifties. "Excuse me, is anywhere else around here open?"

"No." The woman collected the glasses in front of him. "Just us."

"Bugger."

On the other side of the pub, Middleton's hair caught the light and gleamed like a fishing lure. "Are you sure there's nowhere else?"

The woman gave him a scathing look. "It's a Wednesday. In Bendigo."

"Right." Ty's words were coming out in that blurry, distorted way that said he was drunk, but not nearly drunk enough. He wanted to go to bed without a single thought in his brain. "Can I have another drink, thanks?"

The woman looked as unimpressed as Ty felt. "You come here with that sustainability convention?"

"Yeah."

"You going back tomorrow?"

Ty knew what she was saying; *don't you have work in the morning, dickhead?* He dredged up his best smile. It felt gummy and insincere. "Just having a night out."

Ty already knew he was far from the man he'd once been, but if he hadn't, the proof was written all over the bartender's highly unimpressed face. "You felt like having a night out alone?" she asked, sounding suspicious, as though this might just be a cover for a murder plot.

"The rest of my colleagues tapped out early. Wives to call. Kids to talk to."

She scanned his left hand. "Hmm."

"I'm single." Just twenty-four months, eight weeks and nineteen hours, but who the fuck was counting?

"I can see that." The bartender looked him up and down. "Bourbon, was it?"

"Yeah, no ice." Ty handed her twenty dollars. "Keep the change."

That got him a smile. Another glance at the bar and Ty prayed the woman would bring his drink back fast. Middleton, it transpired, had found a new way to inspect her friend's tongue ring—by making out with it.

Ty watched her and Buddy writhing against the karaoke machine in disgust. This was a girl who covered her ears when people swore. How was she tongue-fucking in a public bar? In fairness, no one else was paying them any attention. Maybe because almost everyone else in the pub was a student, too busy trying to get their own genitals rubbed to give a shit about Middleton's. Ty scanned the room and with a jolt of unease, realised he was the oldest person there. That seemed to be happening a lot lately. He was the oldest guy in the gym, the restaurant, the cocktail bar, the cinema. There was a reason for it. Most of his generation stayed in on Saturday nights, selected gyms with childcare centres and cafés with aisles big enough for prams. Meanwhile, he stayed in the same circles he'd always been in, not quite out of place, not quite in it, either.

He thought of Veronica, wondered if she'd bought a pram yet, and his alcohol buzz flattened. He knew he should clear out of the bar and go back to his hotel room, but then he'd have nothing to do but lie on his hard yet somehow also spongy mattress and watch the bedroom fan rotate. At least here there was loud music and cheap liquor, and he could distract himself from his life by hating Middleton. Middleton with her husky voice and perky tits. Middleton, who was twenty-five but looked about seventeen. Buddy, Ty could see, was attempting to pull her t-shirt from her skirt and get up her bra.

Good luck, mate I bet she's sewed in. By the way, Middleton, I'm your boss. You're really gonna get felt up in a public bar in front of your boss? And how old is that kid? Nineteen?

However young, he was a good looking little shit. Shaggy blond hair, clear skin, broad shoulders. His arm muscles were almost comically swollen, bulging inside his t-shirt sleeves like hams. They made a pretty picture, him and Middleton. People would pay serious money to watch them fuck, the porn tagline something like; *'big brother nails sister's friend at sleepover.'*

Ty pictured himself, blond hair that was getting too long, blue eyes bracketed with lines. Firefighting had left him with bad knees and his back ached when it was cold. He looked forty-five because he was forty-five. In the porn scenario, he'd be Buddy's dad, home early from a business meeting. He'd spot what his son was up to and—

Guilt rose up inside him like bile. He squashed the thought before it could expand into a full-blown fantasy. *Creep,* he told himself. *Sicko. Pervert.*

Middleton kissed her way across Buddy's cheek and Ty felt invisible lips ghost across his jaw. Middleton was going to suck that boy's cock tonight, he'd bet his right hand on it. She had the perfect lips for blow jobs, pale pink and pouty. Perfect hair, too—thick and grabable. He bet she moaned while she sucked, her tongue humming so the guy could feel it in his balls.

That was Ty's favourite thing. A girl's head in his lap, his fingers running through her hair as her wet mouth bobbed on his dick. He sat back in his chair, trying to remember the last time he'd been blown. A year ago, he guessed, maybe more. Hookups rarely included blow jobs; when a woman took a man home she wanted a ride, not to suck all the stiffness out of his dick. That was understandable, but still, Ty missed head. Veronica never swallowed, but she'd always been happy to suck him dry if he returned the favour. Diminishing thrill-factor aside, the sex was so much better when you were in a relationship. Getting it regular two or three times a week from someone who knew how you liked it beat fumbling around with strangers by a country mile. Still, he had no plans to find himself a girlfriend—no matter how many of his friends insisted he go out for dinner with their cousin's best friend's wife's doctor's sister. He was no good on dates anymore. No good with expectations of romance or nervous, hopeful smiles. The very idea of being set up made him want to leave whatever room he was sitting in.

He studied the couple by the bar. If Middleton blew him, Buddy was young enough to get it up again. Hell, maybe he'd get it up three or four times. Middleton would probably roll into the breakfast meeting tomorrow exhausted and Ty would have to watch her yawn and know she'd spent the whole night getting screwed.

He closed his eyes. "Where the hell is my drink?"

As though she was waiting for him to ask, the bartender reappeared with his bourbon. She had, despite his request, put three ice cubes in it. Ty wasn't surprised. It was that kind of night.

"Here you go." She placed the glass in front of him.

"Thanks."

"No problem. I'm, erm, Sandy by the way."

Ty's stomach panged a warning. Looking up, he saw she'd put on lipstick, and her dark red hair was fluffed around her face. *No. Not a fucking chance.*

Her age didn't bother him—far as he was concerned, consenting adults were all the same age in the dark—but she had a wide, earnest smile like this was a high school disco and he was the teacher she'd had her eye on all year. He didn't have the fucking energy. He just wanted to get drunk enough to go back to his hotel room and pass out. If he was horny, he could always crack open the complimentary moisturiser and wring himself out. It wasn't as good as a blowjob, but it was a lot less messy. Metaphorically speaking. He picked up his drink without meeting Sandy's gaze. "Nice to meet you."

"Are you staying across the road?"

"Yeah, I am."

Sandy rocked on her heels. "Is it a nice room?"

"Nice enough."

Part of him felt guilty about how he was acting. There were better ways to do this. A few years ago he'd have told her he had a physically demanding job and needed sleep, or that he had a girlfriend. Then again, a few years ago he did have a physically demanding job and a girlfriend. Now he was just some mid-level, middle-aged corporate asshole with a borderline drinking problem and an unfinished manuscript, of all the fucking clichés. So he waited for Sandy to read his near-silence as a complete lack of interest and leave him alone. The moment never came.

She leaned closer, her thick purplish perfume surrounding him like an eighties miasma. "I finish up in twenty minutes. Want some company?"

Across the pub, Middleton had her hand in Buddy's hair and was kissing him so deeply she looked at risk of falling into his face. Ty genuinely considered Sandy's offer. He could bed her and make her scream so loud everyone in the hotel block heard it. Then tomorrow when the guys were ribbing him in that half-admiring, half-jealous way, Middleton would know she wasn't the only one who could pull on a work trip. She'd have to look at him and wonder how he was in bed, see him as a guy who could get laid instead of some old man she offered meringues to at work.

For a second Ty was sold, then the stupidity of the idea sank into his bourbon pickled brain like water soaking into soil. Unprofessional, inappropriate, and not to mention tacky. He raised his glass again, downing half the too-cold liquid inside. "Thanks for the offer, but I'm headed to bed as soon as I finish this."

Sandy raised a heavily plucked eyebrow. "I'm saying I can keep you company in bed."

"I heard you."

"Well, you're not gonna turn me down, are you?"

Ty closed his eyes, feeling the dirt and grit that had collected there. Why couldn't anything ever be easy? "Sorry, I'm not interested."

"Why? You got a better offer?"

Ty's gaze jumped to where Middleton stood sucking face with her teen paramour. "No."

"Then why—"

"You a mum?"

Sandy frowned. "What the hell does that have to do with anything?"

"I don't do mothers."

Her mouth fell open. "You can't be serious?"

"I am."

For a moment she stared at him in confusion, then the reality of what he was saying seemed to hit her right between the eyes. "You're an asshole!"

"I know."

"You don't know it enough." Sandy's palms found her hips, her elbows sticking out like the handles on a premiership cup. "Finish your drink and get out of here, or I'll chuck you out."

"Not a problem."

She shot him a look of pure venom and stormed away. Ty felt a twinge of remorse, but the relief was much, much greater. He didn't need a fly-by-night fuck, he needed to start sleeping off what he hoped would be a manageable hangover. He finished his drink, stood and pulled on his jacket. It was a nice coat. A double-breasted wool affair Veronica had found in a boutique store when they were staying in Dublin. He almost choked when he saw the price tag, but she'd insisted he buy it. "You look like such a catch in it, Tyler. Like a handsome stranger you fall in love with on the train."

As he buttoned up, he cast a last glance at Middleton, who was still making out with Buddy by the jukebox, oblivious to him the way she'd been all night, the entire time he'd known her.

Outside, the winter air was sharp as a knife. Ty breathed it in, feeling pleasantly warm and cold, sober and drunk. He lingered by the beer garden, inhaling deeply, wishing he could smoke like the kids around him. He had dropped the habit when he joined the MFB. You couldn't be a firefighter who voluntarily gave yourself smoke damage, but years later he still craved the taste, the smell.

"Have you seen Trigger?" a stringy-haired kid shouted, audible even over the crowd. "He's, like, two seconds away from fingering that chick right at the bar."

Ty paused as all the kids in Stringy-Hair's gang—teenagers far gawkier and more acnefied than Buddy— turned and looked at Middleton through the window.

A Burmese kid with a nose ring groaned. "Fuck me, who is she?"

"No idea." Stringy-Hair sounded wistful. "Trigger just walked up to her and asked if she wanted a drink. I hate that cunt sometimes."

A doe-eyed kid in a beanie laughed and held up his phone. "Don't be jealous. Did you get Trigger's snapchat?"

"He snapchats me twelve times an hour," Nose-Ring complained. "What's this one about?"

"He said if he can get that chick back to his dorm he's keeping his laptop open."

Several boys hooted and Stringy-Hair downed the last of his pint. "That said, we should head back and get comfortable before the show starts."

"Solid plan." Beanie-Baby began tapping on his phone. "I'll tell Trig we'll be ready in a halfa."

Drunk and a member of Gen X, it took Ty a few seconds to realise what was going on. When he did his pleasurable drunk-cold sensation vanished. Buddy was going to cam himself and Middleton fucking, and let all his friends watch. Ty's hands balled into fists. For some unfortunate reason, watching porn with your mates was a male rite of passage, like doing a burnout in your mum's car or discovering soap made terrible lube. But this, what they were planning to do to Middleton, was completely fucked up. He needed to do something. The kids were busy finishing their beers and arguing if there were any chips in the dorm kitchen. None of them noticed Ty enter the beer garden or walk up behind them. He cleared his throat. "Having a good night, boys?"

The group turned, their expressions hostile until they caught sight of him—six-two and built like the metro firefighter he no longer was—their facial features became neutral real fast.

"Uh, yeah." Stringy-Hair gave his friends a sidelong glance. "We're, uh, having a good one."

"Glad to hear it." Ty walked over to where Beanie-Baby was lighting up a big-boy cigarette. "Can I grab a smoke?"

"Sure." Beanie-Baby handed him a Winfield Blue along with his lighter. It was purple and had a topless chick on it. Ty was one hundred percent sure it was meant to be ironic. Kids these days had no fucking taste. He lit up and took a swift drag, relishing the hot prickle in his throat.

"Thanks." He tossed the lighter to Beanie-Baby then stepped back so he had all the little assholes in his line of vision. "I think we should have a chat about your plans after you leave this pub."

The boys looked at one another in drunk confusion. Beanie-Baby laughed. "We're going back to our dorm, y'wanna join us?"

He was expecting his friends to laugh, but they just nudged the ground with their sneakers and looked at their phones. Ty was sure some of them already knew what was happening. He locked eyes with Beanie-Baby. "If you wanna go back to your dorm and have a circle jerk, that's your decision, but you're not gonna do it watching your mate fuck one of my employees."

It was satisfying, watching their faces fall. The most satisfying thing Ty could remember experiencing in weeks. Maybe months. He smiled at the mortified boys. "Here's what's going to happen. You're gonna swear on your sad little lives you're not gonna do what I heard you say you were gonna do, then you're gonna run back to your crusty dorm room and jack off to Pornhub like good little boys, understood?"

There was a spatter of mumbled consent but Beanie-Baby scowled at him. "And if we don't?"

Ty pointed at the CCTV camera fixed to a nearby brick wall. "Then I'll call Senior Sergeant Gerry Handler down at Bendigo Police Station. He's a friend of mine. I'll tell him what you were planning on doing. I'm sure he'll be able to ID every one of you rapey little fucks from the security video."

"It's not rape—" Beanie-Baby began, but Nose-Piercing elbowed him in the ribs. "We were joking," he said. "We wouldn't do that."

"Yeah, the sincerity in your voice is heart-warming." Ty ground out his barely smoked cigarette on one of the wallets sitting on the picnic bench. Beanie-Baby gave a hiss of outrage but was elbowed into silence again.

"C'mon, let's go." Stringy-Hair picked up his phone and shoved it into his pocket. The rest of the gang followed suit, muttering under their breath. Ty watched them go, his anger thrumming like a live wire. From the way they were talking, he'd bet money they'd done this before, the perverted little shits. He breathed deep, telling himself he shouldn't follow them and give them a more physical taste of his fury.

He turned to the pub window and found Middleton still getting warmed up by the boy who planned to exploit her. If he didn't help, no one would, but god he didn't want to talk to her. Not now that he was drunk and alone and had spent so much of the night thinking about sex. Maybe he could just wait till Buddy went to the toilet and king-hit him? Maybe he could text her. Something like *'your boy's an amateur pornographer and he wants to make you a star, so go to fucking bed'* should do the trick.

As he shoved his hands into his pocket, he considered doing the lowest thing of all—nothing. Middleton was a savvy girl, surely she'd notice if the kid started fucking around with his laptop? And if she didn't, that was none of his business. This wasn't a burning building, and he wasn't a firefighter. Not a hero, not a good guy, just a drunk moron who'd singed a kid's wallet and insulted a woman who wanted to shag him.

So leave. Leave.

He couldn't. He couldn't move an inch. Ty sighed and allowed his feet to carry him toward the pub door, his guts twirling like spaghetti through fork tines. Middleton and the kid were still making out when he tapped his employee on the shoulder. She unstuck herself with some difficulty and turned to face him.

When Ty was a kid, he and his brothers had set off a whole crate of fireworks at once. A blistering rainbow had exploded inches from his face, and even though his mum burst out of the house screaming for them to move, Ty hadn't. He'd stayed still, drinking in the colours, watching them burst through the air and set pineapple trees ablaze. Looking at Middleton was kind of like that. It burned, stung, made him immune to his own stupidity. Every time he saw her face, with its upturned nose and lightly freckled cheeks, he wanted to do terrible fucking things to it. Up close he was powerless against thoughts of tearing her out of her high-necked, knee-length clothes and keeping her naked in his bed for a week. Transform her from a good girl into a writhing animal who lived to pleasure his dick.

This was why he never fucking talked to her.

"Um, Mr Henderson?" Middleton said in her throaty voice. "Can I help you?"

Why did she have to sound like that? Like someone was perpetually stroking her to an orgasm? Why couldn't she have a girly, high-pitched voice to match her girly, high-pitched personality? Ty unclenched his teeth. "We've gotta be up early for the seminar tomorrow. Time to go to bed."

Middleton blinked at him. The whites of her eyes were pure milk, the irises a chocolate brown, sweet as her godawful personality. "I understand, Mr Henderson, but I kind of want to stay up. I promise I'll be on time tomorrow no matter what."

She took Buddy's hand and smiled at him. He smiled back at her like he wasn't planning on showing all his friends what her pussy looked like. Ty gritted his teeth. Again, why couldn't anything ever be easy? "That's great, but GGS isn't paying for you to get poked on the company dime. Wrap this up and go to bed. Alone."

Middleton's plaything, whom Ty had been resolutely ignoring, cleared his throat. Up close he had a meathead's face, a broad nose and a thick mouth. "Who are you?" he asked.

Ty straightened his shoulders. "I'm—"

"Oh, sorry, introductions!" Middleton beamed at both of them. "Sam, this is my boss, Tyler Henderson. Mr Henderson this is—"

"I don't give a shit, Middleton. Say goodbye to your friend and—"

"Wait up..." Buddy's dopey expression grew dopier. "Why is he calling you Middleton? Isn't your last name McGrath?"

She beamed at him. "You remembered! All the guys I work with call me Middleton."

"Why?"

"Because I'm the only girl and I have brown hair, and my name's Kate."

Buddy continued to look confused.

"Middleton." She enunciated the word as though to a two-year-old. "Kate Middleton. Get it?"

Buddy stared at her, demonstrating he very much did not get it.

"The Duchess of Cambridge? Prince William's wife? The future queen of England?"

Ty had heard enough. He gripped Middleton's upper arm, ignoring the jolt of electricity that shot up his hand. "We're leaving now, okay?"

"Okay." Middleton pulled out her phone. "Just let me find a picture of Kate Middleton to show Sam."

"We don't have time for this, you need to go to bed."

"Hang on a minute." Sam moved toward him. He was tall enough that he and Ty were eye-to-eye. "Just because you're Katie's boss, doesn't mean you can tell her what to do."

"Yes, it does."

Buddy's forehead wrinkled. "Well, yeah but, like, not when you're not working."

"We're on a work trip."

"Yeah, but like, she's at a pub. She's not at work."

In other circumstances, this might have been funny, but the last of Ty's patience was waning. He tugged Middleton's arm. "You done?"

She shook her head. The fruity scent of her hair washed over him like a strawberry haze. "Hurry up."

"I will, I'll just be a sec!"

Sam looked from her to Ty. He flexed his sinewy upper arms. "Why don't you get out of here? I can look after Katie."

Ty released his hold on Middleton. "Is that right?"

"Yeah, why don't you fuck off?"

For all his big words, the kid looked uneasy. Just like his mates, he was all talk, too green to hold his own, too young to shut his fucking mouth. Ty got a nice firm grip on the kid's neck, one that could be mistaken for paternal camaraderie. "From what I heard, the only 'looking after' you were planning on doing involved your friends and a webcam."

Buddy's face contracted. He didn't look like a big man anymore, he looked like what he was—an overgrown kid with more hormones than sense. "You didn't...I wasn't...how d'you know...?"

"Your mates are drunk, Trigger, and something tells me they'd be shit at keeping secrets even if they weren't."

The kid's gaze darted toward the beer garden. "That was a joke."

"Ha-ha-fucking-ha." Ty tightened his grip on the kid's neck. "Think Middleton'd like to hear your joke Trigger? Think she'd find it funny?"

Buddy glanced at Middleton, who was thankfully still doddering away on her phone, completely oblivious to their conversation.

"Don't look at her," Ty said. "Look at me. Explain to me why you were going to violate a woman for no other reason than it would entertain your fucking friends."

"Come on, man, I wasn't going to do that. We're not even going back to the dorms, we're gonna go back to Katie's hotel room."

"No. You're leaving, and you're never coming near Middleton again, understood?"

Sam looked like he wanted to protest. Ty squeezed his hand, compressing the nerves in the kid's neck, feeling his spinal cord go taut. "I said, understood?"

The kid scowled at him, then nodded.

"Good." Ty let go of his neck. "Now fuck off."

But before the kid could leave, Middleton shoved her phone in their faces. "Here we go, royal wedding!"

Startled, Buddy jerked his head, making Middleton drop her phone on the floor. "Shit, sorry, Katie."

"It's okay." Middleton got down on her knees and began looking for it.

Ty rolled his eyes. "I reckon that's your cue to leave, Trig."

"But—"

"Found my phone!" Middleton thrust the device into the air. Ty looked down to see her beaming at him from her knees. His first thought was of her smiling like that before going to town on his cock. The second was that something about her was off. Her pupils were blasted—big as black holes and shiny bright. "Middleton, are you on drugs?"

"No!" She looked shocked at the suggestion.

Ty believed her, but her voice was blurry and her eyes were gleaming like wet tar. What could she be on? He hadn't seen her drink anything tonight, all throughout dinner she'd sipped raspberry lemonade like a nine-year-old.

A dark thought occurred to him and he grabbed Sam's upper arm, too furious to make it look like anything but a threat. "You give her something?"

"No!" Buddy looked as shocked as Middleton. "Never! I wouldn't even know where to get stuff like that!"

"Don't fucking lie to me, Buddy."

"I'm not! I swear!"

"You know..." Middleton knelt up a little straighter. "You know, it's weird, Mr Henderson, but sometimes when I drink and take Ritalin, I have blackouts. I look normal, but I'm checked out inside. I once ordered a pizza, ate half, wrapped up the leftovers and when I woke up, I thought someone had broken in to my Aunt's apartment and left a thin crust Mexicana in my fridge."

Both he and Buddy stared at her.

"You're on Ritalin?" Buddy asked, echoing Ty's thoughts.

"Yeah, totally. Yeah." Her voice had the dreamy, checked-out quality of the stoned.

Ty released his hand from Buddy's arm. "Why are you on Ritalin?"

"Oh, I need it for my brain!" Middleton wrinkled her delicate nose. "Oh, I shouldn't have told you that, Mr Henderson, please don't tell any of the other guys?"

Ty compressed his eyelids together as tight as he could, hating everything and everyone, primarily himself. He opened his eyes. "Middleton, can you please just get up so we can leave?"

His employee looked down at herself, as though puzzled to find she was still on the floor. "Oh. Maybe."

Ty watched her struggle for a few seconds, then against all his better judgment, extended a hand. She took it, her skin unnaturally soft, the bones in her fingers as delicate as a bird's. Ty knew he was filing that information away for unsavoury purposes and hated himself a little more. As soon as she was on her feet he dropped her hand. "Let's go."

"Okay." Middleton turned to Buddy, wobbling slightly like a newborn foal. "Want to come back to my hotel room with me?"

The kid beamed as though he'd just been handed a free pint. "Sur—"

"No, he fucking doesn't!" Ty snarled. "You can't fuck someone if you're off your head on pills!"

She gave him a sugary 'I'm a good girl' smile, the kind that haunted his jerk off sessions. "I'm fine! The fuzziness goes away pretty fast."

"That doesn't fuckin' matter. Besides, Buddy has a big exam tomorrow. He needs to go home and study, don't you, mate?"

Buddy glared at him. "My name's...yeah, yeah I do have to study. Sorry, Katie."

Middleton sighed prettily. "That's bad luck, good night kiss?"

He smirked. "Sure."

They moved toward one another and the awareness that Middleton was going to suck face with her would-be webcam predator in front of him snapped something inside Ty.

"Okay, we're done here." He bent down, grabbed her around her middle and threw her over his shoulder. Buddy made a noise of outrage but Middleton merely tapped his back. "Mr Henderson, can you please put me down so I can kiss—"

"No. Say goodbye to Buddy."

He felt her body turn in Buddy's direction. "Goodbye, Buddy. Good luck with rugby!"

"I...but...?" The younger man caught sight of Ty's face and fell silent.

"He's really nice," Middleton said as he strode toward the front door.

"No, he isn't."

The remaining patrons were so drunk they barely noticed a man carrying a girl out of the pub but behind the bar Sandy let out a theatrical snort. "You did get a better offer then. Bit young, isn't she?"

Ty thought it better not to respond.

"Who was that?" Middleton asked, as he walked them down the mercifully empty street toward the hotel.

Ty ignored her. "Can you walk?"

"Um, maybe?"

He groaned and hefted her a little higher on his shoulder. He couldn't put her down only to have her collapse, but carrying her like this was a long way from professional; the sooner he dropped her off at her room, the better.

She tapped his back again. "Mr Henderson, I'm not what that woman said. I know I have freckles, but I'm twenty-five. That's super legal."

Ty clenched his teeth and willed himself to walk as fast as he could on footpaths still slick with afternoon rain. Why did she have to call him 'Mr Henderson?' Everyone at work called each other by their nicknames. To the other staff at GGS, he was 'Hendo,' 'Nirvana' or 'Ty.' He didn't want her calling him those things, but hearing her say 'Mr Henderson' in her sexy little girl lisp was worse.

Middleton tapped his back in a line, like she was playing itsy bitsy spider. "Mr Henderson, why're you helping me? You don't even like me. I'm pretty sure you hate me."

Ty stayed silent.

"You know how I know? You never talk to me. You won't look at me. You always schedule jobs, so we never have to go out to sites together. Sometimes I see you glaring at me like you're trying to give me cancer with your eyes. Is any of that ringing a bell?"

Again, Ty said nothing. He had an arm slung across Middleton's thighs, and he could feel the muscles twitching beneath her skin. She had good legs, as far as he could make out through her endless pairings of thick patterned tights and knee-length skirts. Maybe she got them from roller derby. He entertained himself for a second, picturing what she wore when she played. He'd never seen a game, but he'd always had a thing for girls wearing roller skates. Sometimes when he was cranking one out he imagined sitting on a chair and having a girl ride him with nothing but skates on, the wheels spinning uselessly in the air as he fucked her...

"Are you carrying me like this because you used to be a firebag?"

That got Ty's attention. "What?"

"A firebag," Middleton repeated. "Shoot, I mean a firebag."

He heard a soft smack that told him she'd slapped her own forehead. "Fireman," she gasped. "I mean fireman, sorry, I feel weird."

"Ritalin does that to you?" Ty asked, unable to help himself.

"No, I had a couple of vodka raspberries, it's been a while since I've been drunk."

"I didn't see you drink anything."

There was a short pause. "How do you know? Were you watching me?"

Ty clenched his jaw and vowed not to speak again.

"Anyway, back to my original point about you hating me." Middleton's voice was as bright as if they were discussing newborn puppies. "I kind of get why we never talk. I mean, we don't have anything in common. I'm a girl, and you're all 'I'm Tyler Henderson. I'm from Regional Queensland! I never smile!'"

She said all this in a gruff attempt at a man's voice, her body stiff as though she was flexing her muscles. "Or maybe you're just like all the other guys on the crew, and you hate having a girl around because you can't rearrange your testicles in front of everyone anymore."

Ty was so surprised she said 'testicles', he almost dropped her. "That's not true," he told her. "No one resents you being there."

Though they did tend to adjust themselves more freely when she wasn't.

Middleton made a soft clucking noise with her tongue. "You still hate me. Admit it!"

I do, Ty thought. *I hate working with you. I'd love for you to get another job. Just take your long hair and jiggly tits and sweet smile and get the fuck away from me. I had enough problems before I started panting after your ass like a stray dog, and after tonight I'm only gonna have more.*

Silence fell between them as Ty cursed the distance between the pub and the hotel; it hadn't seemed this fucking far when he walked over. Middleton's fingertips traced his back once more, making the hairs on Ty's neck stand on end. "This is a beautiful coat. Where did you get it?"

Distracted by her touch, he said, "Ireland, my ex picked it out for me."

"Is that your ex-fiancée that no one is allowed to talk about?"

Ty said nothing.

"Hmm, well, either way, it suits you. It makes you look like, I don't know…"

A stranger you fall in love with on the train, Veronica's voice whispered in his ear. *My perfect gentleman, Tyler.*

"Sherlock Holmes," Middleton concluded. "Like the Benedict Cumberbatch version of Sherlock Holmes. Only you don't have a sly badger face."

"Right."

They were silent after that. Ty walked as fast as he could and after a few minutes spotted the lights that marked the main street hotel. He congratulated himself on a job well done and patted Middleton's foot. "We're close to the hotel now. I'm gonna put you down, okay?"

There was no reply.

Ty shook her a little. "Middleton?"

No response.

"Shit." He slid her off his shoulder and held her in front of him. Her eyelids were closed, her breathing was even. He groaned. "You can't do this to me, you just can't."

But she had, she'd passed out less than ten meters from her hotel room, and she didn't have a handbag on her. He couldn't rummage through her clothes for a keycard. He couldn't call anyone to take her off his hands. He recalled that quote about how saving a man's life made you responsible for him. He'd already saved Middleton from becoming an involuntary porn star, he couldn't abandon her to the freezing cold. As far as he could see, he had only one option.

He raised a palm to his forehead and hit himself a couple of times, then he hoisted Middleton back over his shoulder and walked toward the hotel. His room was as cold and bland as he'd left it, the bed made, his leather overnight bag on the side table. He dumped Middleton on the hard navy couch and studied her for a moment. Her dark hair was spread around her like a mourner's veil and her eyelids were flickering with the telltale signs of REM. She had very long, dark lashes. Ty stared at her for a beat too long, then walked away shaking his head. Hopefully, she'd wake up after a couple of hours, realise what she'd done and sneak back to her room to avoid embarrassment. If not? Well, maybe waking up in his hotel room after blacking out would finally motivate her to seek employment elsewhere.

Ty flicked on the light, took a piss, and brushed his teeth. He made as much noise as possible, hoping to wake Middleton up, but she dozed on. Unable to sleep naked the way he normally did, he pulled a fresh t-shirt and underwear from his bag and changed in the bathroom. His cock was heavy against his thigh, throbbing with an unwelcome eagerness. Bad thoughts swooped through his head like the fruit bats he could hear chattering outside. He ignored them, dressing and climbing into bed, pulling the cold sheets over his chest. When he closed his eyes it occurred to him that a gentleman would have let Middleton have the bed. He sat up, prepared to change places, then grimaced and fell back against the mattress. No matter what Veronica said, he wasn't a gentleman. Not anymore.

2

Kate had no idea where she was. Most women would be distressed by that, but for her, it was as familiar as donning her old school uniform. When she was a teenager, drinking and smoking sticky lumps of weed was the only thing that numbed her boiling hyperactivity. She had been a fifty-five-kilogram girl with the drug tolerance of a Keebler elf, so she passed out a lot. Once, at a house party, she'd climbed the stairs to the guest bedroom and fallen asleep on the carpet. Brent's mother had found her the next day and they'd both screamed fit to bring the house down. Another time she'd blacked out in the bathroom at a Chinese restaurant and had to be carried out by one of the cooks. Ritalin had proved itself a much better mood-modifier than vodka UDL's or home-grown cannabis, but it lowered her alcohol tolerance even more.

She couldn't quite remember why she'd decided to drink tonight, but it was clear her inner lightweight had decided to re-emerge. She prodded her face and body for injuries and found none. That was good. She was fully dressed. Also good. Her back ached. She felt around herself. She appeared to be lying on a ridiculously hard couch. But where? And for what reason? Had she gone out and crashed at some stranger's place? As her eyes adjusted to the dark she realised the room seemed familiar, familiar and yet somehow new as well...

"Hotel room!" She sat bolt upright. "Bendigo! Hotel room! I was nervous because it's my first work trip! That's why I was drinking!"

She smiled into the darkness, quite proud she'd managed to remember where she was and that she'd found her way back to her hotel suite, safe and sound. But that didn't quite add up. If she made it back to her hotel room, why was she on the couch?

A low grunting moan came from across the room. She looked over and gasped, a little theatrical gasp that sounded like it was for show. There was a man in her hotel bed, or an enormous woman. Or a really big dog.

The thing emitted another grumbling noise, a man, definitely a man. How had he gotten here? Kate patted herself on the head, willing the thoughts to return. Had she broken her years-long dry spell and hooked up? If so, why was she on the couch with all her clothes on? She tried to retrace her steps, think back to whether or not she'd met anyone, but she could only picture the pub; old and dingy with a faded burgundy carpet. She had arrived with the other GGS employees, sitting at the edge of the group listening to the men discuss what was better—chicken schnitzel or chicken parmigiana. Tyler Henderson had been at the head of the group, his face set and his hair gleaming gold. He said very little and drank a lot. He glanced away whenever she spoke.

That he didn't like her always would have hurt. That he didn't like her and she was so hopelessly attracted to him *burned*. In the kind of all-encompassing obsession she'd only ever read about in books, but unlike books, her obsession never went anywhere or did anything. She just got sweaty palms whenever she saw him and it made her work-life very awkward.

Her obsession wasn't even original. *Everyone* had a crush on Tyler Henderson. Women, gay men, straight men, more perceptive animals. It was like having a crush on a Hemsworth brother—it made you basic as hell.

Charisma, Kate had once written in an email to herself, *means people are attracted to you no matter what their type normally is. It means being so compelling you transcend what people think they want and have them want you anyway. Tyler Henderson has that more than anyone I've ever met. Consequently, my crush on Tyler Henderson is lame and I need to get over it right now.*

She'd signed the email and sent it to herself. But despite what she learned in self-development audiobooks, writing it down did not help her achieve that particular goal. If she closed her eyes she could picture him perfectly—tall and handsome as a captain in a military movie. Authority emanated from him like radiation. When he spoke, his words appeared to carry more weight than anyone else's, as though they were made of gold. Everyone looked up to him, everyone wanted his approval. That Kate didn't have it was a huge X beside her name when it came to her GGS status. Ty's dislike of her seemed to predate anything she'd said or done. Her first week with GGS, they were approaching one another from opposite sides of a hallway and she'd tried to make conversation the only way she knew how. She whipped the lid of her baking tin off and smiled. "Hello, Mr Henderson, would you like a lemon-curd meringue?"

First, he had looked at her like she was a penguin that had learned how to talk, then his lip curled with the mild distaste she would come to know well. "No thanks," he said, but his eyes delivered another message. *You are stupid. Lemon-curd is stupid. Meringues are stupid. Stop talking to me and never do it again in your life.*

Kate tried to oblige as much as possible.

It didn't seem fair. Of all the men to instantly hate her, why did it have to be one who dressed like a French billionaire and smelled the way her first orgasm felt? Who had a voice like hot gravel and was so well travelled he made David Attenborough look like her mum? She'd have thought his dislike was garden variety sexism but Ty was famous (in an industry where referring to your wife as 'the old ball and chain' was still considered hilarious) for his progressive views. He frequently shut down regressive conversations with a curt, "if you feel that way, go join ISIS." He was even, it was whispered in the darkest of office corners, a *socialist*.

Why would a socialist hate her so much? She loved sharing. That was what the lemon-curd meringues were all about. Kate exhaled, bringing her attention back to the mystery man in her bed. She needed to focus on something other than Tyler Henderson. She tried to replay her time at the pub. She'd sat there for hours while the men around her drank steadily and she'd been so bored she'd secretly ordered a vodka raspberry. No one noticed so she'd ordered another one, then another one. Once she was pleasantly buzzed, she'd gotten up and started playing the pinball machine. It had a dragon on it. She'd been feeding the slot another dollar when...

The image of young guy burst into her mind—a nice smile, curly hair and massive shoulders. "Aha! Rugby Boy!"

The man in her bed let out a groan.

"Ooh, sorry!"

Rugby Boy groaned again, and Kate clapped her hands over her mouth. She remembered now. Rugby Boy had reminded her of the guys from home, sweet and countrified but without the surfer's tan and sea-salt hair. He offered her a drink with such puppy dog eagerness, she'd said yes without even thinking about it.

As the night wore on and she became tinglier with alcohol, Kate had decided it was time to try again and that if Rugby Boy tried to kiss her, she would let him. He tried. His kisses had been toothy and a little too wet, but he was confident and attractive, and his body was as hard as stone. She decided she wanted to go home with him. That was where her memory reel ended, but Kate could pretty much piece the story together from there. She and Rugby Boy had come back to her room, one or both of them had decided she was too drunk for sex, and then she'd offered him her bed as a consolation prize. It was kind of unchivalrous of Rugby Boy to have taken it, but hell, this was meant to be a one-night stand. What could you expect?

Kate studied the man-bulge in her bed. It was a shame they hadn't consummated their encounter, they might have had fun together. She had been thinking about sex all day. She'd have loved to blame that on ovulation, but the truth was being in such close confines with Tyler Henderson made it hard not to think about sex. There was something strangely intimate about seeing him in jeans and a plaid shirt, socialising with other men and nursing straight liquor in a pub like a cowboy. As she kissed Rugby Boy, she'd thought she'd felt his gaze on her. The mere idea had gotten her ridiculously excited. She knew how weird that was, she had hoped sleeping with Rugby Boy might go some way toward helping her with her dumb crush.

It still might. Maybe you just need to get into that bed and show him you're sober and up for it?

It would be so unlike her, but that made the idea more appealing, not less. Why couldn't she get into bed with Rugby Boy and see if he was still keen? Previous experience with any and all males said he would be.

Careful not to make too much noise, she stripped off her shoes, tights and skirt and crept toward the bathroom. There, she rubbed a little hotel toothpaste on her tongue and wiped away the black mascara smudges under her eyes. She wished she'd unpacked her bag so she could reapply concealer but she didn't want Rugby Boy to wake up and find her rummaging through her bags like a possum in a compost bin.

Studying herself in the mirror, she pushed her shoulders back and tried to strike a sexy pose. She looked like a kid in her mum's high heels, like she was pretending to be the woman she actually was. All her life she'd been, in the words of her friend Maria, *very cute.* There were infinitely worse things to be, but sometimes she longed for obvious signs of womanhood—big boobs, round hips, a butt of any kind. Still, there was nothing she could do about that, aside from spending all her money injecting loads of foreign materials into her body, but screw that. Robbed of big tits, Kate tousled her hair (her favourite attribute) and pouted her lips (second favourite). Then she removed her bra and shot her mirror-self her sultriest look. With some nipple action happening under her t-shirt, she looked kind of slutty, which she supposed was as good as it was going to get.

The main room was dim, the only light source moonlight filtering through the curtains. Rugby Boy was sleeping on his side facing away from her. She slipped into the bed and wrapped an arm around his cotton-covered middle (he'd gone to sleep in his t-shirt, how adorable). Rugby Boy smelled amazing, hot and manly in a way that made her light-headed with horniness. Was that from his scent alone, or some kind of muscle memory from all the kissing they'd done at the pub?

The guy tensed, shifting against her. "Unhh?"

"Hi," she whispered. "It's just me. Sorry for being such a mess before. I don't normally get that way."

The Guy let out a grunt of what was clearly resentment, mingled with please-fuck-offness. He probably hadn't been jazzed about going to bed horny while she laid on the couch like a log. Well, she knew just how to make this situation right. Kate slid her hands down his chest and had barely passed his navel when she felt his semi-hard cock. She ran her hand up and down it, gently squeezing the springy flesh. Weird how nothing in the world felt like penises except penises. Rugby Boy let out a muffled groan. His shaft stiffened, forcing her curled palm to expand. Erect, his penis was approximately the width of a baseball bat, properly and ridiculously huge. "What the heck...?"

Rugby Boy made a sound of protest and Kate realised she'd let go. She re-gripped his swollen shaft, slowly beginning to tug. He gave a contented moan and then tensed. "No," he mumbled. "You're... blacked out."

"That was before," Kate said, pleased he remembered. "I promise I'm excellent now. Just let me make it up to you."

A hard-skinned hand closed over hers, pulling her away from his erection. "You dunnoweme 'nything."

It was a little mortifying to be told to let go of someone's dick. Ordinarily, Kate would have stopped. She'd have rolled over and tried to go to sleep, but she didn't want to. She felt uncharacteristically bold. After all, Rugby Boy didn't know her. He didn't know she'd spent her whole life being called a wallflower and a prick-tease. For all he knew, she was Maria, the kind of woman who could seduce a man with her eyebrows and knew exactly what to do with an arm-penis. Her heart racing, she pressed her lips into the back of his neck, where his scent was especially sweet. "Maybe I want to owe you something," she said in a voice so sexy she could hardly believe it was hers.

Rugby Boy's body stiffened against hers. "Like what?"

Before Kate could psych herself out, she slid down the bed, climbing over his hard thighs so that she was face-to-penis with his penis. It was even more intimidating up close, not to mention stretching the hell out of his expensive-looking briefs. Why would anyone have a cock this big? Like, genetically? Surely it was more of a burden than anything else?

Never mind that. Concentrate on befriending it.

She inhaled the warm sweat-and-salt smell, amazed that something that should have been so nasty made her body buzz with excitement. "Can I use my mouth on you?"

"Yeah, but—oh fuuuck."

If Kate's lips weren't occupied, she'd have smiled. For his token protesting, Rugby Boy was silent as she nuzzled him through his underwear. Then he rolled onto his back to give her better access, spreading his arms wide across the mattress. Kate crouched between his legs, kissing and rubbing everything until Rugby Boy pulled up his t-shirt. The head of his cock extended beyond his briefs, lying heavily on his ridged stomach.

Kate was glad they were working up to revealing his whole dick slowly. If Rugby Boy had just whipped out his massive dong, she'd have run away. Now it was kind of familiar to her, it was easier to deal with. She placed her lips around the swollen head and applied a tight sucking pressure.

Rugby Boy grunted like a wounded bull. Still feeling exceptionally bold—and a little bit bratty—Kate released the head of his cock and resumed playing with what was covered by his briefs just to see what he would do.

Rugby Boy didn't say anything but he started breathing hard

enough to blow a little pig's house down, huffing and puffing as his cock swelled against his underwear until it looked fit to burst.

Kate could feel herself getting wet, her body priming itself in a way it had never done when she was with one of the other two men she'd done this with. She knew she was toying with him, but she couldn't help herself, it was so *sexy*. She tugged down his briefs inch by inch and applied light, sucking kisses to his skin before gently licking everything that was exposed like an icy pole she wanted to last hours. She could sense Rugby Boy's growing need, and it made her feel both powerful and vulnerable. At any moment he might reach a breaking point, seize her hair and growl that he was going to punish her for teasing him. Her backside tingled at the thought and she blushed, glad the darkness concealed her face.

Sexually inexperienced as she might be, Kate was and always had been kinkier than a bag of zig-zags. It felt like she'd been born that way, craving things she didn't understand way before she reached sexual maturity. The dad in *Taken* had a particular set of skills, she had a particular set of fantasies. Unlike her, they weren't polite, they weren't nice, and they didn't leave when they were asked. Instead, they dominated her romantic desires so fully she couldn't have an orgasm without thinking about spanking or date a nice, vanilla bank manager called Paul. Her fantasies steered her, full-force, toward men like Tyler Henderson, near-mythical embodiments of male authority who—surprise, surprise—weren't the slightest bit interested in having very depraved sex with her.

In her effort to rid herself of this handicap, Kate had tried celibacy, therapy, self-loathing, and prayer; it was no use. Her kinks were like that weirdly sinister kindergarten rhyme about the teddy bear picnic and the thick dark mud that deterred attendees. Her kinks chanted in her ear; *'you can't go under it, you can't go over it, you have to go through it.'* So, she went through it. Not as proudly as she'd liked, but she went through it. She had an account on a kinky personals website, even though the only messages she ever got were from nutcases and couples looking to have a threesome. She went on dates with nice, attractive guys and when the time came for them to go to bed, she told them what she liked, even though it usually resulted in bad foreplay followed by a ghosting. She understood where they were coming from. That she wanted a man to smile with pleasure as he caused her pain was weird to her, too.

In bed with this big stranger, Kate gave herself permission to pretend. She teased Rugby Boy and imagined him growing frustrated enough to make her comply with his demands, to lay her across his lap and blister her backside. To call her the things she longed to hear. She was so lost in her fantasy that when a heavy hand descended on her head she was so startled she let out a yelp.

"Enough," a rasping voice told her. "Suck it. Now."

Kate had half-forgotten Rugby Boy could talk, but he had a beautiful voice all dark and deep as a marble quarry. She frowned. "What?"

"Happy to play with it, weren't you? Well, my dick's not a toy. You've wound me up good, now it's time to finish what you started."

He pulled his t-shirt over his head, exposing a ridiculously defined chest, then he yanked down his briefs one-handed. His cock slapped down onto his bare stomach—thick as Thor's hammer. "Put your mouth on it."

Kate body thrummed with nerves. Was this really happening? Was she finally in bed with a man who could give her what she wanted? She edged forward, brushing her mouth across his shaft, testing him. Rugby Boy's palm became a fist in her hair. "I told you we're done playing. Wrap your hand around my dick."

A shiver went down Kate's spine. She immediately cupped her hand around the base of his cock. "Like this?"

"Harder. Tight as those little fingers can go."

Kate complied, trusting she probably couldn't hurt him without some kind of utensil in her hand.

"Very nice." Rugby Boy's said in a rasping tone. "Now put your lips around me, I need to come."

She shivered. It was hard to tell if he was playing her game or just being a bit of a dick, but she decided she didn't care. It felt real and that was all that mattered. She opened her mouth and leaned down to start sucking when Rugby Boy put a big palm in her face.

Kate paused. "You don't want me to anymore?"

Her nameless lover lay there, breathing hard, his cock throbbing in her hand. Even in the darkness, she could see a pearly drop was welling at the tip. She bent around his hand and sucked it away. Rugby Boy hissed like a cut snake. "Fuck it."

His rough hand cupped her cheek and urged her mouth onto his cock. Kate swallowed as much as she could. His cock felt like she had a smooth tennis ball between her teeth, one she knew would be far less forgiving of bites.

Oh, Rugby Guy's penis, she thought, sucking hard. *I'm sure you have a long and illustrious career of making women happy in front of you, but tonight, please let it be my turn.*

"Deeper," he growled. "More."

She slicked him down with her tongue and, inhaling deeply, tried to take him deeper. He was so large she was practically unhinging her jaw. Her digestive system, no doubt confused by her attempt to swallow an entire leg of ham, was producing an unworldly amount of saliva. Spit began to run through her fingers, smelling and tasting of toothpaste and raspberry lemonade.

"That's it, that's good." Rugby Boy sounded tense, almost pissed off, and his hand was still tight in her hair. Kate thrilled over those things the way a normal girl might thrill over gentle kisses and soft words. She began to experiment with her grip, using both hands and her mouth. As she played around with her technique, the man attached to the penis was silent, his hand rising and falling with her head. Kate was a little disappointed, she'd been hoping for more dirty talk, but this was okay. It made him seem careless, a lazy lordly type who was content listening to the sloppy sounds of her mouth and enjoying how humiliatingly eager she was.

Her mind, as it sometimes did in these moments, wandered to Tyler Henderson. She didn't know if any real dominant tendencies lay behind his commanding façade, but the idea that they might *did stuff to her.* Whenever she was struggling to finish herself, she slotted him into her fantasies and she was there within seconds. Unable to help herself, she did it now.

"You horny little slut," she imagined him saying as he thrust into her throat. *"You like staring at me? Imagining me fucking your needy little body? This is what you deserve."*

Kate moaned, the razor blade of wrongness grating oh-so-pleasurably against the whetstone of her arousal. She felt kind of bad for pretending Rugby Boy was someone else, but who was to say he wasn't picturing the Hadid sisters or Ansel Elgort or something? She began moving her mouth and hands even faster, needing him to finish, needing to be a good girl.

Rugby Boy's fist tightened in her hair. "You like suckin' dick, huh?"

Kate confirmed her liking-ness with a moan.

"Tell me you like it. Say my name."

Uh oh.

Kate sucked deeper, hoping to override the question with sheer blowjob excellence, but Rugby Boy pulled on her hair so that she released him with a 'pop.' "Is something wrong?" she asked.

"You tell me you like it, right now and you say my name while you do it."

Oh geez. Kate began flipping through a mental Rolodex of possible names. Sean was a common name. Statistically, there was a good chance he was called Sean. Should she call him Sean? No, she shouldn't call him Sean. Maybe she could give him a cute epithet instead. 'I like sucking your cock, babe.'

No, not babe. 'Handsome,' or 'sexy' didn't seem right either. But what the hell did that leave? High Commissioner? Lord and Savior? Mine Führer?

"I'm waiting," he snarled.

Panic rose in her gut and it occurred to her; this was a one-night stand; she could call Rugby Boy what she always wanted to call the men she was in bed with. It might freak him out, but she wasn't going to see him again. And surely, since she was sucking him off, he could cut her some slack in the name-calling department? Kate smiled up at the shadow she assumed was his face. "I like sucking your cock, Daddy."

Rugby Boy's body went rigid. The hand in her hair fell limply to her side. Kate's cheeks grew hot, and she wondered whether she should try to force down her shame using his cock as a plunger, or sit up, wipe her mouth and try to explain that what she'd said had nothing, not one thing, to do with incest.

Before she could decide on either, his hand rose, clasping her hair once more. "Say that again."

Kate's heart leapt into her mouth. Was he angry? Was he going to yell at her? "I-I like sucking your cock."

"Little girl." His voice was icy with disdain. "Say what you just called me again."

But she couldn't. Instead she asked, "Are you mad at me?"

There was a silence more loaded than all the guns in a gun-nut's gun locker. Then he spoke. "No, but I want you to say it again."

"But I—"

"Not what I want to hear, sweetheart." He gently forced her head back, not hard, but firm. His manhandling and the sense of powerlessness it arose in her made Kate quiver.

How did you know? she wanted to ask. *I never told you, how did you know?* But, she supposed in the scheme of things that didn't matter as much as following orders. She swallowed. "I like sucking your cock, Daddy."

Rugby Boy let out a furious growl forced her head down.

"Suck," he demanded. "Put your lips around it and suck."

She opened her mouth and engulfed him like a sword swallower. He moaned and within seconds he was—there was no other phrase for it—riding her face, thrusting into her mouth with a ferocity that both frightened and aroused her. It was all she could do to keep her jaw wide and not to bite him as he worked himself between her lips. He wasn't silent anymore, he was making the hottest noises Kate had ever heard, shallow inhales and muttered curse words as though he both loved and hated what she was doing to him.

It's happening, she thought as she hummed to keep herself from choking. *I met Rugby Boy, and it turned out he's The Boy, the instantly perfect sex partner every woman hopes to meet but never finds. This is how Lief from Deltora Quest felt when he realised he was the king, probably.*

She arched her back, her inner muscles clenching on nothing, and she knew for the first time in her life that she was going to have an orgasm with another person. He didn't have to ask her about her favourite positions or go down on her until his jaw was numb, if he so much as *breathed* on her pussy she would—

"Coming." Rugby Boy reached down and cupped her right breast. "Coming in your tight little throat."

Kate barely had time to moan her eagerness before he convulsed against her tongue, jamming himself as deep as he could and swearing fit to make a nun blush. Kate choked a little but kept swallowing, her need to please outweighing the needs of her soft palate. His taste was hot and clean, like freshly tumble dried t-shirts.

He withdrew from her mouth, his big fingers brushing clumsily down her cheek. "Good. Good girl."

It was a sign of how twisted she was that Kate couldn't remember ever being so proud. She bent to lick him clean, but Rugby Boy pulled away. "That's enough."

He tugged up his briefs and collapsed back onto the bed, his unsteady panting the only sign he'd just violently orgasmed in her mouth. Kate licked her lips. Was it over now? Was Rugby Boy the kind of guy who lost interest the minute he was done? Her one and only ex-boyfriend had been like that, and it had frustrated the hell out of her. Bossy 'you serve me' selfishness turned her on, but there was nothing sexy about almost cracking your jaw open to please someone and getting nothing in return. Maybe he wasn't her perfect sex man after all.

A hairy thigh nudged her shoulder. "Come up here."

Kate clambered up the bed, tracing her tongue over her teeth, trying to clean her mouth as much as possible. Rugby Boy shuffled back so he was sitting against the headboard, then seized her hips and sat her on top of his thighs. "You okay?"

"Yes." Kate still couldn't see him properly, but being this close was making her shy. She cast her eyes downwards, feeling fragile. She'd called a man 'daddy.' She'd never done that in real life before. Rugby Boy stroked her arms, his palms rough as tan-bark. Weird that a student had such rough hands but Kate had never been touched by a rugby player before. Maybe they all had hands like that.

"That was good work," Rugby Boy told her. "Best head I've had in a long while."

She smiled, still unable to look at him. Without warning, he slid a hand between her legs and inspected the state of her underwear. "You're soaking," he remarked, sounding mildly surprised. As though he'd looked out the window on a cloudless day to see it was drizzling. "You want a little something, sweetheart?"

Kate nodded, then a rough finger forced her chin up. "Can't hear you."

"Yes, I want something," she whispered, adoring him more than was strictly necessary.

"Good girl."

Without warning Rugby Boy shoved her wet panties aside and slid a large fingertip through her folds, dipping himself inside her. Kate cried out at the sudden compression of such swollen skin. She gripped Rugby Boy's thick shoulders.

"Yeah, that's it, hold onto me." A broad thumb placed itself against her clit. There was no preamble about it, no fuss. He began to stroke her sensitive nerves with the light, precise brushes of a master painter. "I'm gonna make you come like this, okay?"

No 'try.' No 'do my bests.' Just 'gonna,' like her orgasm was a foregone conclusion. It was presumptuous and cocky and Kate could only whimper her agreement and hope like hell he was right.

Approximately ten seconds later she was riding his hand, gasping and moaning and humping his fingers like the most shameless slut on earth. The sopping wet sounds her motions were creating was embarrassing—but she still couldn't stop. It was like nothing she'd ever felt before. He didn't seem at all concerned that he'd hurt her, that he would fail to get her off. That confidence was so attractive she could barely stand it. When blended with his finger-skills, his scent and the memory of his cock, Kate knew this was going to be the most memorable, sexual encounter of her life. Her engineer brain started whirring, trying to figure out how she could replicate this experience when she was alone, and the answer was—she couldn't, not in a million years, not unless fully automated sex-robots arrived two hundred years earlier than predicted.

"Say it again," Rugby Boy growled, frigging her. "Say it."

This time Kate knew exactly what he wanted to hear. "Daddy," she moaned. "Daddy."

"That's it gorgeous, keep saying it."

Orgasms were like mountains, they had summits. Usually, when Kate was with another person, her arousal didn't leave base camp one. She could carry herself a little higher using Sherpas—thoughts of men like Tyler Henderson spanking her, tying her down and using her as they saw fit–but the idea of reaching the pinnacle was laughable. She never orgasmed, except alone in her bed with all the time in the world and no expectations except her own. Tonight, that was different. Tonight she had wings and was speeding up the slopes in an icy blur. Her body was trembling, sweat beading on her back and between her breasts and she was going to come, she could feel it in her bones. And yet, no sooner had she thought that than the delicious buzz between her legs vanished.

"Daddy." It was an involuntary cry, a plea that he wouldn't let this end without her finding some satisfaction.

Rugby Boy's fingers closed around her nipple. "You horny, sweetheart? You wanna finish?"

"Yes." *Please help me do it, Rugby Boy. Please?*

His fingers curled inside her, thick and unrelenting. "Concentrate, focus on how I feel inside your tight little snatch. Nothing else matters. I'm not going to stop. I'm going to keep fucking you with my fingers until you gush all over me, understand?"

There was something familiar about his words, as though he'd stolen them from a favourite movie, but maybe that was just because they were perfect. Kate was here, living a lifelong fantasy, why couldn't she come? She worked hard, ate her greens, and gave money to Greenpeace, why couldn't she have an orgasm with another person, just this once?

"I understand," she told Rugby Boy, then screwed up the last of her courage. "Can you...keep talking to me please, Daddy?"

"Of course I can." He began to move his fingers faster, his free hand tugging her aching nipple through her t-shirt. Kate closed her eyes, and she felt the gears slowly begin to turn, tightening, galvanising. The potential for orgasm was drumming inside her, and she honed in on it, trying to make herself as aware as possible.

She'd met a hot stranger who liked being called 'daddy' and who knew exactly what to do to turn her on. It was like the universe had conspired to let her come, all she had to do was embrace it. Rugby Boy's fingers bit down on her nipple, and the pain was as lovely as the sizzle of pleasure that shot down to her groin. "I really like that."

He chuckled darkly. "I know you do, I can feel you tightening up around my fingers. You gonna finish all over me, little girl?"

"Yes, Daddy," she said and meant it.

Rugby Boy let out an angry sounding moan. "God, I'm fuckin' hard again."

The wonder in his voice made Kate think this wasn't a regular thing. That was odd, she'd have assumed most young guys could get it up twice. Then again, she'd barely had sex, so what did she know?

As he rolled his thumb over her clit, Kate had a beautiful realisation. As unbelievable as Rugby Boy's finger skills were, they could two-birds-one-stone this situation. She wanted to have sex with him, and if she did, she could try and have the orgasm simmering in her pelvis on his magnificent dick. That would be a double victory. She pressed her mouth against Rugby Boy's ear. "Do you want to have sex now?"

He let out another furious grunt, his fingers pumping deeper. "No."

"But I really want to feel you inside me. You're so big."

"Too bad," he said, but his breathing had become painfully laboured again. Kate was half-convinced this was a test, that he was

teasing her as she had been teasing him. She assumed her most innocent tone. "Please, Daddy?"

Rugby Boy made a noise like a wild animal. "Fuck, you're a greedy
little thing, aren't you?"

Kate, sensing she was about to get her way, added a little more
sugar to her voice. "Yes, and I know it's bad but I want it. I want you."

Rugby Boy muttered something that sounded like 'why isn't
anything ever easy?' Before she could ask, he pulled his fingers from
her soaking slit. "Fine, you want my dick, you'll get it."

Kate bit back a jubilant 'Yesssssss!' "How do you want to do this? Do
you have a condom? I don't think I have a condom."

"Sweetheart..." Rugby Boy cupped her jaw. Kate could smell
herself on his fingers.

"What?"

She felt him shake his head. "Nothing. I'll fuck you, but you'll get
back down there and suck me first. Get me nice and hard for you."

"Yes, Daddy," she said, the word getting easier with each and
every use.

"Good, and take your fucking fingers away from there."

Kate, who hadn't even realised she was rubbing her clit, had her
hand snatched away.

"That's mine." Rugby Boy ran a finger through the wet line of her
cunt. "You don't get to touch what's mine. Now, get me ready."

Kate propped herself on all fours between his legs, almost
delirious with pleasure. Who knew that in Bendigo (population: ha-
ha-ha) there lived the sex partner of her dreams? As she bent down
and took him into her mouth, she began planning excuses for return
visits. Maybe she could schedule an engineering job up here? It was
out of the way, but he was worth it. The question was, would he be
interested? Determined to prove her mettle, she took him as far into
her throat as she could.

"That's it." His big hand braced itself around her jaw, as though
testing how wide she could open her mouth. "Suck Daddy's big
cock."

Rugby Boy calling himself that most treasured and lust-inspiring of titles made sweat break out on Kate's neck. As she sucked she heard foil crackle and her heart leapt. She'd been worried about interrupting all the hotness to ask about condoms again, but it was clear Rugby Boy wasn't going to be a jerk about this. She reminded herself to feel around the base of his shaft before he slid inside her, to make sure it was on. She'd learned about the stealthing movement at derby practise. It was real and it was terrifying.

"Just a little more," Rugby Boy coached. "Just a little deeper and I'll ride your pussy, Middleton."

Kate sucked harder, tasting small surges of salty pre-come. She felt uneasy, as though his short sentence had been a threat. She replayed his words in her mind. *Just a little more. Just a little deeper and I'll ride your pussy, Middleton.*

Middleton. Why would Rugby Boy call her *Middleton*? She had a lot of nicknames, but each one was restricted to a specific group of people. She called herself Kate. Her family called her Katie. Her roller derby team called her Macca, the Australian appellation for anyone with a McLastname. Her derby name was Princess Bleach. Her Aunt Rhonda had called her KJ. Only the guys at work called her Middleton. Only the guys at work...

Kate felt like she'd been plunged into a dunk tank full of nitrogen. She remembered showing Rugby Boy pictures of Kate Middleton on her phone because the nickname confused him, he'd heard it because Tyler Henderson had been there. *Tyler Henderson had been there.*

Kate suddenly knew, knew with every fibre of her being that the guy whose dick she was sucking on wasn't Rugby Boy. She sat up, woozy and terrified.

"What's happening, Middleton?" In the dim light, Kate could see the stranger had a transparent disk of latex pinched between his thumb and forefinger.

He shifted, so the silvery brightness sifting through the curtains revealed his profile and now that she was looking, Kate recognised the nose, the line of his jaw, the sharp cheekbones. She was in bed with Tyler Henderson. Her boss. She'd blown her boss. She'd swallowed her boss's semen. She'd called her boss 'daddy.' She was currently in the process of re-sucking stern, unfathomably attractive, thought she was the scum of the earth, Tyler Henderson.

"Hoooooaaaaaaaah!" Kate scrambled backward on the bed, flapping her hands as though they were covered in wasps. "Hoooaaaaahh!"

"Middleton?" Tyler Henderson glanced around the room, no doubt trying to pinpoint the reason for her sudden insanity. "The fuck's happening?"

But Kate could only moan and say 'hoooaahhh' and wriggle backward. How could she have missed it? Even in the semi-darkness, the broad body was nothing like a twenty-year-old's. It was thick with muscle and hairy across the middle and, "Oh god, oh god, oh god, oh god!"

"Middleton." Ty's voice punched through the air like a Ginsu knife. "Talk. To. Me."

His voice was so familiar, liquid steel and molten lead. Why hadn't she recognised him?

Kate pressed a hand to her chest. "Mr Henderson. It's me, Kate. We're...we're hooking up!"

Everything went quiet. Kate could hear a cacophony of crickets chirruping outside the hotel window. She became profoundly aware of her half-naked body, her insanely wet panties and aching nipples. She'd done oral with Tyler Henderson. Kate hadn't been a proper believer for years but the urge to drop to her knees and say the entire Hail Mary was overwhelming.

Ty spoke out of the darkness. "You didn't know it was me, did you? You thought I was that fuckwit from the pub."

"Er...yeah."

There was another long silence, and Kate would have given anything, anything on earth, to rewind ten hours and instead of going to the pub, fall into a very big hole and die. "How...why are you in my hotel room?"

"This is *my* hotel room." The soft malice in Ty's voice sent a chill down Kate's spine. "I brought you back here after you blacked out and I couldn't find your room card."

The floor seemed to shift beneath her bare feet. Tyler Henderson had known who she was the whole time. Of course he had, he'd called her Middleton, he'd knowingly let her blow him. Kate didn't know whether to be flattered, disturbed, outraged, insulted or any other emotion on earth. "Mr Henderson, I don't think you get it...*I went down on you*. And you touched me. And I went down on you and you came and I *swallowed it*."

More painful silence. Kate wished she hadn't put so much emphasis on the words 'swallowed it.'

Ty pointed a ghostly hand towards the door. "This never happened. Get dressed and get back to your room, right fucking now."

It was hard for Kate to find her clothes in the dark, but she didn't turn on the light and neither did Ty. He remained in bed, silent and motionless as she pulled her skirt up her legs and tugged on her stiff Mary Janes. Her bra was still in the bathroom, but she decided to leave it behind, sacrifice it for the greater good. It felt like Tyler Henderson's hotel room was running out of breathable oxygen. She scurried to the door and all but flung herself into the night air. The door slammed behind her, severing the experience into then and now. She dug her keycard out of her secret skirt pocket and ran toward her room. Her hands were trembling so hard she could barely swipe the card against the door. As soon as she was in her room she picked up her phone, desperate to unburden the horror of this situation on someone else, but there was only one person she could talk to about this, and at two a.m. on a Wednesday night, she'd be a jerk to call Maria. She sent her a message asking her to call once she was awake and took a long, hot shower that didn't go an inch toward making her feel clean or calm. Despite the insanity of what had happened she was still so aroused it hurt. Her body, brought to the very brink of orgasm by her secret crush was taut as an elastic band. She lay down on the bed and ran a finger through her slit, caressing herself lightly the way Ty had, then stopped.

That's mine. You don't get to touch what's mine.

She shivered and took her hand away, not letting herself question why, not letting herself think of anything at all. Instead, she put on her complimentary dressing gown, made herself a powder hot chocolate and settled on the bed to watch *Scrubs*. She had no idea what tomorrow would bring, but she knew she wouldn't be sleeping tonight.

3

D *addy*. The word echoed through Ty's brain, reverberating through the soft tissue. *Daddy*.

He was sitting in a conference room, and instead of focusing on the presentation about interior solar panels, all he could think about was that miserable, dangerous, unforgettable word. *Daddy*.

For more than three decades, he'd been dumbstruck by that word. The word and the idea behind it. Not the notion of being a father, not the desire to have some porn star type cry out 'daddy!' while he did her in the ass. What he wanted was complicated, dark and detailed as a Leng Jun painting.

The fantasies began when he was young, young enough that the idea of him being a dad was ridiculous. They lived and breathed with him, growing as he did. Ty wasn't religious, but his desire to play daddy from such a young age made him wonder if reincarnation wasn't real. It felt like he'd inherited another man's tastes. As though some higher power had said 'Daddy is the word, and the word is Daddy and Daddy is the only thing that will turn your crank. Also, you have a sadistic streak, enjoy that. Amen.'

Getting off on such a massive cultural taboo had always freaked

him out. He grew up thinking he was evil on the inside, like Ted
Bundy or Ivan Milat. He was the school captain, the only guy in
Parratanna school history to make the first tier rugby team at fifteen.
His success—and his hair colour—earned him the nickname 'Golden
Boy', but it had never felt earned. He couldn't kiss a girl without
wanting to pin her down and make her hurt, and what kind of golden
boy did that make him? He started to ignore the chicks who hung
around the club rooms asking if he could give them a lift home. He
pruned back his crushes like rose bushes. If asked why he didn't have
a girlfriend, he said chicks were annoying and the sex wasn't worth it.
It was a pretty misogynist sentiment, but in a small town in the '80s,
people took it as a sign of maturity.

"Good thinking, Tyso," his old man had said, slapping him on the
back. "No need to get tied down to the scrubbers around here. Wank,
study hard, go to uni."

Words had been Ty's only release. He spent hours writing out his
fantasies in longhand, frantically jerking off and then locking the
papers in his guitar case. It weighed heavily on him, his grimy trea-
sure, but it was the only thing that helped him stay sane. The older
he got the more his hormones thrashed like live eels, demanding he
fuck, insisting he fuck, telling him he would die if he didn't fuck.

It wasn't until uni that things changed. Away from his family and
the hot Queensland sun, the idea that he would snap mid-orgasm
and murder whatever girl he lost his virginity to just seemed kind
of...stupid. So he lost his virginity. Then he lost it some more. As he
became more experienced, he learned to pass himself off as a fan of
rough sex. Plenty of girls were into light spankings and bondage and
that was satisfying enough to stave off his darker, less acceptable
urges. He thought of such sex as the beef-paste astronauts ate in
space, nutritious if not actually food. If his girlfriends had known
that, they might have been insulted, but Ty had no intention of telling
anyone about his kinks. He left the bloody meat of his fantasies in the
guitar case he'd brought from Parratanna to Melbourne and was
determined to let them rot there.

That wasn't to say he didn't fuck up. A few times he'd drunkenly initiated role play that went down like a lead balloon, a few lovers found (or went looking for) his porn and didn't like what they saw one bit. The daddy stuff unnerved even the kinkiest of his sex partners. Ty understood that. His preferences lay along the fault lines of multiple taboos: older man/younger woman, incest and abuse of power, domestic violence. Research conducted on early computers told him age-play wasn't unheard of, but Ty couldn't trust his partners would believe him when he said he wasn't turned on by abuse. It had taken *him* years to understand he wasn't turned on by abuse, just the games, just the consensual perversion of it all.

He was a somewhat literate guy—captain of his school debating team—but he didn't have the words to articulate his needs. Not that it mattered, Ty had a feeling he could have been Bill fucking Shakespeare, and it wouldn't have convinced any of his exes to put on a tartan skirt and blow him for pretend lunch money.

The only person he'd come close to having a fulfilling D/d relationship with was Veronica. She'd called him daddy in the sack. Ty wasn't sure how she found out he liked it, he assumed he'd told her when he was drunk. They never took it further than her saying that word, but to have sex while a beautiful woman called him daddy was everything. He'd been effortlessly faithful, so sure it couldn't get any better, then she left him, and that very same week he met Middleton. She was so saccharine and wide-eyed, Ty convinced himself what he wanted from her was pure projection, and yet she'd come into his bed last night and called him that fucking word. Called him that word with the kind of joyful lust he'd waited his whole life to hear and she hadn't even known it was—

"Hey, Boss!"

Ty started, crushing the cardboard coffee cup in his hand and dousing his chest in hot milk. "Shit!"

Jake Holland, a perpetually bewildered redhead commonly referred to as 'Dutchy', winced. "Fuck, sorry boss, I'll go get some serviettes."

He dashed off. Ty attempted to pat himself down with his notepad, meeting the gaze of everyone who stared at him until they looked away. Dutchy returned a few seconds later with an insanely high stack of paper towels.

"Are you right, boss?" he asked, handing them over.

"Fine," Ty lied.

Dutchy dropped his ass into the seat beside him. "Sure. You just look a bit...out of it"

That would be because he was fresh from enduring one of the worst nights of his life. No sleep Ty could have dealt with. No sleep would have made sense. Instead, he'd passed out not long after Middleton left and woken twenty minutes later grinding a hotel pillow. He should have stopped, should have taken control of himself, but his head had been swimming with thoughts of Middleton. He pictured fucking her, her pert tits shaking as he hammered into her slippery little pussy. *"Daddy,"* she'd say. *"Fuck me harder, Daddy."*

Half-asleep and unable to stop himself, he thrust into the bedding. The rough material felt nothing like a woman's cunt but when he came, he did it so hard his whole body convulsed. He soaked his briefs, warm come spreading across his lap and seeping into the pillow. Feeling utterly depraved, he'd mopped up and fallen back to sleep. He woke the same way an hour later, his cock throbbing, his brain sagging with memories of Middleton sucking his dick. Out of sheer desperation, he'd stroked himself in bed, soiling the already soiled bedding some more.

That was it, he told himself when it was over. *I'm done.*

Only he wasn't. After forty minutes, he'd woken up his body primed to fuck a girl who wasn't there. He'd forced his hand away from his cock and gotten up to take a leak. That was when he found her bra. It was exactly the kind of bra he'd thought a girl like Middleton would wear, pink lace with a delicate bow between the cups. He checked the back for her size but the label was so worn the writing had rubbed away. He guessed they were C's, pert and supple beneath her t-shirt.

He brought the lace to his nose and inhaled. Her bra smelled like her skin, like strawberry cheesecake filling and he remembered with a visceral hunger the noises she'd made as she rode his hand; the helpless sobs and whimpers of a good girl pushed to her limits. Ty's self-control collapsed faster than you could say 'lost cause.' He spent the rest of the evening tugging on himself, by the end his dick ached but he couldn't stop. His need was bottomless, every release only making him want more. He should have fucked her. Should have worked himself inside her tender cunt and ridden her while she called him daddy. Now nothing else would do. The truth of that, along with the memories of what he and Middleton had done kept him abusing himself until morning.

When sunlight peered through the thin hotel curtains, Ty's sheets were drenched in sweat and come and the whole suite smelled like raw sex. He made a half-hearted attempt at cleaning up but there was no getting rid of the stains or the smell. The hotel staff were going to think he was an animal.

Ty had dragged himself into the bathroom for a cold shower. When he got out, he saw the icy water had done nothing to remove the shadows under his eyes. He looked haggard as a paperback detective whose case was going very badly. Staring at himself his misery turned to anger. How dare Middleton have thought he was that stupid kid? How dare she suck his dick imagining another man's face? How dare she crawl into his bed and make him think she was tired of fighting the same attraction he'd felt the moment he laid eyes on her? She'd seen right into his soul and she hadn't even known who she was looking at.

Dutchy nudged his side. "You sure you're okay?"

"I'm fine," Ty repeated for what felt like the nine hundredth time. "Shouldn't you be taking notes?"

"We know all this shit already. Flex-panels are no good in our houses."

"Doesn't matter." Ty nodded his head at the woman speaking. "Start taking notes."

Dutchy pulled out his pen, grumbling to himself. Ty watched, exasperated. So far the GGS guys had treated this trip as a chance to get away from their families and drink too much. That was fine, but you needed to do some fucking work as well. Despite everyone in management making that clear, his men resented his every attempt to make them do their jobs. Ty thought longingly of the MFB where the chain of command was fixed, and every man knew his place. This kind of bullshit would never have happened there. He'd wanted to spend the rest of his life in the Metropolitan Fire Brigade, but fate had dealt him a different deck. Now he was treading water in the corporate world where his job consisted of doing paperwork and babysitting a bunch of borderline alcoholics. It wasn't a hard job, overseeing the design of ecologically friendly houses, but it wasn't particularly inspiring.

Ty's mind wandered to his leather overnight bag, where the yellow pads and pens he'd stowed were waiting to be filled with the second chapter of his novel. He wouldn't be writing on this trip, he knew; he was too tired, too wrung out, too concerned he was about to get the sack when Middleton told Johnno what he'd done to her in his hotel room.

Daddy. I like sucking your cock, Daddy.

The spokeswoman for flex panels spoke on and on about their benefits. Ty tried to get his mind out of the gutter and concentrate but that phrase kept coming back to him, repeating itself in his head like a mantra. He was about to go outside for some fresh air when all the hairs on the back of his neck stood up. He turned and sure enough, a mere thirty minutes after the seminar had started, Middleton was here. Ty returned his eyes to the stage, trying to keep his breathing even. She wouldn't come over and sit with him. Ever since the lemon-curd meringue incident she'd gone out of her way to avoid him, a state of affairs he'd encouraged at every turn.

"Middleton!" Dutchy raised a hand and waved her over, drawing the eye of all the people around them. "Over here, come sit with us!"

Ty considered giving Dutchy a dead-leg, but it was already too late. Middleton had caught sight of him and was walking their way. Ty studied her out of the corner of his eye. What he saw did nothing to improve his mood. She looked fresh-faced and perky; even more so than usual. Her waist-length hair was loose around her shoulders and her skin was all but glowing. She'd forgone her usual bulky dress for skinny jeans and a singlet top that exposed her pale shoulders. She was also holding a trendy coffee cup, which meant she was late not because she'd rolled out of bed, exhausted from thinking about their encounter, but because she'd treated herself to a barista-made-latte. Anger rose in Ty's blood like mercury.

"Never seen her in jeans before," Dutchy muttered. "She's got good legs, doesn't she?"

Ty had splintered a hand mirror when he was a kid, smashed it on the driveway just because he wanted to see what it would look like. Who knew the seven years of bad luck his mum warned him about would concentrate itself into this single business trip?

Middleton sat down beside Dutchy. "Hey guys, did I miss anything?"

"Nothing too important." Dutchy tapped her coffee cup. "Any good?"

"Yeah, amazing. It's from the Bluebird café on Main Street. Want me to show you where it is later?"

"Fuck yeah, I'm dying for—"

Ty cleared his throat.

Dutchy went red. "Sorry, boss."

Ty waited for Middleton to apologise, but she just pulled a notepad from her bag and began taking notes. She was wearing pink ankle boots with a pattern of roses on them. Why did everything about her have to be so fucking cutesy? And why could he smell her from two seats away? That strawberry-pie scent that had lingered on his bed sheets long after she was gone.

Ty's overwrought genitals stiffened, and he remembered her weight in his lap, the way she'd squirmed and sighed as he fingered her. He'd been so close to feeling her come, her wet pussy clenching down on his hand as her saliva dried on his cock...

Ty swore under his breath, forcing his attention back toward the woman giving the presentation, repeating her words back in his brain. *By 2029 we anticipate that seventy percent of all households will—*

"Where did you end up last night?" Dutchy muttered to Middleton. "I couldn't see you when I left the pub."

"I was playing the pinball machine," she whispered back. "I left at eleven."

"No, you didn't. I didn't hear you come into your hotel room until two. You're in the room next to me, remember? So where'd you go?"

Brass bands constricted themselves around Ty's chest. Dutchy had a longer nose for gossip than any woman Ty had ever met and Middleton blushed like a milkmaid whenever anyone said anything remotely sexual. If she stumbled now, said the wrong thing, their entire encounter would be revealed.

The end of his career flashed before his eyes. He saw himself carrying a box of his stuff from the GGS building amidst whispers of 'such a fucking cliché.'

Middleton took a sip of her fancy coffee. "That wasn't me. I was in bed. You must have heard the person on the other side of you."

Her voice was smooth, her expression bland as boiled rice. It wasn't just a convincing lie, it was a *perfect* lie.

Dutchy frowned. "But I heard you. I know I did."

Middleton giggled. It sounded like a wind chime being buffeted by a breeze. "Seriously, I wish I was doing something more exciting, but I was watching *Scrubs*."

"Oh." Dutchy looked disappointed. "I thought you might have gone wild for once."

Another crystal-clinking giggle. "I wish."

Ty stared at Middleton. He had been with her in the small hours of the morning, had blown a load in her mouth, and for a second, he, himself wondered if it had all been a crazy dream. If he'd invented the whole thing in his mind. Then her milk-chocolate gaze locked on his and she winked.

Winked.

She winked at him.

The next few hours passed in a haze. Ty stopped pretending to concentrate on the seminars, his entire focus was taken up by the fact that Little Miss Sunshine had fooled him. He'd thought there was nothing beyond the sweetness and he was wrong. No girl who lied as effortlessly as she did was new to dishonesty. No girl who could suck off her boss, then wink at him was as shy as she'd pretended to be.

It took him a long time to untangle why that pissed him off so much. Part of it was ego; he prided himself on being able to see people for what they were; who didn't? Everyone wanted to think they were a good judge of character. But it wasn't just that. He felt disappointed. He'd taken some selfish pride in the fact that he'd corrupted the pure and bubbly Middleton last night—tarnished her just a little. But that was stupid. He'd been beyond irritated by the girl Middleton was pretending to be and he had no right to judge. He was the golden boy with the guitar case full of handwritten pornography, he knew all about concealing the things you didn't want other people to see.

At lunch he waved away invitations to join this group of executives or that cluster of GGS employees to sit by himself and ask the all-important question—could he and Middleton 2.0 take this further? They had chemistry after all, and Ty could admit he'd been fascinated by her for a long time, if in an exasperated *'is there a real person beneath that canary yellow blouse or just a very chipper robot?'* way.

But it wasn't that simple. The daddy-daughter dynamic had two major facets; hard and soft, punishment and cherishing. Ty had always understood the first and never had much use for the second, but Middleton was so delicate it was difficult not to want to protect her. Last night he'd given her plenty of hard, but he'd also found his mind wandering to the soft. He'd wanted to shower with her once they were done, sleep with her tucked into his side, kiss her and make sure she knew what a good girl she was. That disturbed him almost as much as the fact that he'd touched her at all. Wanting to fuck his pretty employee was biology, wanting to cherish her was something else. Something worse.

He glanced at where Middleton was sitting, so fucking young in contrast with the other engineers, like a schoolgirl who'd been brought to a sustainability convention by a time-strapped mother. There were twenty years between them, but side-by-side, people might have easily guessed twenty-five or even thirty. Ty had never wanted to be a dirty old man, parading younger women around, so everyone knew his dick worked. He'd never planned on being single in his forties, but since he had no choice, he could at least avoid looking like a tacky piece of shit.

Forget it. Forget it ever happened and be grateful she hasn't run to Johnno to say she's suing you.

After lunch came a presentation from a hipster RMIT professor who appeared to be suffering from the same Benjamin Button's disease as Middleton. Despite looking seventeen, he was a pretty good speaker, using slides and incorporating music and humor into his talk with something approaching flair.

Middleton, Ty noticed, was laughing at all of his jokes. She was sitting on the other side of the hall, her long caramel-coloured hair swept over one shoulder like a mermaid's. He remembered how that hair felt bunched in his fist while she swallowed his cock, and swore. Suppressing painful hard-ons was going to become a big part of his working life for a while.

Once the boy professor was done talking, the hall filled with excited muttering. The next and final speaker was Manning Turner, former coach of the West Coast Eagles Football Team. What his talk had to do with sustainability, Ty had no fucking clue, but he didn't care, and neither did any of the men around him. As Turner climbed the podium, Ty settled in, knowing that at least for the next forty-five minutes he wouldn't have to think about—

Dutchy nudged his side. "Look, Middleton's made a friend."

Inwardly cursing Jake Holland and the country he'd been named after, Ty glanced over to see Middleton talking to Benjamin Button. She was smiling and tossing her hair the way she had when she'd stood flirting with that big stupid lug last night, only this time Ty didn't have the mercy of alcohol to take the edge off.

None of your business, he told himself. *None of your business, she can flirt with whatever gawky, four-eyed motherfucker she*—

"Is she hitting on him?" Dutchy asked.

"I don't give a shit. Shut up, will you?"

But despite his words, ignoring her was impossible after that. Ty's gaze keep veering to where she stood whispering and laughing and at one point touching the Boy Professor's shoulder. Turner droned on about premierships and club rooms and all Ty could think about was the way he'd left Middleton high and dry last night. What if she was still horny and wanted this Goonies-looking prick to finish what *he'd* started? The idea had his buffet lunch petitioning to return to the outside world. When Middleton pulled out her notepad and started scribbling on it, Ty stood up. "I'm going to have a talk with that girl."

"About?" Dutchy asked.

"Speaking while people are giving a presentation."

The corners of Dutchy's mouth pulled down. "Don't go too hard on her. She's just a—"

"She's *not* a kid. She's twenty-five, and she's here representing our company. Be back soon."

He left before Dutchy could say anything along the lines of 'why the fuck do you care if she's talking? *We're talking.*'

Middleton, with her back to him, didn't see him coming. But the boy professor did. He gave Ty a nervous grin that said he looked exactly as angry as he felt. "Can I help you?"

"Not particularly." For the second time in twenty-four hours, Ty tapped Middleton on the shoulder. "I need a word with you."

She turned, and her box-of-fireworks smile exploded out at him.

"Sure," she said in the honeycomb voice that had, mere hours ago, moaned that his cock was so big. "What about?"

"About talking during someone else's presentation."

"Oh." Middleton's face changed subtly. He couldn't pinpoint how, but it was as though she'd raised an eyebrow one-hundredth of an inch. As though without uttering a word she'd said '*is that really what you're mad about Mr Henderson, or are you mad because this boy professor might fuck me and you can't?*'

Ty looked at Middleton, and Middleton looked at him. Her smile said butter wouldn't melt in her mouth but Ty knew better. Satan himself would melt in that mouth.

"The talking's my fault," the boy professor interjected. "Kate and I got a bit carried away talking about nerd stuff. I'm Patrick Sloan, by the way."

"Tyler Henderson, good talk before." Ty shook the boy professor's hand without taking his gaze from Middleton's. "You ready for that word?"

She blinked at him. "I'm sorry Mr Henderson, but if you don't want us to talk during the football speech, Patrick and I can just go outside?"

Don't you say his name to me, little girl. "It's not just that, there are some things we need to straighten out, Midd—Kate."

Her name sounded strange in his mouth, like a rough chip of wood.

Middleton's sugary smile grew wider. "Sure thing. Lead the way."

Patrick Sloan looked a little put out. "I'll come and find you later and we can keep chatting?" he said, his smile hopeful.

"Maybe when someone else isn't giving a talk," Ty suggested, and the boy professor blushed. A few workers scraped food scraps into ecologically friendly waste bags as they walked through the dining hall but none of them paid him and Middleton any attention. Just a manager and his subordinate, on their way to do official business.

"Where are we going?" she asked.

Ty gestured to a small office left free for upper-level executives like himself to make calls and do work. It was, as he suspected it would be, empty. "Over here."

Middleton stared at him and Ty knew she was wondering what was coming next. He saw the instant she decided she didn't care, turning and striding toward the empty office without another word. Ty watched her go, her pert ass swaying from side to side in her jeans.

Inside the office the blinds were drawn, casting the space into a premature twilight that reminded Ty of the night before. Middleton sat on the desk, her long legs crossed. "What did you want to talk about, Mr Henderson?"

Ty's stomach was heavy, his cock stiffening against his thigh. She knew exactly what she was doing, the beautiful infuriating brat. He pulled the door closed and twisted the lock on the knob. His palms were damp, his fingers shaking.

"Is everything okay?" Middleton's forehead wrinkled like an inquisitive pug's, and though it was entirely out of place, Ty wanted to smile. It couldn't be entirely fake, the sweetness. She was too good at it, she made it feel too real. She must distort what was already there, angling it like a shonky mirror, so it was the only thing you paid attention to.

"Everything's fine, Middleton." Ty walked toward her and was gratified to see her confidence in her sexy pose falter.

She hunched a little and swiped her pink tongue over her lower lip. "Then why did you want to—"

"Talk? Because I have a question for you. Why were you flirting with the boy professor right where you knew I'd see you?"

In an acting manual, Middleton's expression would have been labelled 'lovely confusion.' "I wasn't."

He had always been interested in her, there was no denying that, but now he was downright *intrigued*. Watching her lie so efficiently felt like someone had dropped a thirtieth Hemmingway novel in front of him, its spine un-creased, its pages fresh with the new book smell he found almost sexual. "I thought maybe you were flirting with him to try and push me into doing something."

"Like what?" She made that face again. None of her features moved, but suddenly he felt stupid, oafish, like he was making a mistake.

Fascinating.

Ty changed tact. "Okay, so you weren't trying to push me. The question remains; what are we going to do about this?"

She laughed her twinkly wind chime laugh. "About what?"

"About the fact that I fucked your mouth last night."

And there it was. Middleton's air of delicate naïvety dissolved like sugar in hot water. Her lips parted, and her cheeks went bright red. "I um...I don't..."

A smile creased his cheeks, the sensation so unfamiliar it felt as though they'd been cast in clay. "You do remember that, don't you? You remember that you sucked my cock?"

He hadn't thought her blush could intensify any further but somehow it did.

"I...erm..." Middleton looked down at her feet. "Yes?"

"Good." Ty took a couple of meandering steps forward. "I thought maybe we should talk about it."

She looked up at him, her eyes were wide and he knew she was trying to recover her aura of dizzy misunderstanding. "What would we say?"

"We could talk about you calling me 'daddy.' That was interesting."

If it were possible for someone's head to explode as the result of having too much blood in their cheeks, Middleton would be six feet under. "It's not like that," she said quickly. "It's not about wanting—"

"I know."

"I know that you know." Middleton's eyes were very bright. "You liked it."

A quote Ty couldn't place came into his mind, something about how when you look into a deep, dark place the place also looks into you. He made himself step closer. "I was the first man you ever called 'daddy', wasn't I?"

She glanced away.

"I'm not trying to tease you. I'm not going to hold it against you. I just want to know if I was the first."

"Yes," she told the office wall. "You were."

"Have you thought about me that way for a while?"

Middleton's lower lip continued to quiver, but she said nothing.

Ty thought about the day they met. He'd been sitting hungover and miserable in the staff kitchen. Veronica's ring was burning a hole in his breast pocket and he was trying to come up with reasons why he shouldn't go upstairs and pour a couple of shots of whiskey into his coffee. Then Middleton—though she was months from acquiring that nickname—appeared in the doorway. She looked like an angel, a pure manifestation of innocence, all done up in a pink dress and knee socks. Ty had never, in his life, had such a visceral reaction to a female before, he'd gotten hard right under the scratched IKEA dining table.

"Excuse me," she'd said in her husky voice. "Can you please help me? I don't know the way to the interview room."

Ty had pictured her bent over his desk, crying great fat tears, as he spanked her ass purple. *'Please, Daddy, I won't do it again. I'll be good, I promise.'*

'I don't believe you,' he'd say, *'get on your knees and prove it to me.'*

"Upstairs," he'd croaked. "Interview room's upstairs, on your left."

"Thank you." Their eyes met and the air seemed to crackle between them, heating with the colourless, odourless, and yet completely tangible energy of sexual attraction. In that moment Ty was convinced beyond a shadow of a doubt that this girl, whoever she was, had been thinking what he was thinking. Then she'd skipped away looking like a character in an Enid Blyton novel and he'd felt like the world's sickest bastard. He assumed she was a teenager on work experience and vowed to stay the hell out of her way before going upstairs and pouring those shots into his coffee; one for Veronica, one for his disobedient dick.

A fortnight passed. Ty had *just* begun to reassure himself he would never see the pink-dress girl again when he found out she wasn't a teenager on work experience, she was Kate McGrath, a twenty-three year old civil engineer and GGS's newest employee.

The timing of it all had felt inconceivably cruel. The love of his life had just left him and this impossibly sweet, impossibly young female who riled him up for reasons he didn't understand was in his presence eight hours a day, five days a week. He'd thought it was karmic retribution for all the dirty pornography he'd stuffed inside his Fender case. But now, standing in front of that same girl two and a half years later, Ty knew he'd been right the first time. When they'd met, it hadn't just been him having those fantasies.

"You did think that about me," Ty said. "You felt it too, didn't you? When we first met?"

Middleton blinked up at him, and the air thickened with that same fat, undefinable energy that had sprung up in the GGS kitchen. "I can't..."

Ty stepped forward and put a hand to her cheek. It was velvet soft and sent sparks careening up his arm. "Tell me?"

Middleton's tongue traced her lower lip, soft and pink and plump. "Do you mean in the kitchen? When I asked you for directions?"

He nodded.

"I felt it," she admitted. "I didn't understand it the way I do now, but I felt it."

Ty felt slightly light-headed with relief. "Good."

"Mr Henderson," Kate whispered. "Are you...does this mean you want to do it again?"

So much of him wanted to say yes. The animal who almost fucked her raw last night. The hormonal teenager dying to explore his fantasies with a girl who wanted it the way he did. The pervert who'd lusted after her the moment he saw those knee socks. But there was also the part of him that wanted to wash her in the shower and sleep with her in his arms, the part that had stood alone ever since Veronica left. There was more happening here than the possibility of getting his dick wet and it made proceeding both dangerous and stupid. Middleton was half his age and his subordinate. If things went bad, it could ruin his career, his sanity and just about everything else he held dear.

He let go of her cheek. "We can't."

"But you just said—"

"What happened when we met, it goes that way with people like us sometimes. You can smell it on one another."

"What do you mean?" She said with a trace of little girl sweetness.

"Don't," Ty warned. "You know what I mean. We saw each other, we wanted the same thing. That was pretty damn obvious last night as well, but I shouldn't have let things go so far. I should have turned you down or at least made sure you knew who I was."

"But I was thinking about you," she said. "I was thinking of you even when I thought you were Rugby Boy. I think part of me knew it was you."

Triumph flooded into Ty's veins like a narcotic. He wanted to kiss her, to claim her, to cement the fact that he'd been the one soaking her fucking panties, but then he remembered his realisations of a few minutes ago.

"I'm glad you wanted me," he told her. "I'm glad you don't regret it, but it can't happen again."

"Why not?"

Ty would never have thought it possible but Middleton looked, well, not angry, but *heated*. As though she wanted to shove him in the chest. Her lips were parted and she was breathing hard. Instinctively, Ty knew that if he felt the soft petals between her legs they'd be drenched. She was frustrated and he knew exactly why. Against his better judgment he moved closer to her, standing between her denim-clad legs. "Didn't get you off the way you wanted last night, did I?"

She nodded, worrying at her bottom lip with her teeth.

"You're a clever girl with two functioning hands, why didn't you get yourself off?"

She looked away.

"Because I told you not to touch yourself," Ty realised. "Well, you can touch yourself, you can do whatever you want, but we can't be this stupid again."

"Why?"

"Because it's wrong," Ty managed to say, as he fought the urge to wrap his body around hers and kiss her until she saw stars. "You're my employee, and you're almost half my age."

"You *like* that I'm half your age."

It could have been a shot about older men liking younger women, but Ty knew it wasn't. "It's not about actual age. Me being older doesn't have shit to do with what you want."

Seeing a mischievous smile on that cherubic face, was strange, like hearing a new note on an instrument he'd played for years.

"It doesn't hurt," she said. "It was so good last night, can't we just finish what we started? Just do it once and then never do it again?"

Ty thought of his dad's trailer: older than dirt, its latch would disconnect on any given pothole and send pineapples flying out onto the road. Once, his brother Rhys had been riding in it and *he'd* gone flying out onto the road and broken his wrist. Ty's old man had been too proud—and too cheap—to buy a new trailer until it was necessary and lord, it had made life hard. Ty couldn't do that, he couldn't turn a blind eye to the realities of this situation. He needed to pony up and pay for a new fucking trailer before anyone got hurt.

"We can't," he told Middleton. "I'm too old for you and we work together. You might think you want this, but you didn't get a degree and spend two years busting your ass for GGS to get fired because we screwed each other, did you?"

Middleton frowned, another new and unusual expression on her. "Then why did you pull me in here all alone?"

"Because I wanted to get this situation handled."

"No, you didn't. You came over to me when I was talking to Patrick because you were jealous."

"I was jealous because you wanted me to be."

"No, I—"

"Cut the shit. The jeans, this top..." he brushed a hand over her right shoulder. "Coming in late, flirting with the professor. You were waving the flag and hoping big daddy was going to come over and punish you. You should have seen the way your eyes lit up when you saw me, I could smell you getting wet for me."

He was standing closer to her now, close enough that their noses were almost touching and though he knew it was dangerous he couldn't pull away.

"If you know all that..." Middleton's lips moved infinitesimally, kissing the air between them "...then why don't you do something about it?"

Ty wanted to, wanted to with all his fucking heart and soul. He'd never felt lust like this, sharp and tangible as a spike in his side. His cock was hard, his heart pounding. All he wanted was to show her he was a man of his words. Then he blinked, swallowed, made himself think of Rhys screaming in pain, his wrist bending the wrong way. He stepped backward. "Because it's not worth the risk, and you know it."

She seemed to deflate slightly, as though he'd just pulled a tab in her back. "I...I do know that."

"Good. Then it's settled."

Ty turned to walk away, then remembered something. He pulled open his wallet and Middleton's eyes went wide as hubcaps. "You don't have to pay me, I won't tell anyone."

"It's not for that, it's for your bra," Ty said quickly. "I know lingerie can be expensive."

She frowned. "Why can't I just have it back?"

Because it was wadded up in his hotel bin, covered in bodily fluids. "I, uh, the cleaning people threw it out."

Her face fell. "Oh. Well, don't worry about it, I have plenty more."

Ty put his wallet away. "Fine, then I guess—"

"Daddy." She said it softly, like a birthday wish. Like a secret prayer. Ty froze and as though sensing her advantage Middleton put a hand on his chest. The sensation of her fingers through his shirt was so intimate, it felt as though she'd placed her warm palm on his cock.

"Middleton," he said, every letter a warning.

"Daddy," she repeated. "Why can't you just give us what we both want?"

Ty gently pried her palm from him. "Because you're a nice girl and I enjoyed what we did, but it's not going to happen again."

He turned and moved toward the door.

"Fine," she called, her voice fierce from all he hadn't given her. "Bet you're a bad kisser, anyway."

Ty flipped the lock on the door. "Far as riling a man up goes, Middleton, that's weak as piss."

A moment's silence, and then, "I gave Professor Sloan my number."

Ty's hand froze on the door handle. "Don't you fucking dare."

"A lot of guys don't mind being called 'daddy.' Now that I've done it once I'm sure I can do it with—"

In a heartbeat Ty had crossed the floor and before he could stop, think or consider, he was kissing her, his lips fusing with hers, his tongue sliding into her mouth. It was like sucking on a sugar cube, the sweetness so pleasurable, every taste demanded the need for more. She held back from him, not out of uncertainty, Ty knew, but because she was mad at him for denying her. He kissed her harder, waiting for the moment when she'd stop bratting and give over control. Her tongue was cool against his own, her skull as delicate as blown glass beneath his hands. When she moaned and pressed her body against his, Ty pulled away, clutching a fistful of her hair the way he had in his bed. "You think that skinny motherfucker out there can do that to you, Middleton?"

She was breathing hard, her nipples points against his chest. "No, no one could, no one has..."

Her voice was so needful Ty couldn't help but kiss her again, shoving his knees between hers and spreading her thighs wide so he could step between them. It was manic the way their bodies moved, years of desire focused into a single moment of mouths and hands and needy bodies pressing together.

"You're a Catholic, aren't you?" Ty asked, remembering the rosary beads Stormy had once teased her about carrying.

She nodded and he put his mouth right beside the pretty pink shell of her ear. "If I fuck you, you'll think all your prayers have been answered. I'll make you see god, Middleton. I'll make you think I *am* god."

He kissed her again and this time she was feral, biting and writhing against him. "Daddy, do it to me, please?"

"You don't give me orders, sweetheart. That's not one single part of how this works."

"But—"

Ty slid his hands down to massage her breasts. Desire was slicing through him like a jagged blade, he was losing all control and yet couldn't bring himself to give a fuck. "I'll tell you something for free, little girl; you're lucky we didn't fuck last night. If we fucked, I'd be the last man you ever called Daddy. You'd have to find a new fantasy to play around with because I'd own that one. Understood?"

"Yes." Middleton's eyes were closed, her pale lips flushed with blood. "Yes."

Ty pressed his cock deeper between her legs, making her feel every inch of what she'd never had. "Say it. Tell me what I am."

She moaned it, his favourite, most hated word.

"What do you want?" he asked, but he already knew.

"Please let me finish."

Against so much of his better judgment, Ty found his hands sliding down her body, undoing the top button on her jeans and pulling down her zipper. She shivered as though he was already two fingers deep in her. "Please, please Daddy, finish it."

He tugged her fly wide to reveal pale pink bikini briefs. "Finish what, little girl?"

"My orgas—"

A thunderous round of applause made them both jump. Manning Turner's talk was over.

"Shit," Ty said at the same time Middleton said "Sugar!"

The moment was over, broken. They moved apart, Middleton zipping up her jeans, him adjusting his cock through his suit pants.

"You leave," Ty told her. "Go out and find the others and have afternoon tea."

"What about you?"

"I'll come out in five minutes. I'll say I was on the phone."

"Okay." Middleton paused in the act of adjusting her top. "Mr Henderson—"

"For fuck's sake. I came in your mouth—it's Ty."

And there it was, a crystalline moment in which Ty wanted to laugh, and he saw that Middleton wanted to laugh, but neither of them did. Instead they looked at one another, and just like in the GGS kitchen two years ago, Ty knew they were thinking the same thing, only this time it was—*what the hell have I gotten myself into?* Middleton leapt off the desk and ran toward the door. "I'm sorry," she said, opening it. "I'm really, really sorry.

4

"Alright girls, it's time to stretch!" Maria's voice echoed around the multi-purpose stadium as though she were a goddess speaking on high. There was a general grumble of dissent. No one liked stretching.

"No bitching," Maria snapped. "That means you, Gilly! Hit the floor!"

Kate dropped her ass onto the ground, thinking for the millionth time what a shitty derby coach she'd be. *"Oh, you guys just want to skate around for a bit, do some tackling drills then get ice cream? Go ahead! Please! Here's twenty bucks!"*

She winced as she tugged off her skates. She'd pushed herself hard today and there were gashes on her shins where the edge of her shoes had rubbed her raw. She was drained, her body flickering with rubbery muscle spasms, but despite that she wanted to keep skating. She wanted to skate and skate and skate until she dropped to the floor from exhaustion, unable to think another thing.

Does unrequited love change your biology? she wondered, trying to tease apart her triple knot laces. *Does it make your body work different from the way it did when you thought you stood a chance?*

She recalled, as she had a hundred thousand times, the way

Tyler Henderson had looked when he'd told her she was a nice girl, but it wouldn't be happening between them again. As always, she shuddered with embarrassment. If only she could go back in time and tell her past self not to worry about the meringue incident because one day she would accidentally give Tyler Henderson a blow job and it would make every humiliating thing she'd ever done look as insignificant as the earth from Pluto. Or just show up, slap her past self in the face, and say 'never suck anyone's penis again!'

Maria skated up to her side with a whoosh. The coach of the Barbie Trolls was an imposing woman; six feet tall with blue-black hair and arms covered in 1950s burlesque-inspired tattoos. When she played, her derby name was Frida Killho. Seeing as she was a gorgeous, bisexual, Mexican-born painter, it suited her down to the ground. "What's wrong, Katie?"

Kate forced a smile. Maria was a good friend and a great mentor, but two weeks had passed since Bendigo and she was still in no state to talk about Ty. "Nothing."

Maria looked utterly unconvinced. "Are you injured?"

"Just a bit sore."

"Your family? They're not bothering you again, are they?"

"They're fine, *everything* is fine."

Maria rolled her eyes. "Don't waste your breath, I know you too well. What about work?"

You're a nice girl and I enjoyed what we did, but it's not going to happen again. "Work's...fine."

Maria narrowed her espresso-dark eyes. "I see. A problem with work. Does this have anything to do with the text message you sent me at 2 a.m. when you were in Bendigo begging me to call you? And then when I called you, you attempted to pass it off as a drunken accident?"

"No," Kate said, trying to keep her voice even. "That was...about fondant."

"Fondant?"

"Yeah, for strawberry jewel cupcakes. I was thinking that I'd start preheating it in the microwave instead of using the double boiler method because—"

Maria pressed a gentle finger to Kate's mouth. It smelled, and tasted, like rosewater hand cream. "That's enough. After this you and I are getting a coffee."

"What about your kids?"

Maria made a noise that sounded like 'apishhh.' "Marco can watch them for another hour. We'll have a coffee and you can tell me all about what's bothering you, okay?"

"Okay," Kate agreed, ridiculously relieved. "That would be good, thanks."

Maria smiled. "It's what I'm here for my love, now come."

In the stretching circle, Kate's teammates discussed their plans for the weekend. General offers were made for people to join them at Goth yoga class, gastro bars, and in Rapunzel's case, a field in which some pretty decent mushrooms were growing. As always, Kate stayed quiet. She wanted to attend Goth yoga classes and drink peach blood cocktails and maybe find out if Ritalin and shrooms went well together, but the offers felt so generic. Non-specific. What if they didn't want her there? What if she showed up to these events and it was so uncomfortable she had to quit the team afterward?

Kate had joined derby hoping to find her girl gang, but the reality never jived with the fantasy *Whip It* had promised. Not that it was *Whip It's* fault. Women didn't like her, they never had. Not her mum, not her sisters, not any of the girls she'd gone to school with. They could smell the wrongness coming through her skin like garlic. She was an oddball. The kid your parents made you invite to your birthday party.

At twenty-two Kate had joined the Barbie Trolls hoping her therapised and thoroughly medicated brain would allow her to make friends. Unfortunately, her ability to talk to women was as stunted as ever. She was starting to think her isolation had never been about undiagnosed ADHD, that instead she'd had an invisible female-deterring symbol burned into her skin when she was a baby. Like the Mark of Cain, but for chicks.

At least I have Maria, she reminded herself. *One friend is better than none.*

After training, Maria steered Kate into the nearby Tom Thumb café. It was a cosy little one-room place with a wood fire and a dozen mismatched vintage armchairs. Kate sat down on a mint green sofa and stared at the twee latte paintings on the wall. They were all selling for upward of a thousand bucks. "Do you think anyone buys those?" she asked.

Maria settled herself in the candy-pink armchair across from her. "I don't care. Now, what's wrong? And if you tell me nothing I will be forced to spank you."

Kate blushed. Of all the humans walking the earth, Maria was the only one who knew the full extent of her secret kinkiness. She was the kind of person you wanted knowing that stuff, but Kate never quite got used to being teased about what she wanted in bed. She rummaged through her bag for a lip-balm, delaying the moment when she'd have to answer.

"Katie..."

She sighed. "This isn't like usual stuff. You're not going to like this."

Maria folded her arms across her ample chest. "Katie May, are you *selling* again?"

Kate dropped her lip-balm. "No! God no!"

Unless you counted Tyler Henderson trying to give her money for her bra as 'selling again,' but she hadn't taken it. She wondered briefly what he'd really done to her pink demi—set fire to it, probably.

Maria mimed wiping away terror sweat. "Well, that's a relief. So, tell me what's wrong."

"Afternoon ladies, what can I get you?"

Their waiter was gorgeous. He had soulful brown eyes and a smile that said he was intimately aware of his own hotness.

"I'll have a turmeric latte, thank you darling," Maria said with a flirtatious pucker of her lips. Kate had tried to replicate her pout in the mirror once. She'd looked like a sick duck. "Can I please have a capp—"

"She'll have a hot chocolate," Maria interrupted. "Too much coffee makes you anxious and you're already anxious enough."

"Okay, okay," Kate agreed, knowing it was easier not to argue. "Hot chocolate it is."

They both eyed the waiter as he walked away, his butt was almost but not quite as nice as Ty's.

"So, your work problem," Maria said. "Tell me what it is."

Maria and Ty had a lot in common, Kate realised. They were both sexy, charismatic and fond of short, bursting sentences in which they demanded you give them what they wanted. "I'm going through a weird thing with a guy."

Maria arched a sculpted brow. "Who?"

"I've..." Kate swallowed. "I've told you about him before. He's the hot guy I work with."

The brow rose even higher. "I was under the impression that man was your boss?"

"He's a manager but he's not my *boss*-boss. He didn't hire me."

"But as far as the chain of command goes?"

"Sort of?"

The curiosity in Maria's gaze vanished, snuffed out by a tidal wave of disapproval. "Katie, I know how you are about men in positions of authority, but please don't tell me something happened between you and this person?"

"I...um..."

The waiter swept a tray through the air between them. "Your drinks have arrived, ladies."

"Thank you," Maria said, but she didn't pout, didn't so much as take her eyes from Kate. The waiter seemed rather pissed about this. He unloaded their drinks very quickly and swanned off in the hot guy version of a huff.

"So," Maria said. "This boss of yours, he is giving you signs that he might be open to a sexual relationship?"

I wish. "No. It's worse than that."

"So speak."

"Do you promise not to judge me too harshly?"

"Katie," Maria sighed. "When have I ever done that?"

"I know, but this is different…"

"Enough." Maria pointed a liquid red fingernail at her. She was the kind of woman who always had her nails done, her hair done, her make-up picture perfect. She lived every day of her life as if she were heading to the Oscars. Kate could only boggle at her dedication. Pre-Ritalin, she'd frequently forgotten to put on socks, deodorant and underwear, post-Ritalin, she still had to lay out all her clothes the night before and use an alarm to ensure she brushed her hair and teeth.

"Talk, my love," Maria said. "Or I'll bench you for the next two weeks."

Kate resigned herself to the inevitable. "What do you remember me saying about Mr Henderson?"

Maria's crimson painted lip curled. "*Mr Henderson?*"

Kate ducked her head. "Please don't, he's scary. What do you remember me telling you?"

"That he's scary." Maria held up a hand. "He's scary, older, authoritarian, distant, handsome, tall, he commands the respect of everyone he encounters…" She ticked each reason off on her fingers. "Did I miss anything?"

He has a penis the size of a baseball bat?

Kate decided not to drop the news of her seeing and tasting said penis so dramatically into the conversation. If Maria spat turmeric latte all over her, the orange colour would never wash out. "No, you pretty much nailed it."

"How handsome is this man?" Maria's voice implied such an observation was scientific, able to be placed on a measurable continuum, like heat or your body fat percentage.

"Do you mean like on a scale of one a ten?"

"Yes. And number him objectively, not just because you want to sleep with him."

"Like a nine?" Kate lied. Tyler Henderson was a ten. Anyone who ever met him knew it.

"Hmm." Maria tapped her nails against her latte glass. "If you had to pick a celebrity he resembled...?"

"Maybe like, Michael Fassbender?"

"That's very impressive."

"You have no idea," Kate said, relieved she seemed to be getting it. "Mr Henderson should always be scowling at the ocean in a big white cable-knit jumper. He's so beautiful, and you know how hot guys can be all peacocky?"

Maria gestured to their waiter, who was staring at his reflection in the side of the coffee machine. "I do."

"He isn't like that, at all. He doesn't go around bragging, even though he's been promoted faster than anyone at work. And he's travelled to all these cool places all over the world. And he's done so many amazing things."

"Really?"

"Oh my gosh, yeah." Kate tucked her knees into her chest. "Did I tell you he used to be a metro firefighter?"

"You did not, no."

"Well he was! He only stopped because he got hurt saving a baby from a burning building. That sounds crazy, right? 'Saving a baby from a burning building.' It's like the universe wants him to be as manly as possible. He's probably also coached a winning football team and led a rag-tag gang of soldiers to freedom in a foreign country."

Kate laughed at her own joke then noticed Maria's indulgent smile and realised she was making a fool of herself. She untucked her knees and stared down at them, waiting for the burning in her cheeks to subside.

"So," Maria said with infinite gentleness. "You're infatuated with this firefighting, globe-trotting alpha male, or who you think this alpha male is, but now something has changed. What is it?"

"We..." Kate shook her head, still unable to believe it. "We hooked up. At the work conference in Bendigo."

Maria put down her turmeric latte.

"It wasn't like that," Kate said quickly. "I got a bit drunk on vodka raspberries and couldn't walk and he brought me back to his hotel room and geez this sounds bad—"

"Yes, it does."

"I really promise it wasn't like that! He put me on his couch, fully clothed, and when I woke up, I thought he was this other guy I'd been kissing at the pub—"

"You were kissing someone else at a pub?" Maria looked astonished, and with good reason. It had been over a year since Kate had kissed anyone, but she didn't want her mentor to get all caught up in that fact.

"Yes, only, it wasn't as promising as you want it to be. I wasn't that attracted to him, and he was like, twenty."

"I see." Maria's nostrils flared, reminding Kate of an angry horse. "So you left the pub with your—I'm going to go ahead and assume he's in his late thirties—boss, instead?"

Kate decided that like the size of his penis, Ty's age was another detail she could leave until much later in the conversation. "He's really not like that, it wasn't as sleazy as it sounds."

"Of course it wasn't." Maria's voice dripped sarcasm. "So he left you on his hotel couch and then...?"

This was the tricky part. "I, erm, got into bed with him thinking he was the other guy and then I..." Kate whispered the rest.

"Pardon?"

"I went down on him."

"You *sucked* your boss' *penis*?"

"Maria!" Kate hissed. "Don't say that—"

"*Me*, don't say that? *You*, don't say that! Please tell me this didn't actually happen?"

All around the café, people were starting to stare. Kate leaned toward her mentor. "It's all right, you don't have to yell. It was fun!"

"*Fun*?"

"Well, yeah... until I realised I was with him and not the twenty-year-old. Then I kind of freaked out, but not because I was upset!

More because I would have tried a lot harder if I'd known I was with Mr Henderson."

Maria pressed a hand to her forehead and muttered something in Spanish. Kate watched her, wishing she'd rehearsed what she was going to say ahead of time. Then again, it probably wouldn't have mattered. She probably could have hired a young Emilio Estevez to tell Maria she'd accidentally sucked Ty's penis and her mentor still would have been furious.

With a final spattering of what were probably curse words, Maria uncovered her face and shot Kate the kind of beleaguered look Dutchy gave her whenever she told him the bakery was out of custard tarts. "So what happened after you freaked out? What did *Mr Henderson* do?"

Threw me out of his room like old towels. "He...took me aside and said it couldn't happen again."

"Good," she said with visible relief. "That's very good. Wait, so then what is the problem? Why have you been so upset ever since?"

Kate wriggled nervously against the couch. "I...well..."

Her mentor's face grew stony again. "He's harassing you, isn't he? Trying to blackmail you into more blow jobs?"

Before Kate could answer, Maria reached for her Coach bag and pulled out her phone. "I know a barrister who works in sexual harassment," she told Kate as she tapped the screen. "Give me one week and I'll make sure—"

"Maria, you're not listening to me! Ty isn't the problem, I am!"

Maria paused, her phone still aloft. "What do you mean, *you* are the problem?"

"Ty is the one being all professional. *I'm* the one who keeps sexually harassing him. I'm the one who wants to give him more blow jobs. And other things."

The admission filled her with so much guilt she pressed her face into her hands. She'd known it was true, but knowing and saying it out loud in a packed café were two different things.

She felt cool fingers run through her hair. "Katie, I'm sorry for getting carried away. Don't be ashamed, just tell me what you've been doing?"

"It's so embarrassing..."

"Still, please talk to me?"

Kate tried to roll her eyes and realised it was impossible with her fingertips in her eye sockets. "It's so ridiculous, I've been asking him if he wants coffee and bringing him proofs for no reason and dressing sexy."

"Dressing sexy?"

Kate looked up from her fingers to see a supremely confused Maria. "I know," she said miserably. "I know it sounds stupid but I blew a month's pay on all these pencil skirts and high heels and boring silk tops and Ty didn't even notice. You know who did notice?"

"Who?"

"All the other engineers. And not in a good way. At first they were like 'do you have a job interview? What's with the dress?' and when I told them I was trying a new look some of them actually frowned at me. I tried to laugh it off, but they were seriously—and I know how this sounds—spooked by it."

When Kate bought her new clothes, she'd hoped she was buying a ticket to another life and she had; the life of a biblical leper. She had no idea why everyone at work was so offended by her wearing neutral colours, but they were. Yesterday, Collins, who Kate had barely even spoken to, eyed her burgundy shift dress and said, "I like your old look better."

"So did you stop?" Maria asked.

"No! I spent way too much money on clothes! But it's like the only time anyone at work can stand being around me is when I dress like a..." Kate struggled to think of a word.

"Cabbage patch doll?" Maria suggested. "One of the girls from that band Emmy likes, what is it called again?"

"High-Five," Kate said miserably. "Maybe, I'm just not sexy."

Maria scoffed. "That's not true and you know it. You present your-self a certain way on purpose. You want people to think you're girlish and sweet and helpless."

"I know," Kate said, looking at the floor. She'd discussed these things a hundred times, first with her therapist and then with Maria, but change required more than talking. It required years of unlearning fundamental behaviours, unravelling them the way you'd unravel a jumper knitted for an elephant. "I thought the sexy clothes would help with my overall human development."

Maria blew out a loud exasperated breath. "When you change, it should be because you want to, not because you're trying to attract your boss's attention. The other men in your office don't appreciate you climbing down from the good-girl pedestal they put you on. They didn't have to think about you as a sexual being and now they're having a hard time keeping their erections to themselves."

"Maria!" Kate said, aghast. "I'm not wearing G-strings and leather miniskirts, it's just regular office clothes."

"But you're not a regular office girl. How many times do I have to tell you how beautiful you are?"

Kate looked back down at the floor. It was such a cliché, the girl who couldn't take a compliment, but it wasn't as though she thought she was *ugly*, it was that she thought she was strange. Well, she didn't think it, she knew it. You only needed to look at her history to see it was true. No friends, no good family relationships, only one boyfriend who'd broken up with her when he found her little packets of Ritalin. *'So, this is why you're...'*

He couldn't finish the sentence, but he hadn't had to. Kate knew what he meant. *"So, this is why you're weird. Why you talk too fast and boil the kettle ten times without remembering to make tea. This is why you say you need to pee, then sit on the couch for another hour. This is why you're not like everyone else."*

Kate didn't think she was beautiful but she knew that even if she was as gorgeous as Maria, it wouldn't have mattered. Looks were only one part of the attraction/revulsion equation. You needed to be able to walk, talk and think like normal people. When someone looked at you they had to see themselves. She was too odd, too left of center. Her not-quite-rightness was ever-present in the flutter of her hands and the quiver of her voice. She learned to be sweet, because that was the easiest way to be dismissed but she never learned to be normal. She didn't know if that was something she *could* learn.

She reached for her untouched hot chocolate, wondering if that was the reason Tyler Henderson said it would never work between them. If he'd smelled the strange below the sweet and decided to make tracks.

"You know," Maria said loudly. "If you were a civil engineer in an office with more than one female, your colleagues' ridiculous attitudes would be much more diluted."

It was an argument she'd made many times before.

"I know," Kate told her. "But engineering is a tough field, and GGS gave me my first job. I owe them at least another year."

Maria made another irritable huffing noise. "So, has *Mr Henderson* noticed you at all?"

Kate didn't like the way she kept saying his name as though it was spelt 'Adolf Hitler' but she decided to let it go. "No, he hasn't. I thought that would discourage me but it just makes it worse. Today I went to the photocopier outside his office, bent over and pretended to 'fix it.'"

Maria gave her a thin-lipped smile. "Bad girl. Tell me something, during your encounter, did this man control you in the BDSM sense of the word? Could he tell you were a submissive?"

Kate hesitated. Maria was an out and proud sexual dominant with loads of connections to the Melbourne fetish scene. She ran workshops and hosted rope parties and believed some people were born wholly dominant or submissive, the way others were born gay or straight. Kate didn't know where she stood on that. She'd had submissive impulses ever since she was a little girl, but she wasn't sure if she wanted to make the word 'submissive' an integral part of her identity. There was a cloak and dagger aspect to the kink scene, an *'ordinary people will never understand us'* vibe that didn't appeal to her. At times it seemed more like a cult than a fun way to meet people and hopefully get your butt smacked. But she couldn't tell Maria that, it felt too much like a criticism of who she was and what she'd dedicated so much of her time to.

"Yeah, I think he could tell what I was. He was rough with me and I, um, called him 'daddy.'"

Maria stared at her for so long that Kate was glad of the noise of the café. It told her time hadn't stopped. "Is everything okay?"

"You called him Daddy?" Maria said, her face completely expressionless.

"Yeah, he, erm, liked it. I think he might be that way, too. And, another amazing thing, he almost made me, y'know, *finish*."

She expected Maria to look impressed, she of all people knew that was a personal win, but her friend only continued to stare blankly at her. "So he treated you as you imagine being treated in your fantasies?"

"Exactly. It was perfect. He was perfect."

"He's not. No man is."

Kate waited for her to elaborate, but she didn't. She merely tapped at her latte glass again, her features as frosty as a Melbourne morning. That didn't make sense. Maria had found her crying in the bathroom after her first derby practice, and instead of being disgusted that a grown woman was weeping next to the tampon machine, she'd pulled her into the best hug of Kate's life. From that day on they'd been friends. Maria had her over for dinner, took her to sex clubs and helped her set up an account on Kinkworld, a singles site for the sexually complex perverts of the world.

Kate had known she wouldn't like her hooking up with her boss, but she thought Maria would be pleased she'd almost come with another person and had been brave enough to try and make it happen again. Instead, she looked like Kate had told her she was stomping on cats for fun. After several tense minutes she made herself ask, "Are you mad at me?"

"Katie!" Maria took her hand and squeezed it tight. "Of course not. I'm sorry if I seem strange. I've had a long day."

Kate smiled, relieved there was an explanation. "That's okay. So, what do you think I should do?"

Maria let go of her hand and settled, businesslike, back into her chair. "These clothes you're wearing to work, the way you've been acting, you're trying to tempt *Mr Henderson* into touching you again, aren't you?"

Kate felt her cheeks burn. "Yeah, um, pretty much."

"I'm not surprised."

"Really?"

"We both know you've craved a man like this your entire life. Now that you've got one in your sights, there's no going back. What is your HR policy about workplace dating?"

Kate didn't even pretend she didn't know the answer. "There's nothing in my contract about having sexual relationships with your colleagues and nothing in the employee guidebook. I don't think there's ever been enough women at GGS for it to matter."

Maria made a noise somewhere between a huff and a snort. "So sleeping with him would just be frowned upon and bad for your career and reputation?"

"I know, trust me, I know," Kate said. "I've told myself all of this and worse, but it doesn't stop me from wanting him. I can't think of anything else. I feel like I'm going crazy."

"And you won't consider getting another job?"

Guilt squirmed in Kate's stomach like a particularly unhappy tapeworm. "No."

"Well, then there's only one choice. You need to stop this. Now. No more bending over or sexy clothes unless you want to wear it because of how it makes you feel, understood?"

Kate nodded, feeling miserable. She'd been expecting this, but it didn't make hearing it any easier.

"If you want to begin a sexual relationship with this man," Maria continued. "You need to go to him as an adult, proposition him and then let him make up his mind."

If Maria had suggested she walk up to Ty and punch him square in the face, Kate wouldn't have been more surprised. As it was, she choked on her lukewarm hot chocolate. "Are you serious?"

"Yes. If I told you to stop trying to seduce Mr Henderson and let things go back to the way things were, would you do it?"

"Yes!"

"Really? Or would you continue dressing provocatively and bending over in front of this controlling, authoritative man until he snaps and fucks you on his office floor?"

God, even the mere suggestion made Kate feel like someone had turned on a washing machine in her lower abdomen. "Probably that second thing."

Maria smiled icily as she folded one long leg over another. "Sexual attraction is one of the most powerful forces on earth. Your body will keep trying to get you into his bed and if you're not careful, it could do a lot of unnecessary damage. You need to take your attraction out of your office and into one of your homes, or better yet, a hotel."

Kate pictured herself checking into a hotel with Ty, smiling knowingly at one another before slipping into a locked room to do unspeakable things. The image had a glossy, surreal quality, as though she were imagining herself sleeping with an Oscar award winning celebrity.

"So, how do I approach him?"

"You said he likes what you like; is he on the scene?"

Kate imagined the look on Ty's face if he was made to attend one of the campy fake-slave auctions Maria took her to. "I don't think so."

"Is he the kind of man who thinks such things are silly?"

"Very much so."

Maria huffed. "Is he on one of those dating apps? Tinder or Blumble?"

"Bumble," Kate corrected. "No, I heard him tell a guy that dating apps are too much work."

"Lord, well then it'll have to be your workplace."

Kate began to process and discard ways of approaching him at work. Email? Too risky. Wait in the car-park? Creepy. Telegram? No idea how they worked. Trick him into going to a meeting in which she was the only other attendee? Also creepy.

It was only when she heard Maria say her name that she realised she was zoning out.

"I'm sorry, what was that?"

"Oh, Katie." Maria checked her gold Cassio watch. "It's getting late, how about you come back to my place for dinner?"

Kate hesitated. She'd been looking forward to going home, having a long hot bath and watching the football, but Maria had taken the time to talk to her she'd feel so rude if she just bailed. "Okay, sounds good."

Maria paid for their drinks, swatting away Kate's proffered twenty dollars and they left the café. It had been twilight when they entered the café, but it was pitch black now. They walked toward Maria's BMW and Kate was suddenly glad she'd accepted the offer of dinner; it would be warm at Maria's place and whatever her husband whipped up it would be better than what she had lurking in her fridge. Baking aside, she wasn't a great cook.

As they reached her car, Maria turned to her, her mouth tight as if she were tasting lemons. "How old is Mr Henderson, by the way?"

Oh dear. "He's forty…"

Maria raised her eyebrows. "Forty?"

"Forty…like…erm, five?"

A long stream of Spanish swear words filled the frosty air.

5

Kate's hands were shaking. Beneath her desk, her patent leather shoes were tap-tap-tapping on the floor. *Breathe,* she told herself. *Just breathe. You're ready, you can do this.*

It was a quarter to six. She'd deliberately stayed back an hour working on her monthly status reports because hell, why not try to look like a champion employee before you tried to convince your boss to have sex with you?

The entire floor was quieter than Kate had ever heard it. There was no music, no laughter, no vacuum cleaners humming. All the staff, down to the cleaners, had punched out. Not Mr Henderson, though. Ty was notoriously one of the last people out of the building at night, the one who set the alarms. Kate wasn't sure why, but working late meant he was allowed to take alternate Fridays off. She'd heard he rode his motorbike down to the Mornington Peninsula to spend the long weekend soaking in hot springs and having sex with a load of glossy MILFs. She wasn't sure if she believed that, though. The guys she worked with tended to talk about Ty as though he were James Bond, a larger than life character living a sexy narrative that they, with their paunches and bald spots, could only imagine.

Sure, judge your colleagues for eroticizing the life of Tyler Henderson, that's fair.

Kate's palms had begun to sweat. She groaned and rubbed them along her skirt. It was an old one, calf-length and covered in a pattern of bananas and monkeys. She'd paired it with one of her new water-silk blouses in the hopes of looking whimsically sexy.

Despite her promise to Maria she hadn't fully reverted back to her old style of dressing. It wasn't to flirt—the consensus among her colleagues was still *'your clothes have changed and so have you, man'*—she wore the new things because she felt different when she had silk against her skin. Sexier. More confident.

Her phone buzzed on her desk. She picked it up and saw a text from Maria.

Good luck Katie, try to be brief and call me as soon as you're done xx

Kate sighed. If she screwed this up, the last thing she'd want to do was discuss it. Maybe she could switch her phone off and pretend it died. Although, knowing her luck, tonight would be the night someone stabbed her at the 307 tram stop and she wouldn't be able to call for help.

Worry about getting murdered later. You need to pump yourself up to tell your hot boss he should ignore all good sense and workplace ethics and sleep with you.

Her pep talk did nothing to improve her mood. Her palms were still sweating and white spots kept bursting behind her eyes. As she closed down her computer, she became sure she was going to faint. She had a harder time staying conscious than most people. Alcohol blackouts aside, she'd spent her childhood passing out from plain old fear: at scary movies, the baboon enclosure at the zoo, during her school performance of *The Wiz.* Doctors told her parents it was something she'd grow out of, but she'd still collapsed when her neighbour jumped out at her from behind a bin last year. She'd woken up to find herself in a puddle, surrounded by hot paramedics who thought she'd wet herself. That had been bad enough. If she collapsed in front of Ty, she was officially joining a nunnery. In Gstaad.

Of course *thinking* about collapsing in front of Ty only made her breathing shallow and turned her tongue into a piece of dry toast at the bottom of her mouth.

I can't do this. I'm like one of those fainting goats, only less cute. Ty's going to laugh in my face.

She'd taken her mid-morning Ritalin a little later than usual, hoping to extend its effects into the evening. It didn't seem to be working and taking another one wouldn't help. Ritalin wasn't the equivalent of a line of speed the way most people seemed to think it was. It didn't get her stoned, and it didn't pep her up, it just cleared away the static-y fuzz that blustered through her head, and made her motivated enough to see most tasks through to completion. Valium might have helped, but she didn't have any Valium.

She racked her mind for something, *anything* that could help snap her out of her panic. Her brain handed her bits of generic self-help advice and affirmations, blue light and calm visualizations. And then it landed on something new: Rapunzel.

Rapunzel was the Barbie Trolls' prize blocker and mushroom picker, a six-foot-three lesbian with a partially shaved head and three tongue piercings. She had a white-gold braid even longer than Kate's and was incredibly, almost unnaturally, self-assured. She also slapped herself in the face before derby bouts and advised the other players to do the same. "Not hard, mind," she said. "Just quick repetitive taps, like a boxer."

Kate had never seen any merit in hitting yourself but nothing else seemed to be working. She raised her hands to her face and tapped her cheeks a little. It did nothing but make her feel silly. Then, she heard Rapunzel's voice, deep and salted with the accent of her Manchurian childhood. *"That's pathetic. You really want to fuck this guy?"*

"God, yes," Kate said aloud.

"Then hit yourself harder. Your face isn't made out of post-it notes, you'll be fine."

Grimacing, she slapped herself harder, once, twice, three times. When she pulled her hands away, she was surprised to discover she actually felt calm. Her tongue was wet again and the white spots weren't popping behind her eyes anymore. Rapunzel's technique had worked. Kate reminded herself to thank her, then realised that would make her look insane.

There was less than five minutes until she was due to see Ty. Needing something to do with her hands, she pulled out the folded piece of paper she intended to give him.

It was a bit high school, but she'd decided a note was the best way to proposition him. She would walk into Ty's office, say hello, place the note on his desk and then leave. She would not linger saying things like 'obsessed with you,' 'can't stop thinking about you,' and 'would literally stab someone in a non-essential organ to hook up with you again, Mr Henderson. Please have sex with me, or I will die.'

The note was short, sweet and to the point; *I know you told me to forget what happened in your hotel room, but I can't. I want more. If you're interested, look up my profile on Kinkworld. My user name is @LolaJones.*

She felt silly even writing the word 'Kinkworld' to Ty, much less directing him to her profile, but it would explain everything so much better than she could. The alarm she'd set on her phone began to chime, soft bells increasing in volume. Kate turned it off and tucked her note into a tiny side pocket on her skirt. There it was perfectly positioned so she could pull it out and hand it smoothly to Ty, like a flight attendant giving a passenger a microwaved omelet.

"Now or never," she told herself. "It's now or never."

Kate knew exactly how many strides it took to get to Ty's office—two hundred and nine—but today there seemed to be half that. A quarter of that. She was near him in record time, hearing strains of what she knew was blues music came through his open doorway. Ty loved the blues. It was one of the many arbitrary, stalkerish things she knew about him. She felt the sickening lurch of dizziness and slapped herself as quietly as she could. Her vision immediately sharpened. Though she was sure Rapunzel never intended her pre-derby routine to be used this way, it was quite a discovery. Maybe Kate could make her some muffins and act like it wasn't a gift for teaching her how to control her wayward brain.

Kate straightened her lace headband and forced her legs to carry her into Ty's office. For a panicky moment she wondered why he wasn't there, then realised he was hidden by his huge computer monitor. The top of his blond head was visible, so was a big hand drumming the top of his cordless mouse. He gave no indication he'd heard her come in.

Kate opened her mouth then closed it, her heart fluttering against her ribs like a panicky hummingbird.

I can't do this, she thought and took a huge step backward.

"Middleton," Ty's computer said. "What are you doing?"

He didn't sound angry, just mildly inconvenienced, as though she were a door-to-door salesperson trying to sell him cleaning products. Kate swallowed. "I just..."

Her voice was a thing of ridicule, so girly and crackly it was embarrassing. She swallowed again, trying to wet her throat and sound more like a grown up and less like a Disney mouse. "I wanted to ask you something?"

"And that is?"

"I was wondering...I was thinking..."

"Yes?"

She let out a soft wheezy breath. Maria hadn't prepared her for this. Nothing had prepared her for this. The top of Ty's head was more intimidating than a gang of youths loitering around a train station at night. She couldn't just hand him a folded up note like they were in primary school. Why had she ever thought that was a good idea? As of now, her mission was over. She stared around Ty's office for something she could talk about instead. Desks? Lamps? A big swirly painting by some abstract artist Ty had probably had sex with? Then her gaze fell on the only thing in the room more disturbing than a sex-painting, a fancy crystal tumbler full of brown liquid. *Jackpot.* "I just wanted to say, you shouldn't be drinking at work. It's really unprofessional."

That got Ty to move out from behind his monitor. "*What?*"

Dear lord, what was wrong *with her?*

"Erm, nothing," Kate stammered. "Except...except you're not

supposed to drink at work. It's a violation of our HR policy, you know, like why we can't have beer at the Friday barbecue?"

Ty stared at her as though he'd never seen something quite so ridiculous in all his life and now that he had he needed time to process it. Despite her terror, Kate couldn't help noticing he'd had a haircut. The shorter style brought out the hard planes of his face to perfection and emphasised his eyes. For someone who could glare better than Clint Eastwood, they were a surprisingly warm shade of blue, like a favourite pair of jeans, faded and so comfy she could sleep in them.

"You came here," he said slowly. "To tell me off about drinking at work?"

"Erm, yeah," Kate said, figuring it was too late to back down now.

"I see." Ty raised his tumbler to his mouth and took a slow, deliberate swig.

That's just mean, Kate thought. "Okay, now that we've talked I should probably head home. See you tomorrow!"

Ty bared his teeth in something that definitely wasn't a smile. "Before you go, Middleton, I want you to tell me something."

"Yes?" she asked nervously.

"If you're so concerned with workplace practices, why is it every time I turn around, I'm looking at you bent over in a skirt so tight you couldn't slide a piece of paper between the fabric and your ass?"

Kate's legs got that watery I'm-going-to-collapse-underneath-you feeling. God, what was happening? She was supposed to slink in, drop the note on Ty's desk and slink away, leaving him with nothing but a great view of her butt and the uncontrollable urge to check out her Kinkworld profile. How in the hell had it come to this? "I don't... this isn't about me doing that to you. Not that I'm doing that to you, I'm not doing anything to you. Or anyone."

Ty sighed, picked up his tumbler and drained the whole thing before putting it down with a clunk. "Shut my door."

Kate stared at him. "Do you mean...with me on the other side of it?"

Another, even more cumbersome, sigh. "I mean, shut that door so that you and I are alone in the same fucking room and hurry up about it because I'm getting impatient."

Without thinking, Kate turned and shut the door. The latch clicked neatly into place, sealing her in a confined area with Tyler Henderson.

"Middleton." His voice was rough and smooth, smoke and raw honey. "Walk your ass over here."

Kate's body prickled all over and again she obeyed his words before her brain could even process them, taking small, neat steps towards him the way she had when she was the flower girl at her sister's wedding. The air between her and Ty seemed to surge with an energy that grew stronger with each forward pace. Music poured from his computer, mingling with the electric air, a woman with a throaty voice singing about the devil in a way that felt both prophetic and highly appropriate.

"So..." Tyler Henderson said, tugging his tie so the knot loosened around his neck. "Here we are again."

"And that's...where, exactly?"

"You know exactly where. Look at me."

She looked at him, or rather his chin, which was as far up as her line of vision could go.

"You came waltzing in here to ask me to turn you out," Ty said quietly. "The least you can do is look me in the eyes."

Kate inhaled, and with all her remaining strength, managed to meet his gaze.

Ty's irises weren't the colour of lived-in denim anymore, they were the bright blue of an electrical fire. As their eyes locked she felt a surge arc through her body, excitement so all-encompassing she could barely breathe. He was giving her a look no boss would give their employee unless they wanted a one-way ticket to sexual-harrassmentville. It said she'd been a bad girl and he wanted to punish her for it. Kate's nipples went stiff against her bra, dampness saturated the cotton between her legs. Ever since Bendigo she hadn't been able to get herself off and yet now, without Ty doing or saying anything, Kate knew she could have shoved her hands into her panties and been there inside a couple of strokes. It was black magic. Evil magic. "W-What now?" she asked.

"Now, we discuss why you're here." Ty reached beneath his desk and pulled out a bottle with red wax around the rim. He filled his tumbler slowly, as though he had all the time in the world. The thin trickle of liquid sounded as loud as a waterfall. A white spot burst in front of her eyes and if she could have gotten away with slapping herself, she would have.

Ty took a swig of what she assumed was whiskey, wincing slightly, as though it was a strong but necessary medicine. "So," he said again. "I tell you it's a bad idea for us to fuck each other and you decide a good way to respect that decision would be to wear fuck-me clothes to work and show me your ass at every given opportunity. Walk me through that reasoning, Middleton."

Kate said nothing. Heat was prickling all over her, as though her blood was trying to force its way through her skin like sweat.

"Gone shy, have you?" Ty asked. "You weren't nearly so shy when you bent over the printer without any panties on."

And she'd been silly enough to wonder if he'd noticed. She licked her upper lip. "I'm sorry."

"Oh yeah?" Ty put his hands behind his head and reclined in his chair. "I don't believe you. I think you enjoyed getting me all cranked up, knowing I couldn't do anything about it."

Kate could barely believe her ears. He'd given no indication, none, that he'd so much as noticed her new wardrobe, let alone that it had gotten him hot and bothered. "I promise I wasn't—"

"Don't play dumb."

Kate remembered they were alone, that the entire floor—maybe the whole building—was empty. Her heartbeat thumped inside her ears. "I'm not playing dumb, I don't know what you mean."

"So you didn't come here tonight to ask me to screw you? And you haven't been wearing sexy clothes to work because you want me to change my mind about the two of us and plant my dick between your legs?"

Kate opened her mouth, then closed it again.

Ty gave another world-weary sigh. "What am I gonna do with you, little girl?"

The words were uttered in the same dark tone men spoke in Kate's mind when they announced she was going to be spanked. She extended a foot backward.

"Don't move," Ty said calmly and she froze. "I—"

"Don't speak either."

She pulled her lower lip into her mouth, everything inside her was suddenly very still.

Ty tossed back his drink, reached under his desk for the bottle and refilled his tumbler. Dimly, Kate tried to memorise the shape, the colours on the label. She didn't like any hard liquor but rum, but she'd go to Dan Murphy's and buy a bottle just to taste the way he tasted right now.

Ty took another swallow from his tumbler and swiped a hand over his mouth. "You came here tonight looking to get your little off-limits pussy played with, is that right?"

"No, I—"

"Don't lie." Ty's blue eyes were hard as stone. "Don't lie to me and don't try and explain what I already know. Just answer the question."

Kate licked her lips again. She'd done this so many times in the past hour, they were starting to grow puffy. The lips between her legs felt exactly the same way only wetter. Her fear of disobeying him was melding into the excitement of knowing this was all in his hands, that he could use her as he wished, command her to do anything he wanted.

"Yes," she heard herself say. "I came here for that."

"I know." Ty tapped the rim of his tumbler in time with the music, *clink, clink, clink.* He was looking through her into nothingness, weighing something up in his mind. Kate wanted to argue her case but she just stood there, still and silent. Waiting.

Ty ran a hand through his hair, the gold strands falling like waves of wheat. "When you decided to experiment with clothes that get my dick hard, you know what you did, Middleton?"

Kate shook her head.

"You went from being the office sweetheart to the girl everyone pictures getting dressed in the morning. If I broke up one conversation about your legs, I did it a million times."

Kate inhaled. Surely that wasn't right? Not only had she not caught anyone perving but you'd think that response would have inspired some of the guys to be nice to her, not act like she was carrying blood-borne pathogens.

"Wasn't enjoyable," Ty said, unaware of her confusion. "Wasn't fun watching every other fucker in this office pant after you. I didn't appreciate it one bit. Don't appreciate much of anything you've done since I told you you weren't getting my cock. So here's what I'm thinking..."

He rapped a knuckle on the desk, the sound sharp as a starter's pistol. "Take off that ridiculous skirt, lie your ass across my lap and we'll see what I can teach you about obeying orders."

Silence. Except for the guitar music swelling from Ty's computer, Kate couldn't hear a thing. Not her own breathing, not her heartbeat, nothing. "Wouldn't we get in trouble?"

He shrugged. "*If* we got caught, but seeing as you've done everything but hire a skywriter to spell 'fuck me, Tyler Henderson' in the clouds, I assume you're willing to take that risk. Now lose the skirt and come lie on Daddy's lap."

The word was like an electric shock, a vibration zapping her cheeks to nipples to clit. Before she knew what was happening Kate's hands were moving, her fingers fumbling with the catch, her zipper unknitting itself. Ty's smile when he saw what lay beneath her monkeys and bananas skirt was almost gentle. "You little prick-tease."

Kate looked down at her frilly white panties, her knee length black socks and Mary Janes. It was a bit *evocative*. She was half proud of herself for anticipating that this might happen, half terrified of what was coming next.

"Middleton," Ty said. "Come and get spanked before I decide I'm better off tying you to my desk and doing things to you that'll make you wish you never had the guts to come here."

Kate flinched. It was as though he was reaching into her mind and pulling out one of her prized fantasies, the one where he fastened thick manacles around her wrists and chained her to his office chair. She would lay by his feet like a pet, naked and content, and when he needed sexual gratification, he'd yank down his fly and urge her mouth onto him. She would happily suck even if he was on the phone or dealing with a client, she would do it as though it was her only purpose because it was.

For a moment, the possibility of doing in it real life hung before her like a beautiful moon, then fear burned up her insides. The good-bad dichotomy of such fantasies couldn't be erased. It was aching desire with self-loathing forever snapping at its tail. It was hard having such dark wants, it would be even trickier to share them. Having a depraved sexual encounter with Ty was all she ever wanted, but she couldn't help thinking this wasn't the right time. He might be drunk or confused and there was no way of knowing if someone from work would find them...

Ty stood up, reacquainting her with how tall he was, how handsome and insanely intimidating. He pointed as his desk. "I'm done watching you quiver on my carpet like a scared rabbit. Bend over the desk right now."

Kate's ass cheeks tingled. "What are you going to do?"

"What I wanted to do the minute I met you. Get over here."

It was strange, that moment. As though after hours and hours of sensory panic, her body had to plunge for new responses. Kate looked at him, beautiful and terrifying and felt the calm of knowing exactly what to do. She took a deep breath. "Mr Henderson, I really want to play with you, but I can't right now. I came here because I wanted to give you something and until I do, I don't think we should, um, *get down to business.*"

Ty didn't look angry, but his face changed. Something previously opened, closed. "What did you want to give me?"

Kate bent over and pulled the little wad of paper from her discarded skirt. "This."

"You wrote me a note?"

"Er, yes."

Ty shook his head, a faint smile tugging at his lips. "Hand it over, then."

She strode toward him painfully aware of her bare thighs, the saturated material between her legs and placed the note on the edge of the desk.

"I should go," she said, wondering if it would look silly if she backed away while facing him so he wouldn't see her butt.

"Middleton," Ty's voice was slightly strained. "What the hell is going on?"

Kate licked her puffy lips for what felt like the millionth time. They were cracked now, she'd have to slather them with pawpaw cream once she was back at her desk. "I want you and I think you want me, but if we're going to do this we should do it properly, with rules and a safe word and a room that isn't where we work. That's why I wrote you the note."

Ty closed his eyes. "Go, then. I'll read your note and I'll tell you what I think."

Kate dutifully backed away. When she turned so her ass was exposed to him, Ty made a noise that might have come from a riled-up bull. "Are you trying to drive me out of my goddamn mind, Middleton?"

Something in his choice of words sparked a fire in her. She looked at him over her shoulder. "You know my name isn't Middleton."

"Then what am I supposed to call you?"

"That would depend on what we were doing, *Daddy*."

Knowing she would never in a million years think of a better exit line, she scooped up her skirt and slunk—actually goddamn *slunk*—her ass out of Tyler Henderson's office.

6

As he picked up the bottle he'd been absently pouring from, Ty realised it was damn near empty. He held it high as he trickled the last of it into his tumbler. It gleamed as it caught the light, like a butterscotch river.

He was drunk again. At work no fucking less. Although, if he was honest with himself—and you could be honest with yourself when you were drunk—he wasn't that surprised. When he'd walked through the front doors that morning, he'd already been thinking about the bottle in his desk, the big comfy couch in the staff kitchen, and the change of clothes he kept in his closet.

Ever since his fiancée left, Ty had been having solo slumber parties in his office once or twice a month. The cliché of the workaholic sleeping at his desk wasn't one he enjoyed, but fuck, some nights he just couldn't handle going home. He'd bought his place cheap when he was in his twenties, a moldering townhouse by the beach. He'd fixed it up while he slept in the kitchen, the only room that didn't leak. It had been his pride and joy, his sanctuary from the world. Then Veronica had moved in and he'd let her make her mark; paint the walls, buy new furniture, turn his downstairs study into a gym. Some nights it was too hard to come home and see her books still stacked on his shelf, eat at the Magnus Oakwood table she'd picked out, look at the breakfast nook she'd painted sorbet yellow even though he'd told her it looked like an alcoholic's piss. She'd laughed, when he said that, laughed and told him, '*You're an asshole, Tyler now come over here and kiss me.*'

GGS was only five minutes away from Ty's favourite Chinese place, and it had no memories of Veronica embedded in its walls. He could relax here in a way he couldn't relax at home. Gave him a shorter commute in the morning, as well. The only issue was the hangover he always had the next day. It wasn't the alcohol—although there was always plenty of that—it was the guilt, the voice in his head that said he was being a coward.

Just buy some fucking paint, he told himself. *Buy some paint and chuck out the fucking table.*

But that was hard and sleeping at the office was easy and easy had a way of presenting itself as the best option at the end of another long, miserable day. Tonight Ty had almost convinced himself to go home when the text had arrived from Georgie. As soon as he saw the row of scowling emojis, his stomach had shrunk to the size of a gumball. It was exactly the news he thought it would be.

Medusa had her baby, Georgie had written. *Pics are doing the rounds on social media if you want to avoid. Come over for dinner tonight, we can drink to Veronica's formerly sound vagina xxx*

Ty had laughed, but he didn't reply. He couldn't spend the night with Georgie and her husband talking about Veronica until he felt even more frustrated and pathetic. He also couldn't go home and look at that piss-nook. So, he'd waited until everyone had left for the night and started drinking.

He and Veronica had met at a rooftop party on New Year's Eve. Mutual friends had tried to set them up for months, and when he finally saw her Ty wished he'd agreed to it sooner. They ate oysters and drank champagne, he kissed her at midnight and fucked her at three in the morning. He'd had a good feeling about the year ahead.

Veronica's wild spontaneity had been a balm to the wounds that forced him to retire from firefighting. He had no time to be depressed when he was flying to Thailand or hiking to the tops of unknown mountains up north. Veronica had loved champagne, big parties and travel, he loved not talking about his problems and being anywhere besides home. They were a match. He remembered when she told him she loved him. They'd been in a tiny bar in Spain, her lips had been stained burgundy with Tempranillo.

"I love you, too," he'd said, and for the first time, no voice in the back of his head asked if he *really* meant it.

A few months later, Veronica moved in with him, mingling her record collection and coffee mugs with his. He'd been forty then and she'd been thirty-two, and they'd been so happy, so wrapped up in one another, they made all their friends sick with envy. Ty started saving up for a ring.

They were eighteen months in when Veronica asked, in an offhand voice, if he wanted to have kids. They'd been eating dim-sum in front of the TV, and she hadn't even turned to look at him. Lulled by the casual setting, Ty had told the truth far more bluntly than he usually would. "Nope."

Veronica laughed. "That simple, huh?"

"Yup. Never wanted 'em. Can't understand why people do, to be honest."

"Is it...do you think that's because you don't know any kids?"

Alarm bells had gone off then, the loud clanging ones that called the crew to attention in the fire house. Ty muted the TV. "Veronica, I have six nieces and nephews, and half our friends have kids. I *know* plenty of kids and I was joking before, I can understand the appeal. It's just not something I want."

"Why?"

Ty had scratched his head, trying to give himself time to phrase it right. "You know me, babe, I like sex and reading books on Sundays, going to lunch and ordering another bottle of wine just because you can. I want to see movies any night of the week and travel on a dime. Kids feel like they were specifically designed to stop me from doing what I like to do."

Panic welled in Veronica's ocean-green eyes. "You can travel and do fun things when you have kids!"

Ty had felt like the world was falling out from under his feet. All this time and he'd never asked. Why hadn't he asked? Why had he assumed she felt the way he did?

"Babe," he said as gently as possible. "No, you can't. Just ask my brothers, ask my parents, ask *any* parents. To be a good dad, I'd need to want it more than I want anything else and when I think about having a baby..." He shook his head as the usual claustrophobia rose up inside him, thick and full of cold mucus. "I know it's not for me."

"But...that can't be right." Veronica shook her head so fast her hair looked like a blonde cloud.

Ty took Veronica's hand. "I love you more than anything and we should have talked about this before now, but if you really want to be a mum, I don't know if what we have can work."

The panic Ty had seen on her face when he told her he didn't want kids was a sun shower compared to the monsoon that came after that. They'd talked for five hours, and by the end, Veronica promised she didn't want kids, either. They were loud and smelly and would make her pee when she laughed. She'd only been asking out of curiosity. A part of Ty had known she wasn't telling the truth, but then she'd opened her dressing gown and told him to kiss her and he'd fallen for the oldest trick in the book: distraction by way of tits.

In the following weeks, Ty could feel the issue pulsing under the surface of their relationship, like the yellowish pus inside a pimple. It came to a head in the cab ride home from her friend Deidre's birthday party. Veronica, drunk and on painkillers, had cried so loudly people in other cars kept turning around to look at them.

"Why won't you let me be a mum?" she wailed. "Everyone thinks we'd have the most beautiful babies."

"It doesn't matter what everyone thinks," Ty said through gritted teeth. "Please, can we talk about this at home?"

"You're a heartless bastard! You're unnatural! Passing along your genes is the point of nature!"

"So's dying of cancer but that didn't stop us from inventing chemo."

The cabbie had let out a small snort of laughter. It didn't help.

"Oh, you're so smart, aren't you, Tyler?" Veronica screamed. "So fucking clever. Well, you know what? Maybe *you* can decide not to have kids, but I can't be a woman and not have a baby!"

That had hit a personal nerve. One that made him forget his vow of five seconds ago, that he would be calm in the face of her anger.

"What about Georgie?" he bellowed. "You know she can't have kids. Does that mean she's not a woman? That she and Dave should just kill themselves because their lives are pointless?"

He shouldn't have brought up Georgie; his girlfriend had hated his best friend from the moment they met. Dropping her name in an argument was tantamount to glugging gasoline all over an open fire.

"Oh, perfect Georgie," Veronica screamed with predictable fury. "Of course you'd bring up perfect, perfect Georgie."

"Don't start that again. She's my friend, and she's—"

"Irrelevant! *I'm* not infertile, *you're* not infertile, we have a choice and do you know what I think? I think if you really loved me you'd want to have babies with me." Veronica slapped her palm against the cab window. "Let me out! I want to go back to the party!"

Though every single cell in his body longed to let her go, Ty convinced his drunk girlfriend to stay in the taxi. They drove home in a thundercloud of angry silence and as soon as the car hit their driveway, Veronica sprinted into the house.

Ty pulled out his wallet and the driver, a middle-aged Indian man, had turned to look at him.

"I was you once," he said. "Now I have four children. I love them, but believe me when I say, get a vasectomy."

That night, Ty slept on the couch. The next day he'd gotten as far as calling a doctor's office when Veronica came out of their bedroom wearing his old rugby jumper and a look of deepest remorse.

"I love you," she'd told him. "I love you more than I've ever loved anyone. I'm not going to give you up for some baby that'll just wreck my vagina. You're enough, Ty. You're more than enough."

And so they'd gotten engaged.

Six months later, when the date had been set, and the venue booked, Veronica started acting strange. She got edgy whenever he mentioned the wedding, worked late a lot and saw friends for coffee dates that lasted hours. Ty was apprehensive, but told himself she needed space. Maybe he felt guilty over the baby issue. Maybe he just didn't want to know what he already suspected to be true. It was Georgie who blew Veronica's secret wide open. She spent a week tailing her and discovered the 'friend' Veronica was having coffee with was Colin Boyle, another PR jockey at her firm. Turned out they weren't so much *having coffee* as they were *getting a hotel room in the middle of the day.*

"It's not physical," Veronica had sobbed when Ty confronted her. "Colin just understands my situation."

As it turned out, Colin Boyle, with his bovine face and chemically whitened teeth, wanted babies, too. Ty got his diamond back and within eight weeks, Veronica had another one. A better one. She was married nine months later in a beach side wedding just like the one they'd been planning. Their mutual friends all swore to him it was terrible.

"The oysters were off," Henry said. "And Colin's teeth looked like someone was shining a black light over a cum-stain. Good luck to them, I say. They deserve each other."

And perhaps they did. Once his initial betrayal burned away, Ty could admit he and Veronica were far from the perfect couple. She was good at PR, his ex-fiancée, and the outside had always looked more heartwarming than it ever felt. Still, Ty longed for the first few months of their relationship, not just because of the travel or the sex but because he'd been different back then, when he thought he'd met the woman he could love for the rest of his life. He missed that comfortable delusion and the man who had believed it. That man felt like a brother who'd moved overseas for work and never, ever called.

It had been hard, leaving the MFB but the death of his engagement had bled the last of his hope out of him. For six months he ate, drank and fucked more than he had when he was nineteen, until even debauchery felt monochrome. When that happened life itself became boring, a copy of a copy of a copy. The only new thing was his ever-increasing contempt for a perky civil engineer who wore floral headbands and baked blueberry cheesecake muffins.

Before Bendigo, his attraction to Middleton had been a somewhat safe bet. She was cute, but she didn't seem real to him. She was too preppy and one-dimensional and perfect. After Bendigo, it was harder to resist, but it felt good, like ignoring office birthday cake when you were trying to lose weight. It left him feeling righteous and smug, and people were starting to notice.

"You're seeing someone, aren't you?" Georgie had asked him over dumplings, pure hope sparkling in her eyes.

"My right hand," Ty told her. "My left when that gets old."

Georgie wrinkled her nose. "Overshare."

"You asked. And you shouldn't ask. You know I'm done with all that shit. I'm a bachelor for life now, like Batman."

"More like the Unabomber."

"Whatever. Point is, I'm single."

Georgie sighed. "Tyler, lie all you want. We both know you're a lame romantic at heart. If you're really not seeing anyone, please let me set you up with Millie."

Ty rolled his eyes. "Goddammit, no!"

"But she's an entomologist!" Georgie pleaded. "*And* she teaches Pilates in her spare time!"

She raised and lowered her eyebrows as though teaching Pilates was the single most erotic thing a woman could do. Ty poked her with his chopsticks. "No."

She prodded him back, leaving two small soy-sauce stains that looked like a colon. "Fine. Close the door on love if you must, but at least get some action. When you don't get laid you go all sad around the eyes."

She had a point. Not about his sad eyes, but about getting laid. As he'd sat drinking at his desk after work Ty decided it was high time he flew to Sydney to fuck the schoolteacher he met in a bar last year. He'd gotten as far as checking the flights and wondering if she'd wear a big pink jumper and let him call her 'Middleton' when the original —well not the original, but *a* Middleton—was standing in front of him, in clear defiance of his order to leave him alone. Her reason for being there was obvious and in that moment Ty's resistance had crumbled. Why go to Sydney when what he wanted more than anything was standing right in front of him.

Fuck it, he'd thought. *Let me rub that sweetness all over me. See if I can't make it seep in.*

But no sooner had he given in than she'd handed him a note like girls used to in Secondary School and vanished. Ty still hadn't opened it. He was scared of what he'd find written inside and half convinced it would be *'Do you like me y/n?'* A note. He offered to give her the sex they'd spent years craving and she'd given him a *note*.

As he finished the last of his whiskey, Ty found himself logging into Facebook. There was no need to search for the picture he wanted to see; with five hundred likes and ninety-two comments, it was right at the top of his feed. Most of Veronica's friends were in PR and, understandably, very into social media.

Ty held his phone close to his face, drinking in the image of Veronica and her baby. It had been Photoshopped, that was the first thing he noticed. His ex's skin was silky smooth, the tiny scar between her eyebrows nowhere to be found. The kid looked like every other Caucasian newborn Ty had ever seen, a reddish meatball with eyes. He squinted harder, confused by the fact that he felt nothing. He was looking at the woman he'd hoped to marry, and she was holding the son she'd had with another man, a son she'd pushed out of the body he'd once loved so thoroughly, and he felt...nothing. No pain, no sense that he should have been the one taking that picture, tilting the camera slightly to the right so Veronica's cheekbones would look better.

It's over. I didn't stop her from getting what she wanted, he thought. *Maybe now I can get what I want.*

He stood up and went to the bathroom for a piss. When he returned the first thing he saw was Middleton's note lying in the centre of his desk. He picked it up and opened it. To his relief the message was neither gushing, nor full of *Fatal Attraction*-style threats. She'd written that she wanted him and if he wanted her, too, he should look at her Kinkworld profile.

Ty had no idea what the hell Kinkworld was. It sounded like a porn website. Dimly, his alcohol-soaked brain wondered if Middleton was moonlighting as a porn star. He scowled, then realised he was being ridiculous. The woman could barely look at him. There was no chance she was getting paid to screw on camera.

Occam's Razor, Henderson. What's the logical conclusion here?

The logical conclusion was that she wanted to show him something embarrassing or sensitive. Maybe Kinkworld *was* a porn site, and she wanted to show him a video she liked. That would be a trip. Ty pulled his laptop out of his backpack and turned on his mobile phone hotspot. He'd had to fire employees for not restricting their porn habits to their goddamn phones where they belonged, he wasn't going down the same way.

His first glimpse of Kinkworld was a little disappointing. It wasn't a porn site but some kind of medieval-looking Facebook done up in black and purple. There was no search box where he could type in Middleton's pseudonym, only a banner that encouraged him to create an account so 'kinky people from all walks of life can get to know you and "get to KNOW you," wink-wink.'

Ty hesitated. He hated social media and only sheer force of necessity had forced him to get a Facebook account. But it looked like the only way to gain access to whatever Middleton wanted to show him was to create a profile. He decided to make one, reassuring himself that if he had to 'friend' her or answer any questionnaires or give over his credit card, he'd just quit his job and never speak to her again.

Creating an account only took a couple of seconds. He threw in a fake name, Brian Merchant, confirmed his email address and phone number, and he was there. Banners of naked women suspended in ropes greeted him and—joy of all joys—a search box appeared in the right-hand corner. He typed in @LolaJones.

Instantly the screen displayed a tiny thumbnail picture of a woman's torso. Fat purple letters asked, *is this who you were looking for?*

"Here's fucking hoping," Ty muttered.

He clicked on the picture and the screen redirected. What came up resembled a profile page on LinkedIn, only full of information that if publicly known would ensure you never got hired again. The thumbnail picture was bigger now; a woman in a high-waisted skirt patterned with daisies, her long brown hair arranged so it covered her breasts.

Middleton. Ty would have known it even if she'd not directed him here. She had a tiny beauty mark on her collarbone he recognised. He felt a hot pang of jealousy that she'd put a picture of it on the internet for anonymous perverts to ogle, then remembered he was one of those perverts and decided to get down to business. He skimmed her description as quickly as his drunk eyes would allow. It announced @LolaJones was straight, interested in casual and long term relationships and was twenty-five-years-old. Ty knew that already, but seeing the numbers was always a sock in the guts. He paused, trying to remember what he was doing when he was twenty-five. Living in a cockroach-infested share house in London, training to be a chef during the day, running wild through the city until dawn. Middleton was twenty-five and she was trying to have sex with him.

"You knew that already," Ty reminded himself. "Keep going."

He scrolled down and began to read the short bio below the description.

Hi, I'm Lola,

"Middleton," Ty muttered. "Your name is Middleton, Middleton."

I guess you could say I'm a girly girl.

"I do say that. Frequently."

I like romance and kisses, cupcakes and books where men carry women in the rain. You name something twee, and I probably own or like it. That being said, I'm also a young professional with a lot of socialist, tree hugging and feminist opinions and if you can't reconcile those two things, please don't contact me.

Ty blinked, surprised by her choice of language. He'd never heard Middleton refer to herself as a socialist or a feminist. Outwardly she looked like a woman who played into the helpless 'I can't see a spider without screaming' stereotype of femininity.

I'm interested in meeting new people, especially if they're sexy, sane and interested in spanking me. Check out the list of kinks at the bottom for more...

Abandoning the bio, Ty scrolled to the bottom. Middleton's kink list was extensive.

Spanking, lingerie, bondage, handcuffs, high heels (wearing), anal sex (curious about) and—

Ty's heart pounded against his rib cage.

—daddy-daughter role-play.

He blew out a breath and stared up at the ceiling of his office. Just reading those words made his blood pump faster. He wanted to message her on this bizarre sex-Facebook and tell her to meet him in the nearest motel. Tell her he was game for it all, every last kink and he could help her fuck her way through every fantasy she'd ever had. But that wasn't how he should play this. He'd already tried to seduce her tonight, and she ran. She was willing, but she wanted him to know more. Ty scrolled back up and kept reading her bio.

You might have noticed I didn't put baby girl, submissive, masochist or spanko next to my role. Not to sound whiny, but that's because I don't like those terms. My fantasies aren't just about pain, submitting or spanking and they're not about pretending to be a literal child. What I like is compli- cated, I think it will depend a lot on the man I'm with because so much of what I want involves giving way to what someone else wants.

"That," Ty said. "Can be arranged, Middleton."

When I imagine daddy-daughter play, I imagine entering a state of mind in which I'm entirely innocent and the man I'm with corrupts and disciplines me. To me, this is power play, not a desire to experience incest or genuine trauma. I'm NOT into the extreme aspects of age-play or daddy- daughter kink (infantilization, pacifiers, baby-talk, or nappies). I consider myself more of a submissive with a twist. So if you're looking for a chick to roll around in a crib, drink juice boxes and watch Peppa Pig, I ain't your girl. If you want to pretend I'm in need of tender loving care...or punish- ment, let's talk.

Lola.

Ps. If all your pictures are of inanimate objects/cartoons I'm going to assume you're a married weirdo.

Pps. No one wants to have a terrible threesome with you and your girl-friend. Hire a pro and quit hassling single girls. Life is hard enough for us already.

Ty found himself grinning at his laptop. He could hear Middleton's voice in this profile but it was so sharp and no-nonsense it was as though a tougher sister had taken the keyboard on her behalf. He understood then, what she wanted to show him. She wanted him to understand that she was ready and willing to be everything he wanted in a play partner. To know he wasn't actually corrupting her because she was already aware of, and exploring, her fantasies.

That rattled him, the idea that she'd discussed doing this with other men. Then he remembered the way she'd responded in his hotel bed, how she'd told him he was the first man she'd ever called daddy. She was still green. Maybe it made him a pig, but he was glad about that. He wanted to be her first, show her how good it could be.

And, what, prep her for the next man?

"Don't think about that," Ty muttered to himself. He re-read her profile. Everything she'd written resonated with him—especially the plea to not misinterpret what she wanted as a desire to live out trauma. She was far more eloquent than he'd ever been about the subject. Though she clearly wasn't totally comfortable with her desires, her profile didn't hint at any of the shame he'd carried around since puberty. Maybe it was easier for the masochists, Ty thought. Wanting pain and humiliation couldn't be fun but wanting to *cause* harm was downright fucking terrifying. It made you turn yourself inside out, looking for evidence that you were a scumbag, a sinner, a murderer-in-waiting.

It was that thought that stopped him from hitting the 'message' button. He scrolled upward to the banner he'd glanced at when he first logged in. Big purple letters said the website had eight million members.

Ty sat back in his chair. Eight million people? Eight million fucking people who knew they weren't alone. Eight million people free to date perverts who found their needs not only tolerable but hot? Jesus fucking Christ. When Ty was twenty-five, so much as hinting at his desires on a first date would have resulted in a face-full of wine and a suggestion he get sterilized. Now people were free to wave their freak-flags from the turrets of websites like these. Ty thought of all the young men like him, who instead of stashing niche pornography and staying virgins out of fear would grow up having interesting sex with girls who wanted what they had to give. His mouth was suddenly as sour as an old lemon.

If he'd been born twenty years later his whole life would have been different. He would have grown up regarding his kinks with Middleton's wary acceptance. He'd have spent his twenties and thirties dating like-minded women, maybe married a girl who regarded big purple bruises on her ass as nothing more traumatic than love bites. The realisation was a bitter pill to choke down on what had already been a fairly average Friday evening.

Ty closed his laptop, walked out to the staff kitchen, and got himself a glass of water. He drank it, trying to swill the acidity from his mouth. As he did, he caught sight of himself in the darkened window and was shocked as always by how old he looked. He gave his reflection a weary smile.

"It's over," he told himself. "You're the age you are and there's nothing you can do about it. You'll have to start now."

He returned to his laptop and scanned Middleton's profile one last time. He noticed she had multiple pictures linked to it. Clicking on them he saw they were sexy in a non-explicit way; Middleton in a flowy white dress, Middleton in one of those half t-shirts girls wore, then an image that almost stopped his heart: Middleton in a pair of denim cutoff shorts and roller skates.

"You bad little girl," Ty whispered. How many times had he imagined her in roller skates and the whole time she'd had this picture up on the internet where any Kinkworld asshole could see it? He scrolled down and began to read the comments. Some of them were pure idiocy: *'you're like a rai of sun5hine, wanto come to my palce and fck?'*

written by the cartoon avatars she'd requested not to contact her. Other comments were more troubling. Young men in expensive suits saying things like *'you're exquisite, I promise I can give you everything you're looking for and more. Inbox me.'*

Those comments made him seethe. How could a man claim to give Middleton everything she was looking for, let alone fucking *more*? They didn't know who she was. They hadn't met her, smelled her, watched her for two years imagining exactly how they'd make her beg for mercy before they made her come.

So do something about it, asshole.

Ty stared at the purple 'message' button, pressed it and began to type.

Middleton, you want to do this, these are my rules:

At work we don't talk, we don't have lunch, we don't so much as look at each other if it's not relevant to our jobs. In bed, you'll do whatever I want. You'll get a safe word and a chance to tell me your limits, and then every-thing else is in my hands. We'll go into specifics if you agree to what I've laid out. You've got twenty-four hours to respond or I'm deleting this account.

He wrote his name, swore, deleted it, and then signed off *'Your boss.'*

7

It had been a year since Kate had gone on a date. Not, she kept telling herself, that Ty coming over was a date. In truth it felt more like she'd hired an escort to show up at her door, screw her, then leave. At least she assumed that was what was going to go down. Ty's messages had been sparse, nothing but the barest bones of details.

I'll be at your apartment at 7 pm tomorrow. Be on your couch watching TV. Wear something girly, something you don't care about ruining. I read your limits, that's not a problem, none of those things interest me.

Kate had breathed a sigh of relief of that. She'd hated every second of typing 'blood play, needle play, scat, urine, weapons of any kind, fisting of any form, vomit and breath play' but it had been worth it to know he didn't want to put his hand in her butt and wee on her.

Pick a safe word and send it to me. You say that word, the show stops. You don't say it, I'm gonna take every little plea out on your ass.

Kate had sent him a safe word—"roses"—and proceeded to spend the next forty-eight hours alternating between hot flushes and cold sweats, barely able to eat and constantly checking the time. After work she'd cleaned her aunt's apartment, mopping the hardwood floors and wiping down every surface until it shone. This was followed by a freak out because the place looked and smelled like a hospital so she tried to mess it up a bit by burning candles and leaving used tea cups everywhere.

At 6 pm she showered, rubbed on cocoa butter, and put on her chosen outfit. It had taken her most of the night before to find something cute that didn't mind dying for the cause but she thought her final choice, a velvet leotard in dark plum and a pink skirt, was a good one. The colours brought out the golden tones in her skin and the material was worn enough that she didn't care if Ty tore them off her.

Ty had no opinions on hair or makeup, so she pulled her hair into a high ponytail, dabbed pressed powder on her cheeks, and painted her toenails rose-pink, waving her hair dryer over her feet so it would dry quicker. After a consideration of the temperature, and the crookedness of her pinkie toes, she threw on black knee high socks and Mary Janes. She re-did her ponytail into a loose plait which she slung over her shoulder. Usually, this kind of pedantic frippery would have taken her an hour, but she was so wound up she still had twenty minutes until Ty arrived.

She put on Patti Smith. She turned off Patti Smith and put on Beyoncé. She turned off Beyoncé and tried to listen to an audiobook on successful living. She turned the audiobook off. She forced herself to eat half a peanut butter sandwich then brushed her teeth again.

As she re-examined herself in the bathroom mirror, Kate thought she looked like a dorkus extraordinaire. She fiddled with her plait and tried not to think about how Dutchy once described Ty's ex-fiancée as 'Scarlett Johansson with better tits.'

She couldn't compete with that. The only celebrity she'd ever been compared to was Kate Middleton and no offence to the Duchess of Cambridge, but if men were offered a choice between her and Black Widow, everyone knew what the answer was going to be. She applied mascara and added a touch of gold eye shadow to her lids, and dark powder to her brows. She covered her waterline in white eyeliner and was just contemplating her hair curler when she forced herself to step away from the mirror. No amount of bathroom trickery was going to make her face look like Scarlett Johansson's face. She needed to stop before she went full Bette Midler in Hocus Pocus. Her phone beeped, telling her there were ten minutes until he arrived.

Her palms sweating freely, Kate unlocked her front door. For Ty's proposed role play to work, he needed to be able to let himself into her apartment. It wasn't a risky move. There was a security desk on the ground floor, and you needed a code to use the elevator. Still, knowing the door was unlocked made Kate feel unexpectedly vulnerable. She texted Maria to let her know Ty hadn't cancelled, and their sex date was going ahead.

Maria texted back right away. *Good luck, munchkin. Remember to use your safe word if you need to and take a bath afterward and call me. Enjoy this experience for what it is! xx*

"What is this experience?" Kate asked herself.

Unable to answer that question, she sat down on the couch and turned on her aunt's TV. Ty wanted to interrupt her while she was watching something, but as she flipped through shows, she was confronted with the one decision she hadn't analysed to death: what to watch. She didn't want anything that would distract her or ruin the mood, but as she scrolled Netflix all she could find were sexy Viking shows and period dramas. Nothing that fit the bill. Panicking slightly, she turned over to regular TV and on one of the secondary channels found a reality show about young Brits living together. Kate remembered versions of this show from when she was a teenager; it had no plot aside from the sexy cast members getting drunk and talking crap about each other. It was perfect.

She lay on the couch with her feet dangling over the arm the way she had when she was a kid, and watched the cast prepare for "the most epic night out of all time, motherfuckers!" She felt a bit sad. When she'd been stuck at home with no friends and no partying prospects, this show had made her feel both better and worse. Tonight she let it take her back, let it make her feel small and helpless and young.

I'm home alone, she told herself. *I'm home alone and he'll be here soon.*

Ty hadn't given her a much of a role play backstory—in fact he'd barely given her an abstract, but Kate had fleshed out her character in the manic hours that passed since Ty said he was coming over. She was Katie, an only child living with her mother in the heart of Melbourne. Her parents were divorced, and she attended a hoity-toity grammar school. Last year, her mother had left her to go to Morocco with her friends and returned with a tan, a suitcase full of designer clothes, and a brand-new husband.

Katie didn't like him. He drank too much and was so big it felt like he was in every room of their apartment at once. She didn't think he was *that* handsome, but all her mother's friends raved about him. He was—Kate decided after some consideration—a lawyer, a big shot lawyer with a rakish smile and fancy suits. She'd seen him in a towel once and been shocked by the hard lines of his body, the hair that covered his chest. Thinking about it made her feel odd, all tingly and heavy in her belly. Sometimes she felt like he knew that. He had a habit of smirking at her when they were alone, staring as though he could see all her secret thoughts. Katie wished he would leave. Just go away and leave her and her mother alone, but he never did.

As she rehashed her backstory, goosebumps broke out on Kate's skin. Ty had set the stage for this fantasy but it had everything she liked: corruption, violation and of course, a man she could call daddy. There was only one thing she wanted that Ty hadn't specified; after-care. The thought of being held by him was almost as erotic to her as the thought of sex, but it was very hard to type that out in purple letters on a Kinkworld correspondence. She'd decided to play the situation by ear. Maybe a post-sex Ty would cuddle her of his own accord? Who didn't like cuddles?

Kate crossed her legs, trying to dull the throbbing sensation between them. It felt like she had an extremely warm butterfly in her pants. Ever since she'd walked into Ty's office, excitement had made a hormonal teenager of her. She was changing her underwear three times a day and still feared strangers and dogs would smell her increased arousal and know what a skank she was.

"*Mary, I swear to fookin Christ I'm gonna fookin hurl!*"

Kate refocused on the TV to find one of the girls puking violently onto a street corner. She wrinkled her nose. Maybe this show wasn't the best backdrop for her first encounter with Ty, but the thought of finding another one this late in the game filled her with panic. She needed time to smooth the fabrication-life over reality like laminate paper, to do it so perfectly you couldn't see the bubbles.

Her phone beeped again, informing her it was seven in the evening and Ty would soon arrive. She exhaled, trying to control her panic. She wasn't afraid, but she felt emotionally naked, exposed to the bones of who and what she was. She pressed a finger between her teeth and bit down, willing the pain to keep her from passing out.

Minutes passed like hours as she watched the TV without seeing a thing. A few times she thought she heard footsteps, but it was only the beating of her frantic heart. She tried to calm herself with breathing exercises but when she well and truly heard someone striding toward her front door she yelped like an anxious Chihuahua. She had just enough time to arrange her features into some version of normalcy before her front door swung open and Tyler Henderson was inside Aunt Rhonda's apartment. She guessed he was wearing motorcycle boots. What else could make his tread so ominously heavy? There was the sound of a bag hitting the floor and a loud masculine groan, as though Ty was stretching his back.

"Katie?" he called out in his molten stone voice, and she shivered, wetness welling inside her folds. Hearing him speak inside these familiar walls was more exciting than she'd thought possible. If he left this would still be the most sexual she'd ever felt with another person.

"Erm, hi," she said, her voice hoarse from hours of silence.

Her pulse spiked as he strode toward her, his footsteps like hammer strikes. He was behind her, Kate could feel his eyes on her body, examining, inspecting. She chewed her knuckle, trying to keep her eyes on the TV where two of the British girls were pole-dancing in a bar.

"There you are." His voice was a low rumble, cultured and amused. "Have you had a good day?"

"It was okay," she said around her finger.

Ty made an impatient noise and, to her complete shock, strode off. She listened as his footsteps headed toward the kitchen, as though he'd been inside her aunt's apartment a million times. She heard the fridge door swing open and then the distinct twist-hiss of a beer bottle. Ty must have brought his own. She didn't have anything in her fridge but apple juice and milk.

"Where's your mother?" Ty called out.

Another shudder rippled through her. "She's working late."

That didn't seem like enough, so she added, "She said I can get Thai for dinner."

"Did she now?" There was a sound of a zipper being undone and material being hefted onto Aunt Rhonda's marble bench—Ty's motorcycle jacket, Kate was sure. "Did she say when she'd be back?" he asked.

Kate pictured her fake mother, so different from her real one, with long, carefully maintained hair and a high, botoxed forehead. "Not until late. She's having dinner with someone from work."

"Right." A shadow fell over her as he leaned across the back of the couch. "You didn't answer my question before. How was school?"

Kate's belly drew tight. It felt as though she were at the zoo and a tiger had paced toward the unbreakable glass. You were safe, but you couldn't tell that to the part of your brain that was screaming *Tiger! Tiger! It's gonna eat me!*

"Are you going to answer me?" Ty asked.

"I'm fine," Kate managed to squeak around her knuckle. "How are you?"

Ty chuckled, his shadow juddering across her body. "You're still scared of me, aren't you, Katie?"

Kate forced her finger out from between her teeth. "Why would I be scared of you? You're just some guy my mum married."

He laughed again, raising his shadow arm to take a drink from his shadow beer. "That's all I am, huh?"

"Yes." Her knuckle had returned to her mouth as though pulled by magnetic force.

"Katie." Ty's voice was soft. "I thought your mother talked to you about putting your fingers in your mouth when you talk. It gives people the wrong idea."

Blushing, she immediately removed it. "S-Sorry."

"That's okay." Ty's voice was edged with a severity that made Kate think she'd been right to pretend he was a lawyer. "Just try to understand what it does to men to see a pretty girl sucking on her fingers."

Fear and revulsion washed through her, even as more warm wetness soaked into the panel of her leotard. She half raised her hand to her mouth then lowered it again. Ty chuckled. "Good girl. Now, are you going to turn around and say hello?"

Kate inhaled, then rolled over to look at him. *Oh my gosh.*

She'd chosen a lawyer, but perhaps a biker would have been more appropriate. There was nothing refined about Ty's beauty tonight. His hard jaw was unshaven, his eyes lit with malicious need. It sharpened his handsome features, making them blunt and menacing. His black t-shirt displayed every muscle in his powerful chest. This man wasn't the handsome protector she'd unwittingly cast him as—he was a beast capable of bad deeds and brute force. Adrenaline spiked through her body, and though she'd wanted to say "hello," she found she couldn't say anything at all.

Ty smirked at her, revealing a pointy incisor. "I asked you a question before. Are you scared of me?"

He leaned closer and Kate wriggled back into the couch. Funny how just a few inches was the difference between respectful distance and an invasion of space. "No. I'm not scared of you."

It sounded like a lie.

"Good." Ty leaned down over her and kissed her on her cheek. The skin where his lips touched her burned. She could smell expensive cologne mingled with leather and sweat. Her whole body prickled with the delicious violation of it; a tender kiss from a man who was much, much too close.

"There," Ty said. "That wasn't so bad was it?"

Kate shook her head, resisting the urge to rub her now tingling cheek.

"Glad to hear it." Ty's gaze scraped over her chest. Kate wasn't wearing a bra, and her nipples were spiking up beneath the velvet. Her hands fluttered uncertainly again, wanting to cover her breasts or her mouth.

Ty's incisor flashed at her. "You know Katie, part of the reason your mum married me was because she wanted you to have a male role model. I was hoping you'd start thinking of me as your dad."

"You're not my dad," she whispered. Her voice was trembling. It was from excitement, not fear, but the effect was good. "You're my stepdad."

Ty leaned closer, his presence heavy as a tonne of bricks. "I'm more than that. You need men in your life, Katie. That's what I'm here for."

"I have men in my life. I hang out with boys at school."

"The key word there is boys. You don't know the first thing about men. What they like, what they want."

He was so close she could smell the hops on his breath, malty and pleasant. "That doesn't matter."

"Of course it does. Do you want to get married? Have a husband of your own?"

Kate's first instinct was to tell Ty 'no,' but she was pretty sure that was blocking. She'd done improv classes in secondary school; when someone threw up an idea, you were supposed to go along with it, not shut them down. "I guess so. When I'm older."

"Well then, you need to know what men like."

He walked around the couch, his large frame blocking her view of the TV. "Move up. Let me sit next to you."

She swung her feet onto the floor and sat up. Ty settled in beside her. His skin was very warm. Instinctively, Kate pulled her fuzzy peach-coloured blanket from the back of the couch and moved to wrap it around herself.

"Not so fast." Ty seized a corner and tugged it away from her. Their eyes met, and Kate was struck by how different he looked. Normally his expression was neutral, perhaps a little remote but not unkind. He was grinning now, but it only served to make him look downright *mean*. His gaze as it fell from her eyes to her lips to her breasts was cold, and Kate knew he was calculating how long it would take to get her out of her leotard.

You're a whiny little brat, his eyes said, *but I want to know what your cunt tastes like and I plan on finding out.*

Kate's belly tensed. She felt fear, but it wasn't true fear, it was like the lemon tartness that made a dessert even more delicious by contrast. "Wh-what?"

Ty's gaze fell lower, from her nipples to her lap. He smirked as though he could already taste the wet place between her legs. "Just looking at you."

Kate's cheeks grew hot. She looked around for a way to change the subject and her gaze fell on the beer bottle in his hand. "Mum doesn't like it when you drink during the week."

He laughed and held his bottle, dark green with a label she didn't recognise. "What your mother doesn't know won't hurt her. Do you want some?"

"I-I shouldn't. Thank you, though."

"You've never had a drink before, have you?"

"Yes," Kate protested, as vehemently as though he really thought this was true.

Ty's smile was a slow, sticky promise of corruption. "Glad to hear it. Now take this."

He handed her the almost-full beer and got to his feet. "That's yours. I'll get another one."

When he sat down again he had a fresh bottle dangling from his long fingers. He tapped it against hers. "Drink up, Katie, you could stand to relax."

His faded denim eyes told her something else. *Drink up because if you do, we'll have a secret and if we have one secret, we can have more.*

It was surreal how different his energy was tonight. This wasn't a man you respected and looked up to, this was a man you'd never leave alone with your girlfriend, who'd put his hand on your lower back during a group photo and then slide it down to your ass as the lens flared. It turned her on. It was shameful how much it turned her on, but there was genuine trepidation there, too. This man was a stranger, and such a compelling one she couldn't help but wonder if he was the real deal, if the detached ex-firefighter Ty Henderson was the sheep's clothing and this man, the wolf inside. Her fantasies were twisted, sure, but she heaped all the pain and humiliation on herself. What kind of man wanted to pretend to hurt women, what kind of man—

Enough, Kate told her panicking brain. *Ty pretending to be this guy is no weirder than me pretending to be this girl. I'm not a freaking teenager, I'm twenty-five, and I'm not being groomed by my sexually depraved step-dad. This is Tyler Henderson, a guy I work with. My real dad lives in Cape Otway and is probably eating a dinner of boiled potatoes and sausages right now. I want to have sex with him as much as I want an anvil soaked in the Ebola virus dropped on my head. This is a fantasy, our fantasy. It looks like he's in charge, but I gave limits and a safe word. I agreed to this. More than agreed to it, I helped build it because it turns me on.*

The realisation that she and Ty were two equals striving for the same goal was so wonderful Kate was galvanised into action. She took a sip of Ty's beer, shuddering at the bitter taste. "Urgh."

He chuckled. "You don't like it?"

"Not really."

"Just keep going. You'll get used to it." Ty laid his arm along the back of the couch, not quite around her, but close. He seemed to be growing larger by the second, as though he were feeding on her nerves. "So, you said you're friends with boys. You dating any of 'em?"

Kate took another sip of beer. Despite the taste, she was glad of it. Drinking gave her something to do with her hands. "Mum doesn't think I should date until I finish school."

"Seeing as your mother doesn't think you should drink until you've finished school, I'm surprised you care."

Kate felt her lip tremble and Ty laughed. "Don't worry sweetheart, I'm not going to sell you out. Like I said, what she doesn't know won't hurt her."

Kate smiled into her beer bottle. "Thanks."

"So, no boyfriends?"

She shook her head shyly.

"Why not? Don't you want to have sex?"

And that was the moment, the very instant the line was crossed. Ty's handsome stepfather had been inappropriate, but now their boat was slipping into deeper more devious waters. Kate turned away from him, letting her hair cover her face. "I, um, don't want to talk about that."

"Why not? Don't tell me you're having sex with guys who aren't your boyfriend?"

"No!" Kate said, at once. "I don't do stuff like that!"

Ty pressed his Kevlar-covered thigh against hers. "Are you sure? I know what boys are like and you wouldn't be the first pretty thing to get talked out of her underwear once she'd had a few drinks."

"I haven't done anything with anyone. I promise."

"Have you ever wanted to?" Ty's voice was soft as velvet in her ear.

"Um, I'm not sure..."

He laughed. "That means you have. You want to be careful about that. Some boys can tell when a girl wants to mess around. One of them might make it their mission to give you what you want."

"But I don't know what I want," she whispered.

Ty leaned closer, his eyes crackling with that electric blue fire. "Then he'll have to decide for you. Most good girls like that, it helps them feel like they're not doing anything wrong."

His gaze fell to her mouth and Kate's lips tingled in anticipation.

Kiss me, she thought. *Please kiss me.*

But Ty didn't lean in and kiss her. Instead, he turned to look at the TV. "What the fuck is this show?"

Katie stared at her TV and was horrified to see that four of the housemates were making out in groups of two. One of the guys had his hand down a curvy redhead's top.

"Oh god," the girl said in her clanging accent. "Ohh god, Danny that feels so nice. You're gonna get me off if you keep doing that."

Kate didn't have to feign embarrassment, her insides felt like they were curling into knots. Ty might not be her stepdad, but he was her boss, and this felt like they were watching porn together. She fumbled for the remote but Ty gripped her wrist, his fingers rough and slightly damp from his beer. "Leave it."

"Okay." Kate tried to tug her hand away but Ty held on for a second, as though to show her that he could. Then he let go, settling into the couch beside her once more.

For several long minutes they watched the show, which seemed trashier and sillier than Kate could ever remember it being. One girl made out with another for a vodka shot, a couple of the housemates had sex in the sauna. She was so mortified and aroused, she drank her entire beer just for something to do. Ty, on the other hand, seemed to be enjoying himself. He was certainly smirking like he was. "You ever go to parties like that?" he asked as one of the male housemates steered a couple of Formula One grid girls into his bedroom.

Kate shook her head.

"Shame. I thought you kids were all about running wild. You don't know what you're missing."

She glanced sideways at him. "Aren't you missing that too, now you're married?"

Ty shrugged. "Not always."

"What does that mean? Does that mean you sleep with other girls?"

"It means I'm a man and I do what I want to do because I want to do it."

Kate stared at him, her scoundrel of a fake stepfather. Her pussy was hurting, actually hurting with want. Why did she like that he was playing such an immoral jerk? Why did the idea of him betraying her fake mother feel so good? Ty took the empty beer bottle out of her hands and placed it on the coffee table. "You're not going to tell on me are you?" he asked.

"I should," she whispered. "If you're sleeping with other girls, that's wrong."

Ty's rakish smile grew wider. "I know it seems that way but things aren't always so black and white."

"What do you mean?"

Ty placed his arm on the back of the couch once more. "I mean that your mother works a lot. Most nights she gets home and she's too tired to be with me."

"You mean you get lonely?" Kate said, deliberately misunderstanding.

"Sometimes." Ty's hand slid down the back of the couch to rest lightly, as if by accident, on her shoulder. "But you're here with me now, aren't you? Keeping me company?"

Kate nodded; the beer warm in her empty belly. She wasn't usually so tipsy after one drink, but lust and an empty stomach had knocked her ever so slightly off kilter. It was helpful. This way she could go deeper into the fantasy, leave behind the last traces of her chattering mind. It was high time this seduction gained traction. She turned to look at him, gaining immense satisfaction from the way his pupils dilated and his nostrils flared.

"Can I please have another beer?"

"Of course you can, sweetheart."

He fetched her another dark green bottle from the fridge and settled back at her side, wrapping a casual arm around her shoulder again. It felt good there, good and safe and warm. He smelled nice too, very manly and strong. Maybe Katie could understand why her mother's friends were always raving about him. Also, the show was much easier to watch with him now that she had beer to drink.

"Are you warm enough, sweetheart?"

Kate smiled. "Yes, thanks."

He tugged her closer, regardless. She was almost sitting in his lap now. It felt nice but it also felt a little wrong. Her mum was always harping at her to spend more time with her stepdad, but Katie had a feeling she wouldn't like this. "Are you hungry?" she asked. "Do you want me to order dinner?"

"Not just yet, sweetheart. I'm enjoying sitting here with you." Her stepfather's hand slid from her shoulder to her arm. "What's this top made of?"

"Velvet."

"It's nice," he said, stroking her delicately. "Very soft."

Another five minutes passed and his thumb began brushing ever so slightly against her breast. At first Kate tried to tell herself it was an accident, but as more and more of his hand began to rub her there, she knew he must be doing it on purpose. Her face grew hot, but the place between her legs grew hotter. She'd never known she had so many nerves beneath her skin or that even the places around her nipples could throb. She knew she should pull away, but it felt so nice. Besides, what would she say? He was her *stepdad* and he was probably just being friendly. It was probably better just to let him do it.

As Kate drifted deeper and deeper into the scene, she found herself drinking much faster than usual. When her second beer was empty her stepdad let go of her breast to take the bottle and place it beside her other empty. "You're getting a real taste for it now, aren't you?"

Kate nodded shyly, the nipple he'd been absently toying with was tight and hard and aching slightly. She wanted him to keep touching her there, but unsure of how to ask, she nuzzled into his side a little. "Thank you for the beer."

"Anytime. Want a little more?" Ty asked.

She pretended to hesitate. "Okay. If you don't mind."

"Oh I don't mind at all, sweetheart." Ty lifted his beer and placed it to her lips. Kate hesitated but then he began to lift the bottle and she had no choice but to tilt her head back and drink. He kept going for much longer than she would have, making her swallow what felt like half the beer. As she drank his gaze never moved from her mouth.

You'll suck me like that, his eyes said. *You'll drink me down just the same.*

He pulled the bottle away. "How do you feel, now?"

"Good, I guess." She wiped the wetness from her lips. "A bit funny."

"Funny how?"

"Just floaty and nice."

"I'm glad to hear that." He leaned in close and Kate noticed that like her, Ty had freckles spanning the bridge of his nose. Unlike her, they were so well camouflaged by his tan, you could barely see them. Yet, the fact that this big impressive man had anything as boyish as freckles made her giggle.

Ty stroked his nose over hers. "You're drunk aren't you, pretty girl?"

Kate giggled again. She was still far from drunk but she'd never been less capable of operating a car or heavy machinery. She was high on this fantasy, stoned on Ty's increasingly forthright touches and her own twisted arousal. "A little bit, yes."

"Good, it's about time you did something fun."

Ty's hand found her thigh and alighted itself there, gentle as a butterfly on a pumpkin leaf.

"Do you really think I'm pretty?" Kate asked, a little proud of herself for framing her insecurities the way a drunk teenager would.

"I do." Ty's hand slid a little higher up her thigh and then down again. Up and down. Up and down. "I think you're very pretty, but I bet you get told that all the time."

"Not really. That feels nice."

"I'm glad." He continued to stroke her leg. Not too quick or too hard, but her skirt was inching up, exposing more and more skin.

"Sweetheart," Ty said, in a conversational tone. "Are you a virgin?"

Does never having an orgasm with someone else count? "Yes," she said dreamily.

"That's good, that's very, very good." Ty's other hand had come into play, cupping her cheek and turning her so she was looking at him, or she would be if she had her eyes open. "Katie, have you ever been kissed before?"

She nodded.

"Did you like it?"

"Yes. I love kissing."

"That's good, baby," he murmured, and then his lips were on hers. This touch was as gentle as all the others, so soft and sweet she sighed, actually *sighed* like a girl in a pastel-coloured paperback. She kept waiting for him to turn rough, to unleash the frustration she'd felt humming inside him from the moment he entered her home. Yet the sweetness just went on and on. Dazed, Katie let him ease her down onto the leather couch and when he knelt between her legs and slowly lowered himself on top of her, she didn't protest. All she wanted was for him to never ever stop kissing her. And then she felt it, the long hot length of him pressing into her stomach and she 'realised' what he was doing.

"No," she said, tearing her lips from his. "We can't do this."

Ty's smile was hard as industrial diamonds. "Relax baby. We're just playing, that's all."

"But—"

He nipped at her lower lip, just hard enough so that she knew it was punishment. "No more talking. Just relax and let Daddy take care of you, the way you were before."

A hot throb ran through her, made worse by the weight of him pressed against her center. All that pressure on such a delicate place. "You shouldn't be touching me like this."

"I know, sweetheart," Ty said, nuzzling at her neck. "But you're so pretty I can't help myself."

Kate smiled.

"That's my girl," he whispered. "Now lie back and let me kiss you again. That's all we'll do, I promise. Just kissing, nice and slow."

Good kisses had always made Kate's brain fog over and Tyler Henderson was an *artist*. By the time he slid his tongue into her mouth she'd barely noticed his hips were rocking against hers. By the time he started teasing her, alternating between deep and wet and light and soft, she barely noticed her hips were rocking back. When he kissed her from her collarbones to her ears, his stubble rasping over her skin, she barely noticed he had a hand inside her leotard and was playing with her braless tits. In fact, Kate was fairly certain she'd let him screw her without a condom, pull out and finish all over her legs if he just kept his lips so soft and sweet against hers. But that wasn't what happened. Ty's hand began tugging harder at her nipples, his hips *grinding* against hers like they were crushing wheat into flour with their pelvis bones.

"You're enjoying this, aren't you?" he asked, his voice coarse as sandpaper.

"No," Kate moaned trying to buck him off. "Y-You can't touch me like this!"

Ty rubbed her breasts, weighing each in his palm. "Seems I can. Seems you like it."

In his Kinkworld messages Ty suggested they start out slow and then he'd get rough.

I know you're not opposed to pain, he'd written. *How do you feel about pretending you don't want it?*

Forced seduction, they called it in BDSM land. Struggling until you couldn't struggle anymore. Kate agreed, smiling a little at the thought of resisting Ty, a man she'd so far resisted like a custard resisted a nail. It didn't seem funny now that he was bearing down on her, his hard cock pressed between her thighs, teasing her about how much she wanted it. It was scary and a little humiliating and insanely, insanely hot.

Ty's fingers pinched at her nipple, making her cry out. "That's it," he said. "Now lie still and don't piss me off."

Kate disobeyed, pushing hard against his shoulders.

"If that's how you want it, sweetheart." Ty brought what felt like all his body weight onto her, locking himself firmly between her legs. His cock was hard against her pussy and when he rolled his hips, everything lit up like a sparkler. Kate couldn't help it. She whimpered in a way that could only have indicated excitement.

Ty laughed. "You little liar, saying you don't want it while you rub up against me. I bet your little good girl pussy's throbbing, isn't it?"

"No," Kate lied, now so wet her thighs were slick. She pressed a palm to Ty's forehead, noting the softness of his hair even as she fought to free herself. "This is bad."

Ty shoved down the front of her leotard, exposing her breasts. "Yes, it is, sweetheart. And it feels good to be bad, so enjoy it."

Without warning, he bent forward and drew her right nipple into his mouth. Kate screamed. "No, please stop."

He released her, his gaze black with impatience. "Either you shut up and take it or everything will get ten times harder, understood?"

Kate nodded and he lowered his mouth to her nipple once more, moaning as his tongue traced her. He was as good at that as he was at kissing, sucking her first hard and then soft, laving and gently scraping his teeth over the swollen bud. It felt like she had a billion nerves inside that peak, all of them firing at once. Lubrication surged between her legs and she began to worry he'd think she'd wet herself.

The TV was still blaring but Kate wasn't absorbing a word. She hadn't needed a sex-friendly show, after all. The screen could have been playing a clip of impending Armageddon and she wouldn't have noticed. All her awareness was in her nipples, her cunt and the pulse, pulse, pulse of blood in her ears.

How long they stayed that way, Kate didn't know. Until she was soaking and shuddering with need and moaning so continuously it might have been her native tongue. It hurt to want him this much, to have her nipples sucked until they were crimson, to have her swollen labia crushed against Kevlar jeans, but it was a good pain, a sweet pain. Given a choice, she probably would have stayed there forever. But it wasn't her choice. Ty gave her right nipple an extra hard suck then released it with a *pop*. "I think it's time I got to work on your cherry, sweetheart."

Genuine fear rippled down Kate's spine, less because she was immersed in her character's fake virginity—more because she was finally, finally going to have sex with Tyler Henderson, an event she'd built up to such mythical proportions it felt like he was suggesting she leap of a cliff and fly.

"Please don't," she whispered.

"Sorry, baby I've gotta know what your pussy feels like, but don't worry..." Ty ran his tongue over her nipple, the sensation crude and somehow more obscene than him sucking them like they were peppermint candy. "...I'll be gentle."

"You can't do this to me! I'll...I'll tell my mum!"

Ty licked her other nipple, a slow leisurely stroke. "Tell her what?

Tell her you've been wet for your new daddy since the day I walked through the door?"

"I'm not! I haven't—"

"You think I haven't seen the way you look at me?" He dropped his mouth to her neck and began planting small, somehow mocking kisses on her sensitive skin. "You think I haven't noticed how you're always blushing and ducking out of whatever room I'm in? I bet you've spent hours rubbing yourself raw thinking about me."

Kate, who knew this to be true, felt a fresh surge of delicious humiliation. "I don't want to do it. I don't know *why* I do it."

Ty smirked down at her. "Don't worry, sweetheart, Daddy likes making your pussy tingle. He likes that you want him to kiss you like a prince in a storybook."

"No—"

"Yes," Ty whispered. "And it's okay. Daddy's happy to kiss you like that, but he'll fuck you like a dirty biker fucks a roadhouse whore, too."

Before she could protest, he'd cupped his hands around her breasts like circles, bent his head, and began to suck her with such force she cried out loud. A thick syrupy feeling cascaded from her breasts to her groin, and she found herself gripping Ty's shoulders, chanting *"oh god, oh god, oh god."*

She'd had a friend—well, more of an acquaintance— at uni who swore she could orgasm from nipples stuff alone. That news had made Kate feel very inadequate. She felt enough pressure to orgasm during sex without the added pressure of orgasming from having a mouth on her boobs and yet now, illogical as it sounded, she might actually achieve that impossible goal.

Ty is dry-humping me though, she thought in some foggy corner of her brain. *Maybe that's what Angie meant. Nipple stimulation* and *dry humping at the same time.*

One of Ty's hands was between her legs now, flirting with the lines of her leotard. One fingertip passed lightly over her velvet-covered cunt and she jolted as though she'd been electrocuted.

"That's it," Ty muttered. "Doesn't it feel nice, giving Daddy what he wants? First he'll make you come in your panties, then he'll see about fucking your tight little snatch."

Kate whimpered, her clit burning, her pussy clenching in on nothing. "Please, I don't want to do this."

"How many lies are you going to tell tonight?"

"I'm not—"

"You're soaking wet. I've never felt a pussy so wet in my life."

"But—"

"I've heard you hovering outside your mother's bedroom door at night, wishing I'd take care of you the same way I take care of her."

Kate pictured herself doing just that, how disgusting and messed up it would be. And yet the wrongness coursed through her blood like chemicals far more volatile than Ritalin, getting her higher than she'd ever been. "Ty. Please."

He bared his teeth. "My name's not Ty, little girl. Call me what I am."

Kate opened her mouth but the word wouldn't come out.

"Fine." Ty seized the waistband of her skirt. "Just remember you asked for this."

With that he tore the material from her body, the worn cloth barely protesting as it reduced itself to shreds. Though she'd been thoroughly warned, Kate couldn't help but moan her horror.

"Shut up." Ty balled up the cotton and threw it aside. "You could do with less fucking clothes."

Then he frowned, his fingers tracing the crushed velvet covering her stomach. "What's this?"

"A-a leotard?" Kate asked, a little confused.

"I thought it was a top," he said, sounding much more like her boss than her fake perv stepdad. "Girl clothes are so fucking wild."

His hand brushed over her navel and Kate squirmed uncontrollably.

"Oh, sorry!" he said, pulling his hand away. "I didn't mean to tickle you, sorry!"

The wide-eyed horror on his face was such a strange contrast to what they'd been doing, Kate couldn't help but giggle. "It's okay, you just surprised me."

Ty gave her a rueful smile. "I had no idea it was a one piece."

"I'm sorry, I should have chosen something more practical."

"No, I like it," he said quickly. "I just wish I'd known it was tugging on your pussy this whole time, if I'd known I could have done a lot more with it."

She flushed, very aware she was half-naked and lying beneath him. "I'm...you still could?"

"When you go red like that, it goes all the way down to your tits," Ty said conversationally. Then before she could die of mortification, added, "I wanna keep going. You?"

"Yes, please."

"Good." He bent down and kissed her again, fast and businesslike, an agreement between equals. It warmed some part of her that she hadn't known needed warming. She didn't have long to enjoy it, Ty seized a fistful of the material at her stomach and pulled it tight. The velvet constricted, drawing up between her legs, compressing her most sensitive tissues.

"Please, stop!"

Ty tugged the material, so it pulsed against her clit. "Call me 'Daddy' and I'll think about it."

Kate drew her lips into her mouth and bit them for good measure.

"Have it your way." He released her leotard and cupped her cunt in his palm. "I'm going to play with this now. Moan if you want to."

He shoved the soaked velvet aside and traced his fingers along the source of her wetness. He wasn't rough as she'd expected him to be, but the gentleness was more unnerving. "Wet," he said, gazing down at her. "Wet and red as a shiny new apple. What a little slut this virgin is turning out to be."

"I—"

Ty clapped his free hand over her mouth. "That's enough talk out of you, sweetheart."

With his gaze locked on hers, he began to slide first one, then two fingers into her damp pussy, easing her apart with exquisite slowness.

Kate gave a half-hearted attempt at closing her legs, but Ty only forced them wider with his knees. "No escape Katie, not until I've gotten what I want."

Kate let out a low frustrated whine, her insides were hot, and her vision was shimmering like a mirage. She'd been on edge for so long now, too long. Her orgasm was welling up inside her, tight and full and slippery. She needed more. "Get off me," she told him.

Ty didn't even answer, just curved his fingers in a way that made her scream with pleasure.

"You're an-an asshole!"

"Oh yeah?"

"You're making me do this."

"Maybe," he said in a measured voice. "But you knew what you were doing with your puffy lips and your long hair, teasing my cock day in and day out just because you could. You're getting exactly what you deserve."

Ty's fingers began to work faster, he was now so deep it was almost painful, almost and yet entirely not. As he rubbed inside her, Kate did something she did in almost all of her fantasies—she started to cry. That first burst of feeling was like an orgasm in and of itself, wet and clean and pure. For a moment she tried to contain the outpour, worried Ty would stop, then she remembered his promise that without her safe word, nothing would stop. Absurdly reassured, she let her tears fall freely.

"I'm sorry," she said, not knowing exactly why. "I'm so sorry."

Ty's face was even meaner than it had been before. "Not sorry enough. But you will be, now call me Daddy."

More tears ran down Kate's cheeks, and all she could think was that he was so good at this. So good, better than she'd ever hoped for. "No. I don't want to do this."

"Too bad, I intended to fuck you the minute I laid eyes on your jailbait ass. Call me Daddy, and it'll be our little secret. Don't, and I'll fuck you anyway, then I'll tell your mother all about it."

"No!"

"I will." Ty's breath was hot on the side of her face, his fingers massaging deep within her pussy. "I'll tell her that her cute little daughter got drunk and said she wanted to know what an orgasm felt like. She'll believe me, you know she will. Now say it."

"Do me," she sobbed. "I want you to do me."

"That's a good start, now the rest; who am I?"

Kate rolled her head from side to side, wanting to answer but unable to shape the word with her lips and tongue. "Please..."

"Say it."

Ty's fingers clamped down on her nipple and the jagged nail of pain was just what she needed to get it out. "Daddy!"

Ty's fingers tightened. "Who's daddy?"

"M-My daddy."

"That's my good girl." A grin, all the more sinister for being plastered on that beautiful, all-Australian face. He leaned back and pulled a condom from his pocket. Kate closed her eyes. They both knew the man he was pretending to be would have taken her bare, but since there was no chance of that, she pretended she couldn't hear the sound of latex rolling down his shaft, pretended he wouldn't take precautions to protect them both. Ty's cock rubbed her entrance. With her eyes closed, it felt as broad as a concrete bollard.

"You ready?"

"No."

"That's too fucking bad." Ty spat in his hand and slicked himself down. "Hold still."

Despite his cruel words, he didn't go fast. He moved gently, allowing her delicate folds to expand. She was so wet he slid in much easier than she'd have expected. Soon it was better than easy, it was... amazing. She hadn't been counting on that. Sex had often been uncomfortable for her, a primal but rarely pleasant experience. This was something else. There was the fantasy, but there was also the delicious satisfaction of being split open by Tyler Henderson, her gorgeous boss. She never wanted to believe that her feelings for him would make sex better—especially when her feelings were so lame and unwarranted—but she couldn't deny the fact when it was staring her in the face. Or entering her vagina. He was less than halfway inside her before she began arching her back trying to take him deeper. Ty chuckled and pressed a palm to her abdomen. "Easy, girl."

A few more slick pulses and he was there, fully seated within her.

"Oh yeah, that's nice," he groaned, thrusting deep. "Nice pussy."

He withdrew and plunged in once more, grunting like an animal. Kate squeezed her eyes shut. It felt raw but good, realistic. As she stretched to accommodate him, he picked up speed. One of his feet was planted on the floor so he could fuck into her more deeply. He was still fully clothed, still wearing his motorcycle boots.

"No," Kate moaned. "Please stop."

"I can't. This is what girls are for, sweetheart. This is what you're for." Ty pressed his thumb to her clit and began to rub slow, damp circles the way he had in his hotel bed in Bendigo. "I'm gonna make you come now, not because you'll like it, but because I want you to understand what a dirty little slut you are."

Kate's cunt throbbed. His touch was gorgeous, but it was his words bringing her closer than she'd ever been with a man in her life. She closed her eyes, trying to drown in the midnight blue moment. Her distorted leotard was cutting into her thighs, her chest, and her back like a beautiful straitjacket.

A slut's straitjacket, she thought deliriously. *Pinned down with all the good parts exposed.*

"That's it," Ty muttered. "You're clamping up now, you can't help it. Next time you won't fight me so hard, will you? You'll remember how good it felt to get fucked and you'll spread your whore legs as soon as you see me coming."

As Ty continued his stream of dirty talk, as he thrust and rubbed and played her body like the violin, Kate realised something awful—she couldn't come. She could feel her orgasm welling up like nectar, pooling hot and heavy in her middle but it refused to spill, refused to reach any kind of climax.

She began to rock her hips against Ty's, slow at first, then faster, so that he moved faster. Then they were fucking like animals, their bodies slapping hard against one another. Sweat budded on her forehead, the back of her neck, her underarms, and inside her thighs. It was so good, he was so big and talented, but she couldn't get there. She'd spent years wanting to sleep with Ty and now it was happening and he was so perfect and handsome and hung and fulfilling her wildest fantasies and she *still* couldn't come. She couldn't do it. If she ever could have done it with someone, it would have been with Ty, but she couldn't do it. She was broken. Tears burst from her eyes again, but this time they felt oily and unwelcome.

"Whoa! Easy, baby, easy." Ty's hips slowed and he cupped her jaw. "What's wrong?"

I was crying before, Kate thought. *How does he know this crying is different?*

"Middleton, talk to me."

"I'm fine," she said, rubbing her hands over her forehead and cheeks so he would think she was wiping off the sweat not the tears. "I want to keep going, can we keep going?"

"We'll keep going when you tell me what's wrong." Ty pressed his forehead against hers. "Was I too rough with you?"

"It's not that."

"Then what?"

She inhaled deeply. "I just...I can't finish. I keep getting close, but then I start thinking and the feeling goes away. I don't know what to do. I feel like I'm taking way too long and you'll get bored and..." She let her voice trail off, embarrassed.

Ty smiled, it was wide and warm—the nicest smile she'd ever seen him wear. "This isn't a problem; if you're close, you can get there. You need to relax."

"But—"

"But nothing, we've got all night. Trust me to do this for you."

He slid his hand between them, but he didn't rub her clit; he forked his fingers around her folds and pressed. Everything between his fingers plumped up, the feeling pleasurable, but less intense than direct stimulation.

"Feel nice?"

Kate closed her eyes. The midnight blue of her orgasm was back, swirling behind her eyelids like the painting in his office. "Yes."

"Good." Ty stroked in and out of her slowly. "You feel my cock?"

"It would be very hard not to."

He chuckled. "Just relax. Relax and feel me, feel what I'm doing to you. Don't think about me. I'm doing exactly what I want to be doing. Just concentrate on your body, on how I feel inside you."

"What if I take too long?"

"You won't. I could stay inside you all year and not get bored. Just take your time and come."

Kate smiled at the thought of having Ty's body against hers for three hundred and sixty-five days. Then she thought of something that might help. "Ty..."

He paused. "Yeah?"

"Can you kiss me?"

"Of course I fucking can." And he bent down and did just that.

Perhaps it did take hours for her to climb Orgasm Mountain again, Kate wasn't sure. She did what Ty asked, feeling him with her eyes closed, trying to think about nothing beyond the sensations in her body. Her pleasure began to throb in big rough spikes, but she didn't try to shove herself to the peak, she rose lazily, circling and circling until finally... "I'm close. I think I'm gonna..."

Ty's fingers drew tighter around her clit, compressing the bud so tightly she felt like it might burst. "Yeah, baby?"

"I think I'm gonna come."

"Good." He bent down and sank his teeth into her neck, his sweat-slick hips pumping hard and fast. "Come, Middleton, come on Daddy's big dick."

It was wrong, hearing her nickname and the word 'daddy' in the same sentence but it was wrong in the best of ways. She arched her back and climax rippled out from her in long, shimmering waves. He didn't stop, so it didn't stop; her orgasm hummed and throbbed through her like a living thing, and she scratched him and chewed her lip and screamed and screamed and screamed. She was no virgin but she thought *this is what sex is. Oh my god, this is what sex is.*

When she was utterly wrung out, her head spinning, Ty withdrew. "Okay?"

Kate gazed blearily up at him. "So good. So, so good. I came."

He grinned. "I got that. You up for a little more?"

She nodded, hoping he didn't want her to go on top. There was every chance she'd collapse into a pile of noodles. But Ty didn't want her to go on top, he turned her on her knees and slid into her from behind, his cock feeling newly enormous.

"Can't tell you how many times I've wanted to do this," he muttered, seizing her plait and winding it around his fist. "Can't tell you how many times I've thought about fucking your sugary little cunt 'til you screamed."

An orgasmic aftershock rippled through her, making her clench around his cock.

"You like that, huh? Well hold on, honey. This is gonna be rough."

Kate barely had time to dig her hands into the leather couch when he drove into her, setting a fast, almost brutal pace. It *was* rough, so rough that their bodies made loud clapping sounds and she had to scream just to relieve the pleasure blaring through her. She couldn't come from the sensation but it was dark and pleasurable and she didn't want it to end. Ty talked as he fucked her, filling her ears with the most wonderful filth, about how dirty and pretty and tight she was. Then his hand tightened in her hair and his thrusts became almost painful. "Fuck, baby, I'm comin', I'm comin' in your little cunt."

Baby, she thought. *That's nice.*

When he was done he didn't collapse onto her the way she'd thought he would. Instead, he withdrew, blowing out a loud exhalation as though they'd just completed a particularly vigorous workout. He smoothed a palm over her back. "How you feeling?"

"Good," Kate said, unsure if she meant it. She was feeling a lot of things and she couldn't seem to untangle one emotion from another.

"That's good. Where's the bathroom?"

"Down the hall and to your right."

"Thanks." He lumbered off without another word.

Kate didn't know what she was expecting, but not that. A little disoriented, she remained where she was for a minute, before realising that kneeling on her aunt's couch with her naughty bits hanging out wasn't improving matters. She stood and adjusted her leotard. It was much looser from Ty's ministrations but relatively intact. She walked to Aunt Rhonda's bar on jelly legs and poured herself a shot of Sailor Jerry. She hesitated, then grabbed another glass and filled that too. If Ty didn't want to stay for a drink, she could always have both. She'd probably need it.

8

Ty sat down on the edge of Middleton's bathtub and tried not to laugh like a crazy man. He'd spent years—decades—picturing scenarios like the one he'd just partaken in, and what he'd just done had eclipsed every fantasy. When he came, Middleton's silky plait wound around his fist, the word 'daddy' ringing in his ears, he felt like all the DNA in his body was being teased apart. He'd had, objectively speaking, a lot of sex, but he'd never had sex like that. Not even close. It was the difference between looking at a painting of a feast and sitting down at the table.

He met his gaze in the bathroom mirror. He looked strange; younger and kind of goofy, like a guy who'd just won his girlfriend the biggest stuffed gorilla at the carnival shooting range. He grinned at himself like an idiot until he felt self-conscious, but he still couldn't make his face go back to normal. He gave up, rubbing a palm over his still-elated expression. "Jesus, this fucking girl."

Middleton had been even more perfect than he'd imagined—both obliging and unwilling, sweet and so fucking filthy. Her nipples were the most sensitive things he'd ever had the pleasure of putting his mouth on, and that snatch? When she came, she'd clenched so tight around him, he'd thought he was going to pass out. Ty shook his head, stupidly proud of himself, then noticed something that made his smile fade. He'd sweated right through his t-shirt. There were damp circles under his pits and a triangle down his back like he'd just finished a spin class.

He probably should have taken his t-shirt off before they got down to it, but he hadn't wanted to show her his scars. They'd be too hard to explain and a complete fucking mood-killer.

And you don't want her to see them. Didn't want her to know she's fucking an old man with a Frankenstein back, did you, Big Daddy?

Ty scowled, his face returning to its usual state in the mirror. He shook his t-shirt in a weak attempt to dry out the sweat, then gave up. He showered before he'd come over, and he didn't smell too bad. All he needed to do was go back into the living room, kiss Middleton's cheek, thank her for the shag, and then clear off.

A little callous maybe, but it was up to him to set the tone for what this was and was not. This was not the start of a relationship; this was not even the start of a friendship. As far as Middleton was concerned, he was cock for hire, a daddy for rent. His job, now that he'd fucked her brains out, was to go home to his cold house and reminisce about the fact that he'd came so hard it had probably shaved a year off his life. Middleton could stay here and knit bobble hats or bake scones or whatever she did in her eerily opulent apartment.

He'd been surprised when she'd given him her Elizabeth Street address. Not a lot of twenty-somethings could afford an apartment in the inner-city unless their folks were the one percent kind of rich. Knowing what she got paid he'd assumed it must be a share house or a tiny one-bedroom flat where flushing the toilet made the walls shake. Before now, he'd dimly acknowledged this place was the furthest thing from a share house, but he'd been too focused on Middleton's pussy to do more than that. Now her housing situation seemed especially bizarre. Her apartment didn't contain a trace of her bubbly, children's TV show host persona. It looked like it belonged to an extremely wealthy hipster who had a particular fondness for nude Amazonians—judging from all the statues and oil paintings.

The place was huge with a newly renovated kitchen and an incredible view. It had to be worth a million bucks, maybe two, maybe three. How in the hell could Middleton afford to live here? Was she supplementing her income as an escort? A drug dealer? Did she live with roommates he'd yet to see any evidence of? He decided it wasn't any of his business, dried his hands on an Egyptian cotton towel, and headed back to the living room.

Middleton was still on her couch, watching that dopey reality TV show. As he got closer, he realised she wasn't actually watching the TV; her huge eyes were glazed, her expression dreamy. Seeing her looking so young and pretty and well fucked made him feel a little skeevy. It also made him feel a softer and an infinitely more uncomfortable emotion right in the center of his chest. He'd felt the same way when she'd looked up at him with tears in her eyes because she couldn't come. It made him want to wrap her up in a blanket—several blankets—and put her on a very high shelf where she could curl up, safe and warm like a sugar glider in its nest and go to sleep. Ty shook his head, wondering if his orgasm had melted an important part of his frontal lobe. "Middleton? I just wanted to—"

She turned to face him, and Ty froze right in the middle of telling her that the sex had been great, they should do it again and he was leaving. Her smile was sweet. Not her GGS 'I'm a good girl tra-la-la-la-la' smile, but soft like a newly opened rose.

"Are you okay?" Her voice was even throatier than usual.

Was he? Ty forced himself to respond. "Uh, yeah, what about you? How are you?"

"I'm cool." She gestured to a couple of shot glasses sitting on the coffee table filled with what looked like bourbon. "Want a drink?"

The thought of her filling up the glass for him gave him a floaty, sad feeling. Like when he saw dead Christmas trees piled in people's backyards.

"Yeah, sure. Thanks."

Middleton beamed as he picked up the glass and tossed the contents back like it was malaria pills. The liquor burned in his throat, and he realised it wasn't bourbon, but rum. Being from

Queensland, he was no stranger to the spirit, but this was unlike any rum he'd tasted before. It had a hot, almost fruity flavor. "What is that?"

"Sailor Jerry," Middleton said nervously. "Spiced rum. I thought... you don't like it?"

Ty put his shot glass down and tried not to pull a face. "S'alright. I'm not much of a rum drinker."

"Oh, sorry, I can get you a—"

"I'm all right."

There was a short silence.

"Um, okay then." Middleton picked up her shot glass and sipped neatly; her overlarge eyes making him think of Margaret Keane paintings—enchanting and a little spooky at the same time. He felt a sudden rush of guilt. She'd just given him the best lay of his life, the least he could do was stay for a drink and not be an asshole about it. "Mind if I have another beer? I brought a six-pack."

Middleton smiled. "Not at all."

He felt another powerful tug of that 'wrap her up and hide her somewhere safe' feeling, and walked toward her kitchen before he could do or say anything stupid. He returned to Middleton's enormous stainless steel fridge and freed another beer from its cardboard cage.

"What's that called?" she asked as he sat down beside her again.

"Pepperwood Ale."

"I've never heard of that." She was still hugging her knees. Ty's hand twitched as he imagined putting it on her shoulders, rubbing her soft, new-peach skin. He took a long pull from his beer. "Did you like the ones you drank?" he asked her.

"Not really."

Ty nodded at the empties on the coffee table. "You drank it quick enough before."

She went red. "That was because...you know...?"

"Because Daddy told you to," Ty said, grinning.

Middleton smiled back at him, her face alight with the same dumbfounded joy he'd seen in the mirror.

She felt it, too, the giddy joy of having the sex you'd spent your whole life dreaming about. Ty hovered on the point of telling her how amazing it had been, then decided against it. "So, this apartment...?"

A layer of sugar crystals settled over Middleton's smile like frost. "What about it?"

"It's not what I expected. Is it yours?"

Middleton took another small sip of rum. "It's my aunt's place."

"Shit." Ty turned around, half-expecting to see an older woman scowling at him from the doorway. "Is she, uh, out or something?"

"No, she died."

Fuck. "I'm sorry."

"It's okay." Middleton's eyes took on the slightly hollow quality of grief. "She had ovarian cancer."

Ty wondered what the hell he should do. He'd been good at this once, comforting people. He'd drunk beers with grieving fathers and held widows whose husbands succumbed to smoke inhalation. He'd thought it was easy, but that turned out to be pure arrogance. As soon as he had heartache of his own—an unwanted diamond in his bureau, motley burns across his back—gone was his ability to console other people. Now whenever he saw someone crying, all he wanted to do was leave the room. Still, Middleton hadn't raised the subject of her dead aunt, he had. Ty cleared his throat. "Was her death hard?"

"No, well, it was awful losing her, but we knew it was going to happen. She had enough time to say goodbye properly, and her friends hosted this weird, amazing funeral. It had fireworks and vodka shots and everything."

"Sounds interesting. So how'd you end up with this apartment?"

Ty had seen Middleton blush before but this was in a league of its own. She looked like someone had thrown boiling water on her face. "That's, erm, kind of a long story and you're probably going soon, right?"

It was the perfect out. All he had to do was agree, chug the rest of his beer and head out into the night. But the fact that she was nudging him out the door only made him more curious. "I've got nowhere to be. If you want to tell the story, I want to hear it."

"Okay, hang on a second."

She stood and walked off, returning with a cheerful red and yellow bottle of Sailor Jerry. She topped up her shot glass and downed the lot in one swallow. Ty watched her, fascinated. "Tricky subject?"

She nodded her eyes bright with rum.

"Should I be worried about you blacking out again?"

Middleton flinched. "No. I'm sorry, by the way. I'm so embarrassed I did that."

"Don't worry about it. Tell me about your aunt."

She cast the bottle a yearning look, then seemed to think better of it and sat down beside him.

"So it's the fifties," she said, holding up her hands as though she were framing the scene. "And my grandparents are Calvinists who hate everything, especially women and having fun."

Ty grinned. "Sure."

"My Aunt Rhonda is born and straight away they know she's different; she's loud and reckless and she never wants to wear clothes. She was also ugly, that's her word not mine, and she always said that when a girl's ugly, most people think she's pointless.'"

Ty found this statement depressingly accurate and didn't know what to say. He drank some more beer.

"Anyway, when Aunt Rhonda was sixteen, my grandparents tried to make her marry this guy whose farm bordered with theirs. He was gross and like, twice her ag—" Middleton glanced sideways at him, her expression mortified.

"It's fine," Ty said, amused. "I know you didn't fuck me because I have the adjoining farm. What did your aunt do?"

"Well, that's the cool part," she said, brightening. "She ran away to Melbourne and became a photographer. She was hired by *Rolling Stone,* and she spent like, the next thirty years travelling the world taking pictures. She never got married, never had kids, she just did whatever she wanted."

Ty stared at her. So Middleton thought it was impressive her aunt never settled down. He'd never imagined that was something she'd find impressive. Would she—

A danger sign flashed in front of his eyes. *Unstable line of inquiry. Avoid.* "When did your aunt buy this place?"

"In the eighties. It cost a mint even back then, but she never wanted to live anywhere else. Melbourne was her favourite city, the first place she ever lived on her own and all that."

Ty remembered his own escape to Melbourne. Stepping off the plane at eighteen and knowing with his first breath of chilly air, that this was a place where he could be happy. "Your aunt had good taste."

"She did. She was a hipster before that was even a thing." Middleton waved a hand toward the gleaming hardwood bar. "Every inch of this place is designed exactly the way she wanted it, sometimes I feel like I'm just squatting."

"So she left you this apartment?"

Middleton's smile hardened again. "I...kind of. That's the other bit of the story."

"You don't have to tell me."

"I will, just..." She glanced at the Sailor Jerry. "Could I maybe have another?"

"Go ahead."

Middleton poured herself another shot of rum and took a sip. "So, you know how I'm from a big family?"

"Youngest of nine, right?" Ty didn't like revealing he knew things about her, but coming from a family with that many kids was just one of those things everyone knew—like if a family had twins or a child in a wheelchair.

"Yeah, there's a lot of us. But then most of my brothers and sisters have kids and my parents have a lot of siblings, too. Aunt Rhonda died with seven brothers, fifty-nine nieces and nephews and twenty-three great nieces and nephews."

Ty whistled.

"Yeah. Our Christmases are *messed up*, but the problem was that when Aunt Rhonda died, all her brothers thought they were going to get so much stuff and then I was..."

Ty read the rest of the sentence in her darting eyes. "You were the only one she left anything to, weren't you?"

Middleton looked relieved. "Yeah."

Fucking hell. "I take it your family wasn't happy about that?"

"No. I thought they were nuts before, but I had no idea. Aunt Rhonda was the only person in our family who had any money and when she left it all to me..." She swallowed. "Everyone was very surprised."

"Why? Weren't you close?"

"Oh, we were so close! She saw a lot of herself in me because we both have..." Middleton cleared her throat. "We had a lot in common."

Ty watched her pick at the neck of her leotard. If he had to guess, he'd say what Middleton's unattractive free-spirit aunt and her dainty, soft-spoken niece had in common involved taking Ritalin, but that was so far from his business it was in another galaxy. "How old were you when you got this place?"

"Twenty-two, but I didn't move in until I was twenty-three. A few of my uncles..." She tugged hard on the edge of her leotard.

"Yeah?" Ty pressed.

"They contested the will," she said without looking up. "They said I didn't deserve the place and it should be split between all of them."

Ty frowned. "What did your parents do?"

"They contested the will, too," she said with a brave attempt at a smile.

"Fuck."

"Yeah, they were pretty mad at me, so were my brothers and sisters. I mean, I get it, they had no money and they thought they were going to get heaps from selling this place and then they didn't get any. I understand."

"Still, that's really shitty, Middleton, I'm sorry."

"It's okay," she said, picking at a small scratch in the couch. "Aunt Rhonda must have known it would happen. She put aside money to defend her will. Everyone's claims were dismissed, and I went from being a student with two pairs of shoes to owning this place."

It was a happy ending but there was no note of triumph in her voice. Ty watched as she pulled her knees into her chest and felt a hot burst of anger toward her mother and father. What kind of people begrudged their daughter the break of a lifetime? Money talked, he got that, but wasn't the point of being a parent to take pleasure in your kids' victories? Ty reached out to rub Middleton's arm, then pulled back as though she were an open flame. Some inner metronome told him if he held her now, it would fuck everything up. He grabbed the blanket on the back of the couch and wrapped it around her, tucking the material into her sides so that only her head remained uncovered.

There, he thought. *Much better.*

Middleton peered out at him from her blanket-y confines. "Erm, Mr Hender—Ty. Why am I wrapped in a blanket?"

"You were shivering. Anyway, I'm glad you got this place in the end."

Middleton smiled at him, painfully adorable in her swaddling. "Thanks. I hope you don't think I'm ungrateful. Getting this apartment changed my life. I could intern while I looked for a job instead of waitressing. It was probably the only reason I got hired at GGS."

Ty didn't want to talk about GGS in any way shape or form. He was almost done with his beer and knew he should think about leaving, but now that she was smiling again, all he wanted to do was kiss her. Whether it was a distraction or his body had just hit its peak recovery time, he could stand to get laid again.

Middleton caught his eye. "What's up?"

"Just thinking about what we did."

"Oh." She ducked her head. "I thought you might be mad at me."

"Why would you think that?"

"I don't know. You've got a very stern face."

He put a knee on the couch and leaned toward her. "Really?"

"Yes," she whispered. "It's intimidating."

"Do you like it?"

"I...maybe?" She looked away and just like that, they were playing again.

Ty moved closer, crowding her body with his own, much larger one. "Are you going to do what I want or do we have to perform the whole seduction song-and-dance, again?"

"Please," she said softly. "You said it would just be once."

"We both know I was lying." Ty tugged the blanket from her body and she cringed, covering her breasts with her arms.

"Uh-uh," he said, pulling them away. "Daddy needs a little something, sweetheart, and you want to make him happy, don't you?"

Her brown eyes narrowed. "You're not my—"

Ty kissed her, cutting her words off at the source. Her mouth was sweet with spiced rum, and he found he much preferred the flavour when he was sucking it from her lips. He also found more evidence that kissing was to Middleton what blow jobs were to him; she couldn't get enough. In a couple of minutes of kissing she was as squirmy as she'd been when his dick was planted firmly inside her. When she was good and needy, he asked if she wanted more and she said yes.

"You okay with rough again?" he said. "Nothing from before turned you off?"

"Not at all," she said with an eagerness that was as hot as it was endearing.

"What's your safe word?"

"Roses."

"Good girl." Ty kissed her, taking it deeper than he had before, glorying in the feel of her lithe body shuddering against his. His cock was hard as a railroad spike, slightly sore but more than willing to go again.

"Let's get something straight," he said when he came up for air. "When we play like this, you'll call me Daddy, understood?"

"Yes."

"Yes, what?"

She looked down at her hands. "Yes, Daddy."

"Good, because we're going to play like this a lot." Ty pulled her onto his lap, arranging her legs so she was straddling him. "I need pussy like most men need water and your new job is making sure I never get thirsty."

"Why don't you find someone else?"

Ty seized the front of her leotard with both hands. "Because other girls aren't half as sweet as you, baby and they don't live with me, either. Trawling bars takes time, and I'm not a patient man, now hold still."

He braced his hands and as he'd hoped, the material gave beneath his fingers, exposing her from tits to hips. She gasped and tried to cover herself, but he shoved her hands away and pressed his mouth to hers, all but forcing his tongue between her lips. She fought him, but within seconds she was moaning again. He played with her cunt through her leotard, rubbing her folds without giving any particular attention to her clit. In a few seconds she was panting and after a few minutes, her hands had tightened around the collar of his t-shirt.

"What's wrong, Katie?" He teased. "Getting turned on?"

She shook her head.

"Well, if that's the case...." He withdrew his hand and she whimpered. The neediness in her voice made him laugh. "Sorry, sweetheart, should have said yes when you had the chance. Now, get on your knees in front of me."

"But—"

Ty lifted her up and placed her on the floor in front of him, a tangle of smooth limbs and bare skin. He grabbed her now-battered plait and wound it around his hand in a way that made her eyes go wide. "Let me make something very clear, baby. I let you give me attitude when your mother's around, but you do that here and I'll spank your ass raw. I don't let little sluts talk back to me and when they do I find ways to occupy their mouths so I don't have to listen to it, understood?"

She nodded and Ty opened his jeans one-handed, and pulled out his cock. Middleton—god bless her—eyed it like she'd never seen one. "It's so big."

Ty grinned. He'd heard that before, but women telling you that you had a big dick was one of those things that never got old. "Ever sucked one?"

She shook her head, her eyes the size of planets.

"Then today's your lucky day. This is part of me showing you what men like. When I'm too tired to fuck, or you've got something to apologise for, you're gonna take me into your mouth and suck me, understood?"

She looked down at his feet. "Yes, Daddy."

She was nervous, he could tell. She'd done this to him before, but he imagined it was different in the dark, thinking it was Buddy's teenage cock she was sucking on. Ty picked up the bottle of rum she'd left on the coffee table and pulled the cork. He took a swig, then held it out. "Open wide, baby, it'll help you relax."

Middleton hesitated, then opened her mouth. He poured a little rum between her lips, and watched her visibly relax. It wasn't the alcohol, Ty knew, it was the order. She liked him exerting power over her, liked him being a prick. That was good, he was more than happy to be a prick. He took another swig from the bottle, then cupped the back of her head and pulled her face towards his lap. "Time for your lesson, sweetheart. Suck me."

"But I don't—"

"Just open your mouth and do it. And keep your goddamn teeth out of the way."

Middleton bent her head and began exploring him with suckling kisses and tentative licks. Ty groaned his satisfaction, slumping back into the couch so he could watch her lap clumsily at him. Considering how competent he knew that mouth to be, he appreciated all the more what a good little actress Middleton was.

He let the blowjob go on for much longer than he normally would, tugging her hair out of its loose plait and playing with it as she tongued him. He tried to memorise the way her mouth looked stretched over his cock, the way her eyes pleaded with him to take her again. She was horny, he could tell from the way she was rubbing her thighs together, but a little suspense never killed anyone and he was busy fulfilling a fantasy he'd had ever since he first laid eyes on her. He stopped meeting her gaze, instead he drank rum and pretended to be watching TV. Intense pleasure-pain glazed over her eyes whenever she caught him and she sucked harder, as though determined to earn his attention. She had a big old taste for humiliation, something Ty was more than willing to work with.

"You enjoying this?" he asked.

She moaned her 'no' onto his cock.

"Glad to hear it." He tugged her hair hard, pulling her mouth deeper onto him. "See, you've got a lot of making up to do for all the prick teasing you've put me through."

Her protest hummed down his shaft.

"It's true, sweetheart. If Daddy let you keep going until you paid off your debt, you'd be sucking his dick until the end of the year. Now blow me harder."

She made a garbled angry sound and he laughed. "Forget what I said before. You can talk all you want while you suck my cock. It feels good in my balls."

Her look of hungry mortification was so satisfying Ty barely wanted to come, but that was hardly fair to Middleton's jaw. After a few blissful seconds, he fisted her hair. "Time to get me off, sweetheart. Put your mouth around as much as you can and suck like you're getting paid for it."

She obliged, taking him deep into her mouth. Her delicate fingers wrapped around the base of his cock and began to gently tug.

"Harder," Ty grunted. "Jerk me harder and stick your ass out, so I've got something to look at besides this stupid fucking TV show."

She glowered at him, but the excitement in her bright brown eyes was evident. Ty tilted his hips towards her and prepared to finish when he realised he was wasting a golden opportunity. He loved blow jobs, but who knew how many times he would get to sleep with Middleton? He should be making the most of it. He pulled her hair. "That's enough."

Middleton released him, wiping a hand over her swollen lips. "Did I...? Was I bad at it?"

Ty had to fight the urge to smile. She really was a fucking dream come true. "No, baby, I wanna put it in you again."

"Okay." She bit her lip. "I, um, don't know if I can finish again."

"Why don't you let me decide that?" Ty tugged another condom from his pocket and patted his thighs. "Come sit up here."

Ty was glad she'd told him she was struggling to get off the first time. He'd paid a lot of attention to what worked and what didn't, and it paid off handsomely. A little licking here, a little grinding there and Middleton was shrieking like a madwoman, babbling a stream of compliments, disbelief and prayers to the lord above. By the end he was hardly doing anything, just watching her bounce up and down in his lap screaming his name. She should have been calling him Daddy, but he felt like he owed her a pass. He didn't know who the fuck she'd had sex with before now but it was clear they weren't worth a wank in a sports sock. She looked like she was tapping into another dimension.

"Does it always feel like that?" she asked, when she was done.

"With me, it will," he told her. "On your back."

He fucked her in missionary, her ankles up by his ears, her tight cunt spasming around him. "Know what you are?" he snarled.

"Yes."

"Say it out loud, bitch."

He'd never come as hard as he did when she whispered that she was a whore, *a dirty, filthy slut, Daddy, so do it harder, please do me harder.*

When they were done, Ty went to the bathroom and realised he was too drunk from all the blowjob rum to even think about riding his bike home. Middleton offered him a cup of tea, which he accepted. She brought it out along with a tray of homemade French vanilla slice. Ty ate three huge slabs of it and probably would have eaten more if he hadn't asked Middleton to put it back in the fridge under the guise of giving a fuck about bacteria.

They watched some more of the idiotic British TV show. Ty had never seen it before, but high on rum, sugar, and pussy, he found himself enjoying how ridiculous it was. A few episodes passed like the blink of an eye and he stopped laughing at the fabricated drama and instead started noticing how good Middleton looked in her tattered leotard. He was out of condoms, and she didn't have any—a fact he tried not to take pleasure in—so they just messed around. He fingered her and she gave him a long sloppy blowjob. After he came he must have fallen asleep, because he jerked awake at an unspecified time to find Middleton watching a documentary on the mysteries of the ocean. She was wearing pyjamas. They were pink and covered in cartoon hedgehogs because of course they were.

"Unicorn onesie in the wash?" he asked.

She gave him an adorable mock-scowl. "Be quiet."

"You know I've never heard you swear. Not when you cut your finger on the slide-ruler, or when that client said you were incompetent for the project *he* fucked up. I thought that was weird but now I know you don't even swear when I'm balls deep in you."

"Yes I do!"

"No you don't. You say 'do it harder, Daddy' not 'fuck me harder, Daddy'."

She blushed pink as her pajamas. "Is that a bad thing?"

"Depends." Ty tilted his head at her. "If I was to, say, kick in your TV, would you tell me to get the fuck out? Or would you just say 'oh golly' or something?"

Middleton screwed up her face. "F-Fuck off."

Ty laughed, actually laughed deep from within his belly for the first time in...he couldn't remember how long. It felt like a rainbow refracting from his torso. His laugh made her laugh and then they were both rolling on the couch laughing until Ty felt tears welling up in his eyes. He wasn't stupid, he knew it was a side effect of the incredible sex, but he didn't care. It felt too good.

"Do you want another cup of tea?" Middleton asked when they were done laughing.

Ty knew he should have said no. "Yeah, and can I eat more of that slice?"

They wound up watching the deep ocean documentary together, talking about how Middleton was terrified of lobsters because one had nipped her on the ankle when she was a kid. She was different here, in her home. Sweet but slightly left of center. Her hands flailed as she talked, and she had a habit of tapping her temples and fidgeting with any object that was close to hand. Again, Ty thought of Ritalin and came close to asking her why she took it but knew it wasn't his place to ask. People had a right to keep their shit to themselves. Besides, he didn't need to hear something that would make him feel even more dangerously tender toward her than he already did.

When the documentary ended, they started watching the next one she'd recorded—*Secrets of the Amazon Jungle*. They were halfway through it, when Ty noticed the light peering through a crack in Middleton's curtains. He checked his phone for the first time in hours and was blindsided to discover it was seven in the fucking morning. He was due at work in less than an hour and he didn't even feel tired.

"You're not coming in today," Ty told Middleton as he pulled on his jacket. "Have a nap or a swim in your enormous tub or something."

She stuck out her tongue at him.

"That's an order," Ty said, working hard not to smile.

"An order from my boss or my daddy?"

"Both."

He felt different, his barriers worn thin by hours of drinking, sex and her sweet, uncomplicated company. As she walked him to the door, Ty pulled her into his arms and kissed her again. It could have easily led to more sex but he tugged her to her bathroom and began to run the water in the big claw-foot tub for her. He left her paddling in warm water, knowing the memory of her naked and wet and happy would power him all through the day.

The sun was still rising when he left her building and it was such a beautiful morning Ty decided to walk to work. He had a change of clothes in his office, and he could use a coffee, something that was impossible to carry while steering through Melbourne's laneways on a motorbike. He stopped by Gordano's and found the usually thriving café pleasantly empty.

"You look a bit worse for wear, mate," Rick, the skinny barista said as he foamed the milk for his latte.

"Yeah," Ty said, thinking about Middleton spread beneath him, the hot clench of her cunt, how cute she looked all wrapped up in her blanket, beaming at him like he'd hung the moon.

"Like to meet the woman who put that smile on your face for the first time in about a million years," Rick said, placing his coffee in front of him. "Must be a hell of a girl."

Ty remembered then. Remembered how everyone at GGS came here, how everyone knew Rick. "You ever meet Charlize Theron, you let me know."

The barista rolled his eyes.

9

A song was stuck in Kate's head. She first heard it on Spotify the day Ty told her to take a day off work; directly afterward it moved into her brain and refused to go away. It was a dizzy little pop number called *Electric Love*. Everywhere she went, she hummed it under her breath, whispering lyrics about lightning and explosive lust. She woke up with it and went to sleep with it and she didn't even care. According to her phone, she'd listened to it seventy-seven times.

Why she liked the song was obvious, as obvious as the loose bottles of Pepperwood Ale she kept buying and drinking with her dinner, but as uncool as both of those things made her, Kate didn't care. She sang her song, she drank her beer, and she was dizzyingly, stupidly happy. For the first time in her life, she had a secret about a man—or at least, one that didn't make her hate herself.

She and Ty had hooked up twice since their first night together. The second time had been more of the same role play; Ty found her in the kitchen 'doing her homework' (finishing some reports. Why not incorporate your excellent work ethic into your sex life, particularly when you were screwing your boss?) and placed a big bottle of lube on top of her notebook. "I need to relax before your mother gets home," he told her. "Take everything off except your panties and meet me in the lounge."

Naked except for her underwear, Kate had sidled into the lounge room nervous as the schoolgirl she was pretending to be. Ty had been reclining in one of her leather armchairs, his thick cock jutting from his jeans like a rudder. He'd helped her slick his shaft with the jelly, then closed his palm around hers, 'showing her' how to give him a hand job. It had been obscene the way her breasts jiggled as she worked, the feel of him thick and slippery in her hand, his look of sneering contempt as he told her to hurry up because her mother would be home soon.

"Are you almost done?" she begged.

"Shut up, or you'll suck the lube off, and I promise you won't like the taste."

When he was close he didn't make her suck or sit on him, instead he ordered her to arch her back and came all over her breasts. Kate had never eroticized that act before, she'd always thought of it as a gross by-product of porn. The reality, at least with Ty, was different. When he coated her skin it felt like she'd been marked in a tangible and incredibly erotic way and when he pulled a hand-towel from his backpack to wipe her up she almost told him no, she wanted it to last. But that would have been truly gross and not because of porn. She let him clean her, and once it was done, he shoved his hands in her underwear.

"You better come fast, little girl," he crooned as he rubbed her clit. "If you don't come, Daddy's going to climb into your bed tonight and fuck you 'till you do."

She got off in about thirty seconds.

Kate's fantasies of playing daddy-daughter had always tended toward the intimate. Her imaginary lovers were stern but affectionate, framing their sexual requests as attempts to correct her behaviour or as 'normal' things that weren't sexual at all. Ty's interpretation of a daddy figure as a scumbag willing to blackmail his way into sexual favours wasn't her wheelhouse, but as soon as he introduced the idea it became all she could think about. She could barely keep her hands off herself. At work, she avoided him just so she didn't get distracted and do something mortifying and/or sack-worthy.

A week ago she'd been forced to endure a two-hour staff meeting with Ty. She spent the whole time doing pelvic floor exercises and afterward, she'd had to lock herself in a cubicle and touch herself just so she could concentrate. To be fair to her that had been the day after her third hookup when the purple and red bruises were just starting to blossom on her ass.

Every time Kate thought about that night, her body temperature skyrocketed. Ty had texted her a few hours before he was due to arrive at her place.

You're getting spanked tonight. How hard do you want it?

She hadn't even needed to think about it.

Hard enough that it leaves bruises.

She'd been making ginger biscuits when Ty burst into her kitchen, six plus feet of hard, angry male. He'd picked her up, pushed her against her pantry door and accused her of taking money out of his wallet. Kate had denied it, but her voice quivered so much it sounded as though she was guilty.

"You're a liar," Ty snarled, carrying her to the marble counter and yanking up her skirt. "You know what happens to little girls who lie to their Daddies?"

"No, please, *stop.*"

Ty picked up the wooden spoon she'd been using and held the handle in front of her. "Bite down," he said and when she did he honest-to-god *tore off her underwear.* Just tore it off like it was wrapping paper.

"Are you going to tell the truth or am I going to have to punish you?" he snarled.

It was difficult to insist you were telling the truth through a wooden spoon but Kate tried. When she did, Ty proceeded to lay sheer raging hell on her ass. This wasn't playful 'you've been a naughty girl' swats, this was his huge hand cracking down on her flesh with enough force to split wood. It was like lightning in reverse, first the noise and then the electric zap of pain. Kate had wanted it to stop, but every strike brought her closer to some undefinable edge she wanted to cross, couldn't cross, *needed to cross.*

She had frightened herself with the pleas that had come out of her mouth, guttural appeals for mercy throttled by the wooden spoon, but Ty hadn't hesitated. Somehow he'd known exactly where she wanted to go and when she burst into tears the sensation was every bit as euphoric as it had been when they first had sex. He'd given her three more slaps that barely even registered then took the spoon from between her teeth. "Did you take money from my wallet, Katie?"

"Yes," she sobbed, tears rolling down her chin. "Yes."

"What did you spend it on?"

"Lip gloss."

He smoothed a hand over her smarting behind. "Will you do it again?"

A tear rolled down her face and plopped onto the counter. "No, Daddy."

"Good. Now you'll go put on that lip gloss and you'll pay me back with your mouth. You'll do it a dollar at a time until you don't owe me anything, understood?"

Kate nodded, so light and floaty it was like she was on drugs. She'd always thought subspace was a thing kinksters invented to make their sex sound better than other people's, but this was different. She hadn't orgasmed, but she'd gone somewhere she'd needed to go deep inside. A peaceful, perfect place.

Thankfully, Ty hadn't made her blow him right away, a task that would have been near impossible in her limp state. He'd carried her to her couch and spread her pliant legs wide. The orgasm she'd had as he thrust inside her was as bright as a summer cloud. Now that she knew she could do it, now that she didn't have to be afraid, it was easy. It was like magic.

Afterward, they ate ginger biscuits and watched another documentary she'd recorded on polar bears. She'd wanted to hug him when the announcer talked about their dwindling numbers and maybe Ty had sensed it because he'd wrapped her very tightly in her peach blanket and given her a gruff kiss on the forehead.

She'd thought, *Tell me this is as amazing for you as it is for me. Tell me you think I'm beautiful.*

He'd said, "That was great, Middleton. I'll see you soon. Stay warm."

The next day, true to all clichés, Kate could barely sit down. She could see why this had been a punishment back when people genuinely thought pain taught kids not to steal and lie. When she checked her ass in the bathroom mirror at work, she was amazed to find it covered in indigo bruises. She'd snapped a picture for her own benefit and decided it was too beautiful not to share. Ty's response came an hour later.

Purple suits you, Middleton. You should wear it more often.

It was the middle of a particularly bitter Melbourne winter, but Kate felt like she'd stumbled into spring. Every morning she woke up with excitement bubbling in her middle and remembered she was sleeping with Tyler Henderson. She laughed at stupid jokes, stopped to smell flowers and ordered things she'd never heard of for dinner. Everything felt new and exciting and silly again. *Electric Love* was in the air and even as she skated around the Northcote multi-purpose stadium at derby practice, she couldn't stop herself from singing the words. At least, she couldn't until Casey Hindley threw an elbow into her side. "Are you singing while you skate?"

"Erm...no?"

"I shouldn't have framed that as a question. I heard you singing while you skate; why are you so weirdly happy?"

Kate smiled weakly. Casey was one of the most popular girls on the team. As a practicing Wiccan, she was perpetually adorned in flowing skirts, flower crowns and protective crystals. She held big parties on the solstice that, through a combination of shyness and Catholic guilt, Kate had never attended. It was a well-known Barbie Troll fact that if you had a secret Casey wanted to know, she hounded you like a bulldog until she had every detail. "I'm not happy. I mean, I am but not for any reason. And no more than usual."

Casey narrowed her large indigo-blue eyes. "Are you on drugs?"

Kind of. "No, why?"

"Because it's fucking freezing in here. My feet and tits and hands are numb, and you're grinning like we're on holiday in the Bahamas."

"I'm not!"

"You really are, the question is why?"

Tambara Oluo pulled up alongside them, her dark skin gleaming with sweat. "She's getting dicked, obviously. What kind of witch are you, Case?"

"Wicca has nothing to do with mind reading!" Casey snapped. She turned to Kate. "*Are* you getting dicked?"

"No! Things are just going well at work, and I like the cold weather—"

"And you're getting reamed in the pussy," Tam agreed. "Who's the guy? Or are you finally letting Rapunzel have her way with you?"

Rapunzel, whose metal studded corset made her look even more like a Viking berserker than usual, skidded up to join them. The waist-length braid for which she'd gotten her name wrapped itself around Casey's neck like a gold rope.

"Fucking hell!"

"Soz about that Case," Rapunzel said, untangling her hair from her teammate's oesophagus. "What are you lot talking about?"

"Macca's getting laid," Tam said, before Kate could respond. "We were wondering if you were doing the honours."

"I wish." Rapunzel winked at Kate. "Fight him for you?"

"I'm not seeing anyone!"

"You're clearly lying." Rapunzel slung an arm over Kate's shoulders. "My advice? Tell Casey about it now. Remember when Hellsy wouldn't show us her new tattoo?"

"I remember Casey skating around behind her, threatening to pull up her skirt?"

Rapunzel laughed. "Exactly. Just confess, mate. Tell her who the guy is."

"But there is no guy."

"Oh, so it's a girl? Even better. You, me, and her, this Friday? I give great third."

Kate usually shied away from Rapunzel's indiscriminate guerilla style-flirting, scared she was being mocked. Today, her good mood was a buffer, reminding her that Rapunzel meant well and said stuff like this to everyone. She ducked out from under her arm. "Thanks, but I'm happy doing things in pairs right now."

"Illuminati confirmed!" Casey poked a quartz-adorned finger into Kate's side. "Speak up, Mac. Who *is* this guy? You've been single for longer than I have, I demand to know who you're fucking!"

"No one, I swear."

Tam slid her arm through Kate's and rolled her away from the group like a gentleman suitor taking a maiden for a walk. "Come on Mac, you can tell me. Is it someone naughty?"

Kate thought about Ty pressing her face into her couch as he hammered into her from behind, snarling about what a dirty little girl she was. "I..."

"It is!" Tam announced.

"Knew it," Rapunzel said, adjusted her corset. "She's got that look lesbos get when they're banging a man. I'd say you're fucking a married guy but something tells me you're too pure to fuck a married guy."

"I am. At least, I hope so." She'd wasted a lot of time wondering how she'd behave toward Ty if his fiancée hadn't left him, and had mentally declared the topic off-limits.

Tam squeezed her shoulders. "I've never known you to do anything naughty before, Macca. I thought you were a virgin."

"No, I just kind of look like one."

Her teammates laughed and Kate felt a pleasurable squirm of happiness. Tam, Casey and Rapunzel were the ringleaders of the Barbie Trolls, and it was kind of flattering they'd taken an interest in her, even if it was because she was screwing someone.

Rapunzel framed Kate's face in her hands. "I don't think you look like a virgin. I think you look like a nun."

"Rapunzel!" Tam scolded.

"A cute nun!"

"Can we please stop off-roading here?" Casey demanded. "Mac, where'd you meet this male? Tinder? Bumble? OkCupid? Christian Mingle?"

"IRL?" Rapunzel suggested. "She looks like the kind of girl who'd get approached IRL in like a park or something."

Tam shook out her ombre hair. "No, not a park, the State Library. They were both reaching for the same copy of *Life of Pi,* and they did the adorable 'you have it, no you have it' thing."

Kate couldn't help but laugh. "You're all wrong."

"So tell us who he is and we'll be right."

At this point, Kate did want to tell them about Ty, if only to stop the guessing, but she couldn't. He was her boss, and she didn't think it was smart to tell her derby term she was sexing her boss.

"Did you hear they're remaking *Tomb Raider*?" she said. "Thoughts? Comments?"

Her teammates soundly ignored her and continued to list situations where Kate could have met her lover—café, hostage situation, when she applied to be a nun, and he's a hot priest, and that's why it's a secret.

Shrilly Temple—real name Gilly—came rolling up to join them. "What's happening here?"

"Macca's shagging someone she shouldn't be," Rapunzel said.

Gilly raised a pierced brow at Kate. "I thought you were asexual?"

"Or a nun," Rapunzel agreed. "Turns out, she's not. Although, now I'm starting to get really turned on about the idea of fucking a nun."

Everyone laughed. As the gossip session continued and the guesses grew more bizarre, she decided, in a warm rush of happiness, to just go ahead and tell them. None of them knew Ty, and if she was honest, she was dying to brag just a little. "It's a guy I work with. It's not a big deal, but you guys can't say anything, okay?"

There was a moment of silence. After all the elaborate speculations, Kate guessed 'a guy I work with' was pretty dull.

"I called it," Rapunzel said and cutting through any and all protests to the contrary she added; "How is that naughty? I fuck people I work with all the time."

Tam wrinkled her brow. "You drive for Uber Eats?"

"And?"

"And fucking people in your car is not the same thing."

"It is, but shut up. Macca, what's this guy like?"

Kate licked her lip, determined not to rant on about Ty's beauty and infinite impressive qualities the way she had with Maria. "He's handsome and blond and a little older than me."

That got her a chorus of intrigued oohs.

"How old?" Casey demanded.

"Erm, in his forties."

More intrigued oohs.

Gilly gripped her arm. "Does he have dad-bod?"

"That depends on...what that is?"

"When an older hot guy puffs out a bit because he's really into Big Macs. Kind of like Chris Pratt in *Parks and Rec*."

Kate did a visual comparison of Andy Dwyer and Ty. "Oh. No, he's a *Guardians of The Galaxy* Chris Pratt. He used to be a metro fire-fighter and he has abs."

The loudest chorus of intrigued oohs yet.

Tam clapped her hands. "Naww, that's amazing Mac. I was hoping you'd meet someone. I was thinking about trying to set you up with my brother."

Kate stared at her. "Seriously? That's so sweet."

Rapunzel elbowed Tam out of the way. "You're only saying that because you haven't met her brother; he's an accountant for Westpac and he's boring as shit. If you were going to suck the dick of someone it should be my brother. He paints street murals."

"Oh, wow—"

"With spray paint," Tam said. "It's basically just organised vandalism. Meanwhile, my brother just bought a house in Thornbury and—"

"I want to hear more about this firefighter," Casey interrupted. "Mac, if you want me to do a romance star chart for you both, I will. All I need is the year, month, day and minute you were both born."

Kate blinked. "Wow, um, thank you. But there is no way I can find out the exact minute Ty was born without him thinking I'm a freak."

"Fair enough, when are you seeing him again?"

"Tonight." Kate's insides squirmed pleasurably at the thought of what she and Ty had planned for the evening.

"Ooh, la, la. Where are you guys going?" Tam asked. "Movies? Dinner? Or are you still in the 'stay home and fuck each other constantly' stage of the relationship?"

"Girls!" Maria's voice was sharp as she strode toward them. "You're supposed to be warming down, not standing around gossiping!"

"But mama bear, we need to gossip," Casey said tugging her arm. "Macca's got a hot firefighter boyfriend."

Maria turned to look at Kate. "Does she now?"

Kate felt all her excitement drain out of her feet into the cold floorboards. "He's not, erm, we're not actually together."

"I see." Maria's eyes were cold.

Aside from a couple of texts, she and Maria hadn't discussed the Ty situation since that day in the coffee shop. Maria had invited her over for dinner a couple of times, but Kate had declined. She had been busy with work, Ty, and training but she was also enjoying keeping her sex life to herself. Maria, she knew, would want to analyse everything down to the bones and remind her Ty didn't really care about her. Kate didn't want that. She understood heartbreak was probably waiting down the line, but what she and Ty were exploring right now was so incredible, so *electric*, she wanted time to enjoy it on her own. That appeared to be backfiring.

Maria opened her mouth and Kate braced herself for her disapproval, when a shrill blast cut through the air. They all turned to see Rapunzel swinging a silver sports whistle through the air. "That was quite loud wasn't it?"

"Yes! Where'd you get that fucking whistle from?" Gilly shrieked

"Found it. Want me to run a warm-down drill, Maria?"

As everyone started swearing at Rapunzel for scaring them, Kate breathed a sigh of relief. She would warm down, then slip away while Maria was busy with the other girls. She had another date with Ty tonight and she didn't want—

A warm hand closed over her arm and Kate found herself face-to-face with an extra irritated Maria. "You told your teammates about Tyler Henderson?" she asked.

So much for her big escape. "No, well, kind of," Kate said. "I told them I was seeing someone from work."

Maria's lips thinned. "*Are you* seeing someone from work? I was under the impression you were having casual daddy-daughter sex with a forty-five-year-old man who happens to be your boss."

"Maria!" Kate glanced around to see if anyone had heard, but mercifully everyone was still bitching out Rapunzel for blowing the whistle. "I didn't mean to tell them about Ty. They guessed I was seeing someone and I panicked."

Maria's fierce expression softened slightly. "I understand you wanting to bond with them, Katie, but telling more people about Tyler is only going to raise your expectations even higher than they already are."

Kate looked down at her pink and black skates. "I know, but I just—"

"We still haven't discussed how this situation has progressed," Maria said. "Are you free after practice? You should come to my place for dinner."

Her heart sinking, Kate opened her mouth to say 'yes, I'm free' when, over Maria's shoulder, she saw Casey and Tam trying to steal Rapunzel's whistle while Gilly filmed them on her phone. All four of them were laughing. They looked so happy, so careless and unlikely to lecture her for sleeping with a gorgeous older man. So Kate did something bad. She smiled at Maria and said, "I'd love to have dinner, but the girls just invited me out for drinks."

It wasn't technically a lie. The team usually went to Rumba Bar after training on Thursdays, she'd just never gone along.

Maria glanced over at the girls' play-fight and frowned. "Are you sure that's a good idea? They'll only grill you about Tyler."

And you won't? Kate shoved the angsty thought aside. "I joined the team to learn how to be friends with women. It's been three years; I think I might be ready to go out for drinks."

Maria didn't smile. "Very well. Come and help me pull out the mats for stretching, please."

She was pissed, but Kate didn't have enough emotional space to feel bad, she needed to confront one of her greatest personal fears. She skated over to the girls whose play fight appeared to be wrapping up out of sheer exhaustion.

"Macca!" Tam said, draping her arm across Kate's shoulder. She smelled incredible, like vanilla and spice. "Did you see me kick this big bitch in the shins?"

"No, but you smell *amazing.*" The moment the dorky compliment left her mouth, Kate was mortified, but Tam grinned.

"Thanks, it's a body butter my mum makes. Hey, want to come out for drinks tonight?"

Kate couldn't believe it was that easy. "Um, okay?"

"Excellent! Do you like espresso martinis?"

"I've never had one."

"So you *are* a virgin." Rapunzel shoved Kate in her side. "And tonight we'll collectively pop your cherry."

Tam gave her a look of disgust. "Don't worry about her. We muzzle her outside the stadium."

Rapunzel smacked her friend on the ass. "You wish. How fucking kinky are you, anyway?"

"Very," Tam shouted back. "You know that."

Rumba Bar courted the derby crowd; they gave players half-price drinks and let them wear their skates on the battered hardwood floors. Kate figured the short shorts and counter-culture vibe was good for business; the place was packed. She crammed herself into a booth between Tam and Rapunzel and despite her plan to eat something before drinking, was sipping an espresso martini in five seconds flat. Turned out they were just cold vodka coffees, but she liked the taste. Despite Maria's prediction that she would be grilled about Ty, the girls didn't even mention him. They started teasing one another about their derby names instead.

"I get that you wanted a witch theme," Rapunzel said to Casey. "But Hermione Maim-Her? That doesn't even make sense."

"You can fucking talk! Your name is just 'Rapunzel.' That's not a play on words, that's just what we call you."

"You try thinking of a play on words about Rapunzel then."

"My derby name is perfect." Tam raised her martini glass as though toasting herself.

Rapunzel scoffed. "You stole it. There are about fifty thousand Foxxy Balboas in America. Face it, the only person on the team who has a cool original name is Mac."

Kate almost spat out her vodka coffee. "Seriously?"

"Hell yeah. Princess Bleach, how'd you come up with that?"

Kate felt her smile stiffen like day-old bread. "I'm, um, the youngest kid in my family. Everyone used to call me Princess."

The rest of the girls at the table gave her big 'nawww' smiles, telling her she'd sounded convincingly cheerful. Kate wondered what they'd say if she told them the term had never been one of endearment.

Her dad was one of those Catholics who took the lords name in vain, plucked two dollar coins out of shopping center fountains, never went to church and invoked his religion whenever the subject of birth control was raised. Child after child he told her mother she'd soon be too old to get pregnant and he didn't need to offend the big man in the sky by getting a vasectomy. Her dad didn't know shit. At the age of forty-seven Brenda McGrath fell pregnant with her ninth kid.

Kate was five years younger than her nearest sister, Claudia. All her older siblings thought they were done enduring screaming, shitting babies. They welcomed her as one would welcome a sex offender into a community swimming pool, which was to say, not at all. Once, when he was drunk, her brother Josh had told her they planned to smother her. "We picked out a blanket and everything, but then mum found out and stopped us."

Kate grew up fully aware no one wanted her to be born. That would have been bad enough, but she'd cried a lot, slept poorly and struggled to make friends. That was the undiagnosed ADHD, but her family didn't know that. They thought she was a brat. Her parents were exhausted by then, completely over the whole child-rearing lark. All they wanted was for her to shut up and stay out of their way. Because she couldn't, because she made things hard, Kate became the little princess. As in, "Suck it up, Princess. Stop crying, Princess. Hurry up, Princess. Mummmm, Princess locked herself in the bathroom *again*."

Kate wasn't sure why she'd chosen Princess as her derby name. Maybe she was trying to reclaim it, maybe the word had been drilled so deep, it was the first thing she'd considered labelling herself when she was asked to choose a name. The only thing she knew was that 'Princess Bleach' was a better derby name than her other childhood monikers; 'Runty,' 'Spaz-basket' and 'Dipshit Magee.'

Mercifully the conversation steered away from derby names and toward who was the most fuckable '90s rock star. Kate sipped her vodka coffee and had just put forward Gavin Rossdale (unfortunate band, gorgeous face) when Casey squealed, "Maria! I didn't know you were coming!"

Kate's stomach dropped. Sure enough their coach was squeezing herself into the booth beside Gilly. "I felt like unwinding so I called my babysitter," she said. "What are we all drinking?"

Another round of espresso martinis was ordered, and the conversation picked up again, this time with Maria at the helm. Soon the whole team was laughing at her stories and discussing sex and BDSM and politics. Kate couldn't think of a single thing to say. She felt irrelevant and completely out of place. She was probably being paranoid but it also felt like Maria was shutting her out of the conversation. When she hit the bottom of her second martini, she excused herself to go to the bathroom and decided she'd leave. It had been silly of her to come to Rumba for drinks, as though she could just make friends with all these cool, uninhibited women. She exited the bathroom stall and walked straight into Maria's velvet-covered boobs. "Sugar!"

Maria barely seemed to notice, her dark eyes were wild. "Katie, are you upset with me?"

Kate didn't know what to say. The obvious answer was 'yes,' but she didn't know if she should say it. Maria looked so upset and really, what had she done? Ask after her, invite her to dinner and then come to the same social gathering Kate had been at. How was that a crime? "No, I'm not."

"Thank the lord," Maria beamed at her. "Come back to the table and hang out with the rest of the team."

"That's okay. I'm probably going to head home."

"Why? I only just got here!"

Kate walked over to the graffitied rack of sinks and turned taps until she found one that worked. "I'm sorry," she said to the Maria in the cracked mirror. "I'm, um, seeing Ty tonight."

Mirror-Maria's smile faded. She walked closer, bringing with her the plum of her perfume and the faint acrylic scent of her freshly varnished nails. "You know it's a vulnerable position you're putting yourself in. Even pretending to be violated can take an emotional toll."

"I know," Kate said. "But it's been amazing. I have zero complaints."

A small huffing noise. "How is he at aftercare?"

Truthfully, Kate didn't know. In all the BDSM books Maria made her read, aftercare was listed as cuddles and kisses, emotional reassurance, and skin-to-skin contact. Kate wasn't sure if watching documentaries and having a few drinks counted, nor did that weird thing where Ty wrapped her really tightly in a blanket, but she couldn't tell Maria that.

"He's great at aftercare," she said with a chirpiness that sounded weak even to her own ears.

Mirror-Maria looked unimpressed. "Very convincing."

Kate sighed. "Okay, I get that I've never done this before and I don't have anything to compare it to, but the sex is great and we're having a lot of fun."

"You're using condoms?"

Kate felt like Maria was hunting for something to get annoyed about. "Yes."

"What about for oral?"

"No. He offered, but I hate the way they taste."

"Is he going down on you?"

Kate winced. That was another danger zone. Ty had never put his mouth near or around her pussy and never expressed any interest in doing so. "Yeah, he uh, loves doing it."

"Really?"

"Oh my gosh, what's with the Spanish Inquisition, Maria?" Kate walked over to the hand towels and tore off a sheet with more force than was required.

"I'm sorry," she said, not sounding it. "I just don't trust this man."

Kate dried her hands and threw the towel in the overflowing bin. "I get that, but you don't need to worry. I think Ty and I are becoming friends."

Maria scoffed. "Friends? Like you were friends with all the boys at your school? Like you were friends with Mr Peterson?"

It took a few seconds for the insult of what she was saying to sink in, but once it did, Kate felt something she hadn't felt in a long, long time. A thin red vein of anger wrapping itself around her like a jelly-fish tentacle.

"No," she said. "Not like that."

She turned and walked toward the door. Maria dashed in front of her and blocked her exit. "Katie, I'm sorry, I shouldn't have said that."

"You shouldn't have," Kate agreed, but the look of agonized contrition on Maria's face bled some of the heat out of her anger. "I get why you don't trust Ty, but you need to understand this isn't like what I did at school or...afterward. This is different. I know what I'm doing now."

Maria took her still-damp hand and squeezed it. "Just give me some time, Katie. Be patient. You mean so much to me, I don't want to see this man hurt you."

Kate made herself smile. She was good at that. "I know."

They shared a slightly uncomfortable hug and Kate went back to the booth to retrieve her sports bag. The other girls were tipsy, and Kate knew her leaving wasn't going to affect them in the slightest. Feeling depleted and headachy from the espresso martinis, she slipped out of Rumba and into the frosty night. She checked her phone and found a text from Ty.

I'll be at your place in fifteen minutes. I had better see those skates tonight, Middleton.

She smiled at her screen, relieved to feel something as uncomplicated as lust. Then, as though her brain was determined to ruin it, something occurred to her. The guys at work had given her another princess nickname—Middleton—and no one called her Middleton more than Ty. Aside from when they were role playing, that was *all* he called her. As she stood on the cold street, Kate wondered why that was. It could have been a quirk, but something about it felt a little strange, the same way him never going down on her, or taking off his clothes when they were having sex was strange. Her own words to Maria echoed in her head. *I think Ty and I are becoming friends.* She shoved her phone back into her pocket, feeling stupid.

10

Mr Peterson was in charge of the Willow Street carpool. When Kate was thirteen, he bought a battered old Kombi Van and offered to drive all the kids on his street to school.

"It's no problem," he told her mum. "I work from home and I'm always going up and back to pick up Deidre; this way it benefits all of us."

It wasn't a hard sell. The other parents were only too happy to give Mr Peterson ten bucks a week for petrol and let him chauffeur their kids, Kate's parents included. They didn't care that their daughter would have literally sat on nails to avoid riding in what her brother Mick had already dubbed 'Rape on Wheels.'

"You'll bloody well take the van and be grateful for it," her mum had said when Kate begged for Rape on Wheels-free rides. "I'm not driving you forty minutes each way because you think you're too good to go with everyone else."

Kate tried to tell her mum it wasn't because of that, it was because Deidre Peterson called her 'Accident' and had once taken a poem out of her diary and read it aloud so that everyone laughed at her. Her mum—who was from a generation that believed bullying was entirely the fault of the spineless victim—snorted and said, "You're not a baby anymore, Princess, you're about to start high school. It's time to grow up."

Her first trip in Rape on Wheels had gone as well as could be expected; she immediately sat on an unwrapped peanut butter sandwich Deidre had put on her seat.

Every kid in the van started laughing, including Mick and her sister Claudia. Deidre then stood up and took a picture of her stained ass with her phone. "Sorry, Accident," she said. "It was just an accident."

For the next forty minutes, Kate fought back tears, wondering what she'd do when she got to school with what looked like a shit stain on the back of her dress.

When the van pulled up at Point Cook Secondary, she'd stayed in her seat as the other kids got out snickering.

"Wagging, are we, princess?" Mick asked as he walked past.

Kate nodded. If she hid, Mr Peterson might not see her and she could go back to Shell Street with him and sneak home. Unfortunately, luck wasn't on her side.

"Katie," Mr Peterson said, sticking his head in the back of the van. "Come on, you need to go to school."

"I can't," she said, pent up tears leaking out of her eyes.

"I know it's scary but you'll have a great time, I promise."

"It's not that. Deidre...I sat on a sandwich. It's all over my dress and it looks like...please don't make me go out there?"

She'd expected him to yell at her, to tell her to suck it up and stop being such a whiny precious princess, but he hadn't. He'd smiled at her. "No problem. We'll get this sorted out in no time. Wait here."

Kate had watched as he jogged toward the front office, utterly terrified he was calling her mum. He wasn't. He returned two minutes later waving a blue and white checkered school dress like a flag.

"It's from lost and found. It might be a bit big, but it'll fit," he said, handing it to her. "Pull down the blinds and get changed, I'll keep watch outside."

Kate climbed out of the Kombi van feeling like the luckiest girl in the world. It was then she saw how handsome Mr Peterson was, with his thick hair and twinkly green-grey eyes. Like a movie star. She'd never really met anyone handsome before and now that she had, she couldn't stop staring. He was so big and hard and *young*. How was he Deidre's dad? He looked more like Kate's brothers than her bald, perpetually scowling father.

"Are you okay?" Mr Peterson had asked.

"Yes," Kate told her shoes. "Thank you."

"Anytime, Katie..." Mr Peterson knelt down and looked her right in the eyes. As they looked at one another, Kate felt something zap from her belly into what her mum called her 'secret place.'

"This afternoon, I think you should sit up front with me," Mr Peterson said. "What do you think?"

Kate smiled. "I think that would be good."

After that, Kate always rode up front with Mr Peterson, mornings and afternoons, five days a week. They'd talked about everything: books, movies, politics, the news. Mr Peterson never patronised her; if she didn't understand something, he explained how the stock market or hydroponics or the Houses of Parliament worked. When he found out she loved studying complex systems he loaned her books like *The Soul of a New Machine* and *The Design of Everyday Things*. As Kate got older, he started teasing her about her nail polish and multicoloured hair, her failed attempts to show other girls she was just like them.

"You're becoming a rebel without a cause, Katie. Soon you'll be too cool to ride up front with me."

Kate had never experienced teasing that didn't come with the rubber band flick of dislike. She liked it. She told Mr Peterson maybe she wouldn't want to sit up front with him because he was an old man and he'd laughed so loud, all the other kids in the van stared.

When Kate was fifteen, she won a statewide geography competition. Upon seeing her certificate her dad had told her it was rigged. "They wanted to give the prize to a girl. That's how things are these days."

When she told Mr Peterson, his brow had furrowed into angry lines. The next afternoon he'd handed her a rose cut from his garden, its stem wrapped in shiny tinfoil and a tiny card that read *Congratulations, Katie! What a fantastic achievement! Love Kane, Jennifer, and Deirdre Peterson.*

That night, Kate had locked herself in the bathroom and erased the names of Mr Peterson's wife and daughter with liquid paper. They didn't give a damn about her, Mr Peterson did. Mr Peterson was the *only one* who did.

Kate wasn't sure why she had the kinks she had. She'd done enough research to know it wasn't as simple as the vending machine theory of 'insert daddy drama, out rolls a can of kinkiness.' It was clear to anyone with half a brain that the abuse-for-kink model held no water. Girls had fathers who abandoned them, loved them, beat them, raped them or were as ambivalent as Kate's dad was and they turned out to be Dommes, subs, bottoms, switches, lesbians, bisexuals or as straight and vanilla as they came. It wasn't that simple.

Still, Kate had to acknowledge that she'd had a painful childhood and that during her formative years, when she was love-starved and desperate for affection, she'd fallen for a much older man she wished was her father *and* her boyfriend.

Before her thoughts about Mr Peterson were explicitly sexual or even romantic, Kate had known she loved him. She'd loved his voice, his hair, the way he said her name. She'd loved his kindness and his sense of humor. When she'd discovered her body in her cramped single bed, Deidre's dad had been in the forefront of her fantasies. Those flickering girlish daydreams hadn't even been about sex. They'd featured things like Mr Peterson laying her down in a big soft bed and saying things like "I love you, Katie. You're the most precious thing in the world to me."

It was embarrassing, really.

She never knew if Mr Peterson was aware of her crush on him. The summer she turned sixteen, the state government funded a legitimate school bus service and Rape on Wheels was decommissioned. Kate had cried in her bed for a week, writing long, rambling poems about the love of her life being snatched away from her. The poems themselves had been histrionic, the 'broken wheel' and 'final jour-

ney' metaphors terrible, but the pain behind them was as acute as
when Aunt Rhonda had died. She'd lost her only ally.

When her grief finally bottomed out, Kate realised she had
another serious problem on her hands—no friends. It wasn't exactly
a new problem, she spent most lunchtimes reading in the library by
herself, but without Mr Peterson's van rides to look forward to it
seemed urgent she find some mates. Kate set about pooling her
resources and found she had two valuable friend-making assets
—boobs.

Boys had never held much appeal for her while Mr Peterson was
around, being gorgeous and talking to her about *The Wheel of Time*
series, but now they took on a new shine. They were nicer to her than
girls and impressed both by her rack and her job at Doughnut King
(she had access to a lot of free, barely-stale, doughnuts).

Unfortunately, the boys she tried to hang around with weren't so
keen on being friends—they kept trying to hold her hand and go in
for unwelcome kisses at the movies. Telling them she only wanted to
be friends irritated them and kissing them back was insanely uncomfortable. After a few months of trial and error, Kate stumbled on a
winning boys-for-friends formula—acting totally freaking clueless. If
she pretended she didn't know what a guy's intentions were, if she
giggled and said things like, 'Which of the girls in our class do you
have a crush on? Is it Rylie? Is it Stephanie?' boys got confused and
stopped trying to kiss her and suggested they go into empty paddocks
and shoot a potato gun instead.

When she perfected the art of acting clueless Kate discovered
another amazing plot twist—the more she played dumb and refused
to become anyone's girlfriend, the more boys liked her. Most of them
were horrible to the girls they actually hooked up with, but they
invited her over to dinner with their parents, taught her to play
HALO and beer pong and talked to her about all the stuff they
couldn't tell their guy mates. It was like black magic.

Being one of the boys got her through the rest of high school, but
Kate always knew it wasn't quite the way it was meant to be. The guys
she hung around with weren't really her friends. They were more like

"friends." There were always strings attached to hanging out with them—laughing at jokes that stung, listening to talk that offended, staying a virgin because they didn't like it when she showed romantic interest in anyone, despite having no romantic interest in her. She was always 'other', the exception to the rule, but part of the rule all the same. Female friendship continued to evade her. Later, she learned girls picked up on ADHD markers better than boys. They sensed the strangeness hiding beneath her lip-gloss-and-ponytail attempts to be like them and backed away as though she was infectious.

Kate wasn't diagnosed with ADHD until she was almost eighteen. Her psychology teacher told her she should be getting much better marks and when Kate showed her all the extra homework she did— the practise essays and questionnaires—Mrs Windsor had frowned and recommended she see a doctor. Kate paid for the psychiatrists visit herself, and sure enough, she had severe ADHD. Severe enough that she'd be on Ritalin for the rest of her life. Severe enough that someone should have noticed when she was a kid, but they hadn't. No one had.

Kate thought about that as her Uber sped her toward Aunt Rhonda's apartment, how she'd grown up feeling so twitchy and weird. How she'd chipped away big chunks of her personality so she could have friends that weren't really her friends. How her first fantasies were about a friendly dad *being nice to her*.

The only person who knew everything about her past was Maria and her mentor seemed to have assigned her a permanent chair in the hall of victimhood. Yes, it was a pretty sad story, Kate thought as the streetlights flashed past, but not one she wanted hanging around her neck like a dead albatross for the rest of her life. She was grown up now, she had her own apartment and Ritalin and a job. Why couldn't she just evolve from the placid half-girl she'd been into something new and bold and brave?

Because you don't have the guts.

The inner voice, cruel as it was, had a point. The habits she'd picked up as a kid ran deep; she apologised even if she knew it wasn't her fault, saw her family every Christmas even though it broke her heart, and never attended a derby event without Maria, despite skating for the team for three years. Maybe her desire to play daughter wasn't about any pseudo-sexual Mr Peterson Freud stuff. Maybe it was as simple as wanting to be the center point of someone else's desires so she didn't have to take any risks.

"God, I'm depressing," she mumbled.

"What was that?" Her Uber driver, a thickset guy with forearms so hairy Kate had first thought him covered in tattoos, turned to look at her from the front seat. "You say something?"

"Um, no sorry. That was nothing."

The driver smiled, it wasn't a nice smile. "Didn't sound like nothing. You having a bad night?"

A nudge of fear in her belly. "I'm totally fine."

"Don't give me that, sexy, talk to me. Are you having boy problems, or is it high school drama?"

The skin on the back of Kate's neck prickled. This guy thought she was in *high school* and he was calling her sexy and asking her about boys. It reminded her of her role play with Ty except that had been a game and this was real life. Saying the word 'roses' to this man would do approximately nothing. She pulled her jacket tight around her neck, wondering what to do next.

"Girly." The driver's voice sliced through the air like a box-cutter. "I asked you a question."

Kate opened her mouth to apologise again, when another hot tendril of anger she'd felt with Maria wrapped itself around her middle. Who was this guy to talk like this? To assume she was a sad teenager travelling on her own at night and try to use that to freaking *flirt* with her? She held up her phone. "Sorry, I'm texting my dad. He's a detective and he's super angry I'm Ubering by myself. I think he's going to come out and meet me once we're at my place. I hope he doesn't take my phone away!"

If it wasn't so sad, the way the driver's face contorted with horror might have been funny. "Sure," he said. "A detective, right. Right, right. Want me to take the next left?"

"Yes, please."

It sucked that the world could be this way, and she'd hardly given the driver a piece of her mind, but as he flicked on the radio and started humming the worst imitation of innocence Kate had ever seen, she had to admit she was a bit proud of herself.

11

The elevator ding was unnaturally loud. Or maybe it felt that way because she was headed toward Aunt Rhonda's apartment in the knowledge that she was going to have filthy, filthy sex. There were two other apartments on her floor. One was occupied by a middle-aged Russian couple, the other belonged to an ancient ex-showgirl gleefully outliving her relatives. They were all nice enough, but they'd skin her alive if they saw her going down the hallway in roller skates. She skated up the hall as quietly as she could. She didn't really need to worry, all the apartments on her floor were soundproofed. Sometimes Mr Petkovic opened his door and marching band music blasted out at a hundred decibels, only to vanish the instant it closed again. Kate had taken comfort in that whenever she screamed for Daddy to fuck her harder. She reached her door and eased her keys out of her sports bag. Ty, she knew, was already in her apartment. She'd given him a key of his own, slipped it into his pigeonhole at work like a criminal. That knowledge would probably make Maria's head explode, but it was safer than leaving her door unlocked and it made scenes like the one they had planned tonight so much more realistic.

Kate slid her key into her door as quietly as possible. The lock turned easily and she tugged her front door open. The unmistakable groans and slapping sounds of sex greeted her.

"Yeah?" she heard a man say. "Yeah, you like that, you dirty b—"

Kate slammed the door shut.

"What the heck?"

Her brain was buzzing with information and all she could think of was Ty bringing another girl to her apartment and having sex with her in full view of her Aunt Rhonda's carnival glass animals. Then she realised that was utterly insane. Since Ty had given her every indication of being sane, there had to be another reason. She re-opened the door, just a crack, and glanced around. A second later she realised Ty wasn't hosting an orgy, he was playing porn through her TV. The voices had the slightly tinny quality of a recorded video and the American accents were obvious even through the moaning. Relief and mortification surged through her in equal measure and she closed her door, needing a moment to collect herself.

Where had he gotten the porn from? Netflix didn't have a secret porn side-channel, was he streaming it on his phone? Had he brought a DVD? Kate knew most people watched porn but the thought of Ty striding into an adult store in one of his nice suits and walking out with a bag of DVDs called things like *Anal Sluts III: The Re-Sluttening* just didn't seem right. But maybe that was the point. From their first encounter, Ty had made it clear he liked playing the immoral sleazebag, an unusual choice from a man everyone praised for being so upstanding and honourable. Maybe it was a release pretending to be the man no one wanted him to be, just like it was a release for her to wallow in helplessness deliberately instead of incidentally.

Her hand hovered over the doorknob. She *wanted* to go inside and experience what Ty had in store for her, and yet something held her back.

"What do you want?" she asked herself

The answer came with embarrassing clarity: Ty on top of her in bed, his naked body warm and reassuringly heavy. He'd thrust inside her with slow, careful rolls of his hips, one big hand cupping her cheek. "Does that feel good, baby? I'm not hurting you, am I?"

"No, Daddy," she'd whisper. "It feels nice."

"Good. I want to make you feel nice." He pressed his mouth to her ear, his hair falling like a silk curtain against her skin. "I love you, Katie, I always will."

As Ty had already noticed, Kate rarely swore. Her mother had been a big fan of the washing-your-mouth-out-with-soap trick, and say what you will about child abuse—it worked. Saying the F-word to Ty that night had given her guilt pangs that lasted days, but in that moment Kate couldn't help herself.

"Fucking hell," she muttered. "*Fucking hell.*"

That fantasy was pathetic. It was a big bowl of sad with tragic sprinkles on top. To think such soppy crap about Mr Peterson when she was fourteen was one thing, to feel that way about Ty, the earth-bound Adonis she was actually sleeping with, was beyond embarrassing. Kate seized the doorknob and yanked her door open. She'd take porn and perversion over that saccharine, painfully female fantasy any day of the week.

The porn was even louder on the other side of the door. She skated into the living room and saw Ty sitting on her couch with a beer in his hand. On the TV an obscenely muscled man was getting a blowjob from two blondes. He was being very ungrateful about it, working a rough fist in each woman's hair and snarling, "*Suck harder you little sluts.*"

The crassness was so overwhelming, Kate had to look away. Ty was so good at getting her into this headspace of erotic uncertainty, making her feel so much younger and more naïve than she was. It was even stronger tonight, with him relaxing in her home as if he owned the place. She shifted in her roller skates, the heavy boots hindering her in a way that felt like bondage.

"That you, Katie?" Ty didn't turn around, but from his voice Kate could imagine his expression, a smirk of pure masculine pleasure. His sex doll was home and he was going to get laid.

"Erm, yeah, hi," she stammered.

She could never call him Daddy when they started playing like this, and it didn't seem right to call him Ty. This wasn't Ty. This was another, meaner man—her brutish stepfather if not the daddy borne of her Mr Peterson fantasies.

"You're late," he said, because that was what they'd planned.

"Sorry, I had derby practice."

He made a meal of slowly checking his wristwatch. "That finished at eight. Where have you been since?"

Kate put her sports bag down on the floor. The clunk, without her roller skates inside it, was much lighter than usual. "Out with my friends."

"And you didn't think to let me or your mother know?"

The menace underlying his tone made her shiver. How did he do it? How did he make her feel guilty for offending her imaginary mum, while he sat watching porn on TV with his boots up on Aunt Rhonda's antique coffee table?

"I'm waiting?"

"I forgot to text," she said. "I'm sorry."

Seconds ticked past with agonising slowness. The girls on the screen moaned and the man swore but Ty said nothing. Kate's nerves began to flutter, her hands and feet and pussy buzzing with useless energy. Sorry was never good enough, but how would her stepfather make her pay? They never discussed the ins and outs of a scene in their Kinkworld correspondences. Kate had a hand in the destination, could veto or suggest certain things, but Ty sat behind the wheel and drove them where he wanted to go. She liked that, didn't she?

Ty sat up, drained his beer, and put the empty on the coffee table. "Come here, Katie."

"Why?"

Tension crackled in the air between them.

"Because," Ty said very quietly. "I want my cock sucked and seeing as you're late, I think it's the least you can do."

She swallowed. The male porn star was now taking one of the girls from behind as the other stroked her hands over his chest. "Okay, but can you please turn that stuff off first? It's gross."

He stretched his arms over his head, making his shoulders flex beneath one of the cotton t-shirts he always favoured when he came to her house. "After all our fun together, Little Miss Good Girl still thinks sex is gross, huh?"

"I don't think sex is gross. I think *you're* gross. Why are you watching this stuff while my mum's out?"

He turned to look at her then, and as always Kate was struck by how handsome he was. Not an unusual or brooding kind of handsome, just *handsome*. Bright blue eyes, thick blonde hair, a stern brow, and a square jaw. She'd never seen pictures of him as twenty-something, but she already knew he was more attractive now. The faint lines around his eyes and forehead lent him the ruggedness of a cinematic cowboy. In looks, he was the perfect all-Australian man, yet such a strange perversion had brought them together. Kate thought of Ty's ex-fiancée. Had she known about this? Had she stood where Kate was standing only with a diamond ring and the knowledge that he loved her? What would having Tyler Henderson's love even feel like?

"I do a lot of things while your mother's out, something you know very well," Ty said scanning her body. His eyes lingered on her tight derby tee. "Is that what you wear to practice?"

Kate tugged at the hem of her short-shorts. "Yes."

"Interesting. So you went out with your little friends after practise, did you? Where to, a playground?"

"A bar."

Ty's upper lip curled into a sneer. "Maybe I'm corrupting you after all. Did you drink?"

"Yes." Kate tried to sound as smug as teenagers always did when they consumed alcohol, as though it wasn't an incredibly mundane adult activity.

"How'd you get drinks? You flirt with the bartender?"

"No, my best friend Casey bought them for me, she has an ID."

She was also twenty-six and far from her best friend, but Kate figured that didn't matter so much in role play.

"Casey, huh? She a dirty little girl like you?"

"No," she said quickly.

Ty's sneer grew more pronounced. "I don't believe you. Maybe you should invite her over some time so I can find out for myself."

Kate knew he didn't mean it, that he was acting like a jerk on purpose, but hearing him talk about other girls, even in the context of this fantasy, stung. Unwilling to let him read that in her face, she bent over to take off her roller skates.

"Leave them on."

Kate straightened up, her heart hammering. "You can't tell me what to—"

"Yes, I can," Ty said coldly. "You know the reason why, go ahead and tell me what it is?"

Kate thought back to their last encounter, Ty rubbing her to the brink of orgasm then stopping, telling her he'd only get her off if she said Daddy owned her pussy. She'd held out, she'd held out at least a dozen times, and then...

"Katie..." Ty's voice was softer than silk. "You look me in the eyes and tell me what I want to hear or what I did to your ass last week will seem like a beautiful fucking fantasyland compared to what I'll do now."

The skin on Kate's backside prickled. She looked down at her roller skates "I have to do what you say because you...because you own me."

"And why do I own you?"

"Because you're my..." Kate glanced up at the TV. The two girls were sitting on the beefy man's face and hips, riding him at the same time. "Because you're my Daddy."

"That's right," Ty said with some satisfaction. "Now take off your t-shirt. Slowly."

Kate peeled her top over her head with what she hoped was sufficient slowness.

"Lose the bra."

She flipped open the catch on her sports bra and let the material fall away. Now she was standing in her fully-lit living room in her shorts and skates, feeling more naked than if she were actually naked. Ty studied her body and she studied the TV. Both of the porn stars were blonde and deeply tanned with breasts like cantaloupes. Was this the kind of woman Ty preferred? His ex had been blonde. 'Like Scarlett Johansson with better tits,' Dutchy had said. As she stood there she felt exceptionally pale, skinny, and bland. She thought about her fantasy—Ty making slow, sweet love to her in his bed—her chest throbbed.

"Touch yourself," Ty said.

"Wh-What?"

"Touch your tits for me. Nice and hard, the way I do it."

She placed her hands on her breasts and squeezed. The sensation sent another sizzle from breasts to groin. Her mind was all over the place but alcohol and anticipation had her body more than ready.

"Very nice," Ty said. "Now skate your ass over here."

Kate skated toward him. She felt a bit guilty for doing it indoors, but Aunt Rhonda had been a huge fan of sexual expression and she probably wouldn't have cared. She stood in front of Ty, expecting him to pull her onto her lap. Instead, he stared at her with frank curiosity. "Is that really your uniform?"

Kate knew it was her boss, not her stepfather who wanted to know.

"Not this." She gestured to her bare breasts. "But everything else is. I wear a lot of protective gear, knee guards, wrist guards, and a helmet."

"Sure." He reached out and brushed the skin below her belly button. His eyes were very soft, almost sad. Kate was on the verge of asking if he was okay when he extended his arms. "Come here."

It was hard work, sitting on someone's lap while wearing skates, but Kate managed to clamber on. Ty stroked her with entitled precision, brushing his palms over her hair and shoulders as though revelling in his ownership. It lasted so long that she closed her eyes, soothed by his touch like an anxious kitten, and when finally he plucked at her nipple, she gasped.

"You're starting to enjoy this, aren't you, little girl?"

"No."

"Liar." Ty's hand closed over the front of her shorts, cupping her sex. "You can pretend all you want, but I know you like it."

Kate struggled weakly against his hold. "You make me have sex with you."

"Maybe at first, but I've woken something up in you, haven't I? You want it now, even more than I do. I can see it whenever you look at me."

He grinned, and Kate knew he was referring to all the meetings in which she'd had to drag her gaze away from his hands, his mouth, the seat of his pants. "I can't help it."

"I know you can't." His hands slid up her torso, cupping her breasts. "I think I'm gonna buy you a nice fat toy. Something you can play with when I'm not here. You can call it Daddy, use it whenever you wish I was inside you."

The thought of Ty giving her something—even if it was a dildo—made Kate's heart clench like a fist. "I don't want that," she lied.

"And what do you want?"

For you to make love to me in your bed, your skin against mine, your weight on my body. "I want you to leave me alone."

"Oh, sweetheart." Ty kissed her hard. It was a kiss meant to claim, his lips and tongue dominating her hers.

"Maybe you do," he said when he pulled away. "I won't leave you alone, though, your pussy's too sweet. Your mouth feels too good around my cock."

"I could tell on you."

Ty bent forward and sucked her nipple into his mouth. "You really think your mother would believe you?"

"Yes, of course."

"Really?" Ty assumed a look of concern. "Alice, I need to get something off my chest. The other night Katie came home and she'd been drinking. She was dressed in...well, let's just say it didn't leave much to the imagination..."

"Stop it," Kate whispered.

"...she came and sat on the couch with me." Ty's face contorted into a pained paternal grimace. "She uh, sat in my lap, if I'm honest.

Then she... rubbed herself all over me. Said she had a crush on me and—Jesus, I'm just a man, what was I supposed to do?"

"You're evil."

Ty dropped his martyred expression and smirked at her. "I am. So if you want to go out drinking with your little friends, you'd better remember to come by here and do right by me first."

As he lowered his lips to hers, Kate was visited by a sharp, unwelcome flash of awareness. Why was she so turned on by her and Ty eroticizing the worst stereotypes about their genders? Man as perverted predator, woman as passive vessel. Kate had read every book on kink and plenty on sexual psychology, she'd discussed it with Maria and the internet at large, but at that moment, the question actually baffled her; *why was she doing this?*

Ty's fingers tightened on her nipples, biting into the sensitive flesh. "Get on your knees, girl."

"No."

"If that's the way you want to play it." Ty slapped his palm into her ass. She'd barely registered the sting before she was lifted into the air and deposited on her knees. He unzipped his jeans one-handed and pulled out his cock. It was thick with blood and glossy at the tip. Too eager to pretend to resist, Kate bent forward to put her mouth on it. Ty pressed a gentle palm to her forehead. "Just a minute."

He picked up the remote and started doing something to the TV. Kate realised he was selecting something to watch while she sucked him off. Another zing sizzled down between her legs.

"There we go." Ty put down the remote and fisted his cock. "Come get it."

Kate looked up at him. Her handsome boss didn't look the least bit civilized now. The TV was flickering over his sharp cheekbones, making him look hard and unkind. She thought of her silly girlish fantasy and shuddered at the thought of trying to fuse it with this uncompromisingly cruel man. It would never, could never, work. This was the way Ty liked to play and she needed to get used to it. She bent forward and sucked him into her mouth like a good girl.

Ty groaned, his hand sifting through her hair. "That's it, deeper now, you know how I like it."

Kate did know. Ty seemed to have a particular affinity for blow jobs. Men's enjoyment of that particular act was well documented, but he almost seemed to prefer them to sex. She'd given more BJs in a few short weeks than she had in her whole life. She guessed he liked the power of watching a woman service the undeniably impressive length of his cock.

As she sucked, the moans on the TV grew more intense, and she could hear sharp slapping sounds, either spanking or sex. The fact that she couldn't turn to look at them made the whole scene more erotic. Ty reached down and cupped her breast. "Fuck, your skin is so soft."

She let out a tiny moan.

"Not as soft as your pussy, though, is it? Soft and wet and tight. I've been thinking about getting you on the pill so I can ride you without a condom. Would you like that, Katie? Feeling me come inside you? Having it run down your thighs afterward?"

Kate's pussy throbbed and without any other way to express herself, she sucked him harder, bringing her mouth further and further down his cock. It was already much easier to do this without choking. She was like the girls at school who made themselves throw up so many times, they could shove a whole toothbrush down their throats. Only less sad, obviously.

Ty's hand tightened in her hair. "That's a good girl. Push your hands inside those shorts and get your pussy ready for me."

She did what she was told, unbuttoning her shorts and sliding her fingertips into her underwear. She was so hot and damp she felt like a rain forest, and the slightest strokes made her shudder.

"That's it," Ty muttered. "Get yourself off while you suck me."

After that, everything seemed to move in leaps. Kate had so much to do—sucking, stroking, listening to Ty's groans and the sounds of porn. She couldn't concentrate on any one thing, her attention leapt from sensation to sensation trying to take it all in. Pre-come began to slick the head of his cock and his motions became rougher. He tugged her hair, forcing himself deep between her lips. As always, the degradation sharpened her arousal. She slipped a finger inside herself and looked up, hoping to see him watching TV and found his gaze fixed on her. His expression was so tender, so infinitely soft, she choked from sheer surprise.

Ty's fist wrapped itself even more tightly in her hair. "You keep your eyes on my cock where they belong, little girl."

Before she could respond, he thrust his hips upward and began fucking himself into her mouth. She felt a slight panic as he bumped against her soft palate and she ceased all attempts to get herself off as she breathed deep through her nose. Ty's gaze was locked on the porn now, drinking it in as he used her mouth. Kate swallowed furiously, trying to keep spit from spraying out of her mouth like a busted fire hydrant. She was barely sucking, just keeping her teeth out of the way and attempting not to choke. Above her, Ty moaned. "I'm gonna come."

Please god, she thought, *I'm only three, maybe four seconds away from gagging, please let me hold out.*

She heard his strangled cry, felt his cock throb as he came but was amazed to discover that she couldn't taste his orgasm. The mess of his semen had slid straight down her throat.

That's one plus to deep throating, she thought, wiping a hand across her lips. Her throat was slightly tender, but she didn't mind. She had swallowed what had to be four-fifths of Tyler Henderson's insane wang and lived to tell the tale; she was a hero.

Ty released her hair. "You okay, baby?"

She thought she'd pushed it down, but as soon as he called her 'baby' it rose again, the desire for him to take her slowly and lovingly in a bed. She hated herself a little for being such a cliché. What they'd just done had been so filthy and hot. Why couldn't she just enjoy that, the way he could? It was like he had strength she didn't, an ability to disconnect that she just didn't possess. Was it because she hadn't had enough sex, or was it really just easier for men? Kate resolved to stop letting her dumb heart get the better of her. "I'm fine."

"Good, that was one hell of a job you just did." Ty stretched his arms above his head and yawned. "Just give me a minute, and I'll sort you out."

"You don't have to do that."

Ty's post-orgasm softness faded like morning frost. "Middleton, take off those shorts and sit on my fuckin' lap. I wanna watch the wheels on your skates spin while I get you off."

A few seconds later, she was riding his hand, his bunched fingers feeling roughly the size of a rolling pin.

"That's it," Ty muttered as he rocked her back and forth. "You like this, don't you?"

"Yes."

"That's because you're a needy little thing now you're broken in. You need dick once a day, or you start to misbehave. I'm gonna have to think up new ways to punish you now I know spanking just gets you wet."

"But—ooh."

His finger circled her asshole, damp and hard. "Have you ever touched yourself here?"

"A little, but I've never had anything inside."

"Figured." Ty slid the tip of his finger just past the ring of muscle. "That feel okay?"

"Um…" The burn was uncomfortable, but it was also nice, wrong, and right just like the games they played. "I think so."

"I won't go any deeper than this for now, but we'll work on it. I'd love to fuck you in the ass, sweetheart."

Kate tried to picture his enormous wang going into her backside and tensed. "Um, have you done this before?"

Ty chuckled. "Yes."

Figured. "How often? And were the women okay afterward? Like could they walk and sit in regular chairs and perform normal butt related activi—"

Ty placed a gentle hand over her mouth. "Don't worry about it right now. We're a long way from that. Just relax and feel what I'm doing to you."

"But—"

"Middleton, I promise if I stick it in your ass, you'll be so ready for it, every inch'll feel like heaven. Now close your eyes and come on me."

Kate closed her eyes and let the sensations take her. She felt the fingers penetrating her, rubbing inside and around her most sensitive areas. She remembered the way his eyes had locked on the TV as she sucked him, the way he'd used her. She felt the press of the roller skates against her feet, clasping her in discomfort as this big hard man forced a response from her body. She shuddered, pressure growing tight in her middle. "Daddy, I think I'm going to..."

Ty leaned forward and buried his face in her neck, the stubble brushing against her as his fingers worked their magic. "Do it, you dirty little girl."

When she was done, Ty wiped his hands on his T-shirt and reached around her to the remote, turning off the porn she'd only dimly registered. "How was that?"

Kate nodded faintly.

"Again?"

"I think I might die."

Ty laughed. There was a warmth to it that, combined with the memory of him gazing tenderly down at her, inspired her to do something silly—she wrapped her arms around his neck and slumped into his chest. She enjoyed a single second of bliss before Ty lifted her up and gently placed her onto the couch. "How are you feeling? Are you warm enough?"

She nodded, knowing there was no reason for the lump in her throat, the hollow sensation in her chest. Ty's palm slid up her leg. "You're shivering, hang on a sec."

He undid the laces on her roller skates and tugged them off her feet, then he took the peach blanket from the back of the couch and wrapped it tightly around her, binding her so tightly Kate felt like a Chinese noblewoman's foot during the Song dynasty.

Why does he keep doing this? Does he think I like it or is it some kind of weird blanket fetish?

Ty stood up. "I'm gonna grab a beer. You want something, or did you have enough espresso martinis at the bar?"

Kate felt a stab of fear. She'd chewed gum all the way home to avoid coffee breath but maybe it hadn't worked? "How did you know I drank espresso martinis?"

A flash of his soft, post-orgasm smile. "I can smell it on your hands. My mate Georgie's addicted to them. Every time we go out she has about five and spends the rest of the night talking like one of those cartoon chipmunks. Rum?"

"Yes, please."

As he left for the kitchen, Kate digested the fact that he had a friend called Georgie. A woman who liked espresso martinis. It was such a little fact, and yet it felt like someone had placed a diamond in her hand. She closed her eyes and imagined the three of them having drinks together. Her and Ty and Georgie, chatting about work and holidays and how she and Ty met...

"Still feel okay?" he asked when he returned from the kitchen with a beer and a small glass of Sailor Jerry.

"Totally." Kate sat up and shook off her swaddles so she could hold the glass. "How do you feel?"

"I'm good." Ty's smile wasn't exactly patronising but you could tell he thought she was cute for asking because of course, he was totally fine. Always and perpetually fine. Something about that flicked at her brain. She took a small sip of rum and felt it trickling into her belly.

Ty settled on the couch beside her, careful, as always, not to touch her. Another irritable flick. She didn't have cooties and even if she did they'd be swimming around in the head of his penis right now, so why was he so uptight about touching her? She bet if science found a way for him to fuck her via some sort of virtual reality/fleshlight situation, he'd take it.

Kate realised she'd just thought the word 'fuck' without feeling the slightest bit guilty. She drank some more rum.

"You didn't mind the porn, did you?" Ty asked, breaking the silence. "I thought it might be good for shock value."

"It was, but you kind of freaked me out at first. I thought you might be having an orgy in my house."

Ty laughed. "I wouldn't do that to you, I promise. Do you want me to leave you the disk?"

"I'm a millennial; I get my kicks on Tumblr—mostly in GIF form."

"Of course." He nudged one of her roller skates with his foot. "So, roller derby. How'd you get into that?"

"I saw a poster about it," Kate lied, not wanting to bring up *Whip It* and her quest for female friendship. "I loved skating when I was a kid. I thought it would be fun and it is. Fun and occasionally painful."

"How does it work, like the competition side of things? How do you score?"

They talked roller derby for a few minutes until Kate, tired of trying to use her fingers to demonstrate blocking and jamming, got her phone and showed him an instructional YouTube video. Watching it required him to sit right beside her, and Kate found herself zoning out to the feel of his shoulder against hers, the smell of his sweat and cologne.

That was when it hit her—in the excitement of her upcoming date, she'd forgotten to take her Ritalin. No wonder she'd spent half the night feeling as loose as a scarf knitted by a ten-year-old. She leapt to her feet. "I have to...pee."

Ty raised a brow. "Okay."

She locked herself in the bathroom, swallowing her pill with water she sucked straight from the tap. Ty was too much of a gentleman to ask but she suspected he already knew she wasn't peeing. It should be easy to tell him she had a totally manageable form of ADHD but what folks didn't know about behavioural disorders could fill a mine shaft. Kate wasn't sure what was worse, the people who thought she was crazy, the people who thought ADHD was invented to sell pills, or the people who wanted to buy her Ritalin.

Or the people like Maria who think you're a googly-eyed flower who can't take care of herself.

"Shut up," Kate told her reflection. "You're always ready with a bitchy comment, but where were you when I needed to be reminded to take my pill?"

The voice said nothing.

"Exactly."

When she returned to the couch, Ty didn't so much as bat an eyelid. "So," he said as she sat down. "Whereabouts are your games played?"

"They're called bouts," Kate corrected with a smile. "And North-cote Stadium."

"Hipster town, hipster sport."

"Pretty much." Kate was struck with a sudden idea. "You know if you want to see a game, I could get you a ticket. Our finals are coming up and there's heaps of night markets and taco trucks and...would you want to come?"

Ty took a long slug of beer before answering. "Not sure that's my scene, Middleton. Thanks, though."

She felt the air cool between them, the electric warmth evaporating into wherever negative romantic chemistry went. Kate picked up her rum and sipped it. She should have been embarrassed but weirdly she wasn't. The man had expressed an interest in roller derby and she had invited him to a bout. He'd said no, which he was at liberty to do, though considering she'd just defied nature to put most of his penis in her throat, he could have been nicer about it.

"I have a question for you," she said without thinking.

"Oh yeah?"

Kate's heart banged a warning against her chest, but she ignored it. "I go down on you all the time, and you've never gone down on me."

Ty's 'you're so cute' smile vanished. The atmosphere between them cooled another degree. "That's not a question."

Kate's hands were trembling, but she wasn't ready to back down, she really freaking wanted to know why he wouldn't do it. "My question is, why haven't you ever gone down on me?"

"Am I not getting you off?"

Ty's voice made her think of rusted axes embedded for centuries in mossy logs. "Yeah, but—"

"Go to some other man if you want your pussy licked, Middleton. I don't do it."

Kate's magical confidence melted away as swiftly as it had emerged. She tugged the blanket across her lap, needing the warmth. How did a guy get away with not giving head in this day and age? Maybe he was just so handsome no one ever demanded it of him. Still, if the old clichés were true and you were what you ate, she would basically be his sperm. It seemed uncharacteristically selfish that he wouldn't return the favour. That he would rather she slept with another man than get that from him. *Prick*, she thought, the word sharp as a vaccination. *Prick*.

"It's not what you're thinking."

Kate turned to look at Ty. "Huh?"

"Me not eating pussy doesn't have anything to do with the taste, or how it looks or being lazy."

"Then why don't you do it?"

"Because..." Ty looked as uncomfortable as Kate had ever seen him. "...it's a submissive thing."

She was so surprised by his answer she laughed. "Are you for real?"

Lines furrowed his handsome brow. "Yes."

"My sister Claudia once faked a pregnancy to get out of the year ten swimming carnival and this is *still* the worst excuse I've ever heard."

"Are you looking to get your backside slapped?"

Kate wasn't done being confused about his vagina prejudice but her body heated at the idea of another round. She chewed her lower lip.

Ty smirked. "Feeling shy, are you? That's okay, we can play like that."

He reached out to grip her hair but Kate held up a hand, warding him off. "Can't you tell me why you won't do it to me? Really?"

Ty opened his mouth, then closed it again shaking his head. "I already gave you my answer, Middleton. We're leaving it at that."

"And what if I decide I don't give head anymore?"

"You'd miss it too much. I see you pressing your legs together whenever you're blowing me. You like it. You like it when I pretend I'm watching TV or drinking beer, too. When I'm acting like I don't know there's a girl between my legs."

Kate looked away, embarrassed to have been caught out. It was bizarre how Ty could be so cagey about some things and so open about others. They had such a bipolar relationship. Sometimes she felt like he knew her better than anyone. Other times it felt like they were strangers who'd happened to see each other come.

Her stomach gave a painful rumble. On days when she knew she was seeing Ty, she was always too nervous to eat. Now she was starving. She needed dinner, something heavy with lots of salt and sauce. She reached over and grabbed her phone.

"What are you doing?" Ty asked with a frown.

"Ordering dinner. Are you hungry?"

"No. I'm good."

He was going to leave; she could feel it in the current of the air, in the tone of his voice. He could drink with her, eat her cupcakes or slices, but it was clear that in his mind an entire meal was violation of their sex-buddy code. Kate's stomach squirmed but she forced herself to open the Uber Eats app and scroll through the options. "All I've eaten today is espresso martinis and your semen. As nutritionally balanced as that is, I need dinner."

Out of the corner of her eye, she saw Ty staring at her, his mouth slightly open. She felt a perverse sense of satisfaction. "Hey, did you know Cookie does Uber Eats?"

"No, I didn't," Ty said warily. Every Melbournite knew about Cookie, they did the best Thai fusion food in the city, and if she'd once heard Ty tell Stormy it was his favourite restaurant, that was just a strange coincidence.

"Well, they do," Kate said in her chirpiest voice. "I'm gonna get

Penang Curry, fat rice, salt and pepper calamari, and sticky rice pudding."

She watched in her peripheral vision as Ty opened his mouth. Closed it. Opened it again.

Come on, have dinner with me, you know you want to...

"Middleton?"

She glanced at him, all casual-like. "Yeah?"

"Can you put down five-spice chicken?"

Kate turned her head away so he wouldn't see her smile. "Sure."

"I can see you smiling."

"I'm not," Kate said, adding five-spice chicken to her order.

Ty made a soft growling noise, like a hostile bear. "I'm gonna beat your ass while we wait for our food."

"Okay."

"It's going to hurt."

"I'm sure it will."

"Then I'm going to fuck you from behind while you bite down on your panties."

Kate licked her lower lip. "Fine."

Ty stood up, unbuckling his belt and pulling it from its loops. "When our food gets here you'll be lucky if I don't make you get the door naked. Now come here."

12

"Who are you sleeping with?" Georgie demanded. The two of them were weaving their way out of Nova Cinema toward the little patisserie where they always got coffee after a movie.

"Fuck, George, don't you at least want to *pretend* to talk about the movie?"

"The lighthouse is sad and so am I. Who are you sleeping with?"

"A gentleman never tells."

Georgie snorted. "You weren't nearly so gallant when we were at uni. Anyone I know?"

"No."

He could feel his friend staring at him. Georgie had intense single-lidded eyes, as meticulous at spotting anomalies in her personal life as they were spotting damaged heart valves in her patients. "You like her, whoever she is, don't you?"

Ty groaned. This focused scrutiny was why he'd wanted Georgie's husband to join them tonight, but Dave hated arthouse films. "They're always about the fucking ocean," he said. "Why are they always about the fucking ocean?"

To be fair, this movie *had* been about a couple finding a baby by the ocean. Ty circumvented a cello player busking behind a woollen hat, hoping that Georgie would take his silence as a hint and drop the matter.

"Tyler. Answer me."

He looked sideways at her. Like Middleton, Georgie looked much younger than she was; her pale skin was as unlined as it had been when they'd met at an orientation party. They had almost nothing in common, the Queensland farm boy and the Vietnamese-born yuppie, but they'd gotten on like a house on fire. They studied together, backpacked through Asia together, even lived together for a while in their twenties before Georgie's cat addiction drove him to more hairless pastures. There had never been any sexual attraction between them. The idea of Georgie calling him 'Daddy' made Ty want to puke and Georgie swore she was still traumatized from the time she'd accidentally seen his dick in the shower. Still, she was his oldest friend, something that had given Veronica no end of grief. That, and the fact he and George once made a drunken marriage pact, agreeing they'd get hitched if they were fifty and single.

As the one to uncover Veronica's cheating, Georgie seemed to think she was personally responsible for finding him another fiancée. She constantly badgered him about dating and now she'd (rightly) guessed he was sleeping with someone, she was desperate to find out who it was. Ty knew he had no obligations to tell his friends—or anyone—about Middleton, but Georgie was crafty. If he didn't throw her a bone there was every chance she'd use her brilliant cardiologist brain to access the information by stealth and uncover a lot more than he was comfortable with her knowing. The sensible thing to do was talk. "You're right," he told her. "I'm sleeping with someone."

Georgie let out an excited squeal.

"*Don't* get your hopes up," Ty warned. "It's just sex."

"That could turn into more!"

"It won't. She's twenty-five and we work together."

"Ooh, risky."

"You would know."

Before she met Dave, Georgie had had a disastrous fling with a twenty-three-year-old nurse. It had ended on what George called 'bad terms' and Ty called 'a clusterfuck.' There had been stalking, threats of libel, and constant drama. Thoughts of things taking a similar path with Middleton made him break out in a cold sweat.

Georgie sighed loudly. "How could such a beautiful man be so clueless?" she asked, clearly referring to the nurse.

"Because his life's passion was skateboarding and he still lived with his parents?"

She made a face. "Yeah, I always forget that. So, how's your bit of fluff, then? Nice?"

Ty eyed his best friend suspiciously. "Nice enough. Don't even think about calling GGS and trying to find out who she is."

Georgie scowled. "Well, when can I meet her?"

"How about never? Unless you feel like stopping by her place and cheering me on while I—"

She punched him hard on the arm. "You're so gross. Fine, so it's not serious and I don't get to meet her, but promise me you're not being a man about this?"

He knew what she was asking, knew why the answer meant so much to her. "I promise. I've been very clear about what this is and isn't. We're having fun and she knows it's not serious."

Georgie visibly relaxed. "Good, I don't want a repeat of The Incident."

Ty reflexively rubbed his eyebrow. "No one does."

In his second semester of uni, he'd slid into some bad behaviour. He'd held the urge to fuck at arm's length for so long that when the dam burst, he had no self-control. It was all too easy for him to take girls to bed, and soon the regularity with which he could get his dick sucked made a pig of him. He screwed two, or three times a day, and still went out to clubs and parties, looking for more. Georgie, who knew he'd come to uni a virgin, let it go for a while, but soon their friendship became strained. She thought he was being an asshole, sticking his dick into anything he could and not giving a damn about anyone's feelings but his own. It was true, he had girls crying outside his dorm so often the spot became known as 'the fountain,' but he didn't care. It felt too good, and as he told Georgie, if girls couldn't handle no-strings sex they shouldn't be fucking him in the first place.

The good times ended the night she came to his dorm room for a study date and found him fucking one of her best friends—the sister of a girl he'd hooked up with two nights before. Georgie snapped. She threw a copy of *Intercourse* at his head, shouted "who the fuck are you?" and ran away, vowing their friendship was over. After a week of intense grovelling on his behalf they made up and Ty promised not to let things get that out of hand ever again.

"You better not," Georgie had told him. "You can have sex with whoever wants to have sex with you, but there's no need to be a cunt about it."

It was a philosophy Ty had tried to respect ever since.

"You know I still can't find that copy of *Intercourse*," Georgie said as they entered Monique café.

"Don't worry about it," Ty told her, inhaling the scent of fresh coffee and warm sugar. "If I fuck up you can always hit me with a hardback of *The Feminine Mystique*."

"True."

They ordered coffee and cannoli and sat at their usual table by the window.

"So what gives the girl away?" Georgie asked.

"Huh?"

"What reminds you she's ridiculously young? Is she broke? Living with her parents? Posts every dump she takes on Instagram? Plays with fidget spinners?"

"I said she's twenty-five, not five," Ty said indignantly. "She's a civil engineer. She has her own place and she likes nature documentaries and making biscuits."

"She's not a bitch?"

"Fuck no. She's sweet as anything, would give you the shirt off her back if you asked. She's a little bit weird but that's part of her charm. She's from the country, one of those big Catholic families."

"Ah," Georgie said knowingly. "So she's batshit in bed?"

"You have no fucking idea."

Ty kept waiting for the day when Middleton wouldn't be astonished by his ability to make her come, but it never arrived. Every time he got her off, she swooned. Her blissful bewilderment made everything they did so much hotter. He felt like a god who'd come down from heaven to teach mortals about sex.

"So," George said, interrupting his wistful recollection of Middleton on all fours. "Is she pretty?"

"Gorgeous," Ty said absently. "Real girly, you know? Long brown hair and freckles. She's shy, you can tell she doesn't know how attractive she is, but when she smiles—"

Ty caught sight of his best friend's smug expression and realised he'd been had. "You're a bitch, Georgie."

She laughed. "I am, aren't I?"

"I mean it. I'm never telling you shit ever again."

"Oh, don't be so dramatic! I only did it because I can tell you're really happy for the first time since Medusa left. If this girl is mature and cute and you like her...?"

"Not going to happen."

Georgie put both palms on the table. "But what if—"

"She does roller derby," Ty interrupted. "You know that game where girls in fishnets and roller skates try to knock each other over?"

Georgie's hopeful expression faded. "Seriously?"

"Yes, seriously. And she..." he struggled to think of something else that would convince her that he and Middleton were a bust. "...she wears headbands with sequins on them."

Georgie looked like the government had declared a nation-wide embargo on coffee beans. "You can't marry a girl who wears sequin headbands!"

"Yeah. No shit."

Their order arrived and they both took big bites out of their chocolate cannoli.

"You never get dessert," Georgie said, bits of pastry flicking out of her mouth. "What's your deal?"

Ty shrugged. He'd been craving custard ever since that first plate of slice at Middleton's place. The taste was bound up in the bone-deep satisfaction of lying on her couch, his lifelong fantasy fulfilled. Although he'd have a hard time explaining that to his GP if his cholesterol shot up fifty points.

"About your fuck-buddy..." Georgie swallowed the last of her cannoli and picked up her second. She always ate like it was going out of style and yet remained rake-thin, another unforgivable offence in Veronica's eyes. "...you're just going to wait for the sex to run out of steam?"

Ty nodded. In truth, he had no idea what he was going to do. Before Middleton he'd been living on a steady diet of irritation and apathy. Now he lived in a parallel dimension where outwardly everything was the same and inwardly things couldn't be different. The smallest things made him feel good—duck curries, good coffee, drinking a beer in the shower, football games where you jumped to your feet and swore at the TV. He was sleeping better, hitting the pool almost every morning the way he had before Veronica left. The reflection in the mirror was frequently as clear-eyed as it had been in Middleton's bathroom. He *was* happier and could understand why people like Georgie would think that made Middleton his dream girl, but they were wrong.

What he had with Middleton worked because it was void of relationship shit. A couple of nights a week, he fucked her senseless, then they watched documentaries and got takeout. They didn't discuss work or politics or whose turn it was to do the dishes. They took a holiday together in the middle of her lounge room and everyone knew holidays had to end.

So where did that leave them? Ty couldn't see the sex running out of steam, it was just too fucking good and even if it did, who knew how long that would take? He couldn't spend years fucking Middleton. He was already far too possessive. His idiotic suggestion she go to another man to get eaten out was weighing on him like a tonne of bricks. The solution was simple—go down on her—but the thought of putting his mouth between Middleton's legs and nuzzling that sweet pink place made him feel woozy. It was too intimate. He couldn't do it to her for the same reason he couldn't spend the night or cuddle. It would shove him over the invisible line separating fuck-buddy from lover, holiday from real life.

"Ty?" Georgie poked him with her dessert fork.

"Huh?"

She rolled her eyes. "Are you officially too old to go to the movies on a school night?"

"Fuck off, you're a week younger than me."

"Yeah, but you have more wrinkles."

Ty shot her a nasty look. "What were you saying?"

"I said, 'if you're really not interested in dating your side piece then be kind to her. Teach her everything you know. I'm sure her future husband will thank you for it.'"

Ty took another bite of cannoli and swallowed without chewing, trying to force down all the things he wanted to say.

"Are you okay?" Georgie, asked, her sharp eyes scanning for whys and hows.

"I'm fine. By the way, I still haven't written another chapter."

That did it. For the rest of their coffee date, Georgie berated him for not trying hard enough with his manuscript, and he was free from further discussions of Middleton and why the idea of her getting married turned his guts to lead.

The next day Ty sat at his desk neglecting designs he should have been proofing and emails he should have been sending in favor of torturing himself with images of Middleton and her faceless, asshole husband—marrying him, fucking him, going to the Eiffel Tower with him and posting dumb pictures on social media. He knew she would date after he was gone, *hoped* she would date even, but something about the thought of her with a husband did his head in.

By early afternoon he had the answer, though he didn't much like it; if she got married, it would be to a man like him. Middleton wasn't the kind of girl who settled. She walked the extra block to get good coffee from Galvano's. She took the time to mark up her designs by hand so that every detail was flawless. Her clothes were always ironed and her patent leather shoes shiny with polish. She served her tea in fancy mugs and her desserts on fancy plates. Now that he'd shown her how good sex could be, she wouldn't want anything less. Her husband would be her Daddy, her last and only Daddy. That shouldn't have mattered, but it did. It fucking *ate* at him.

As he sat, fuming about Middleton's relationship with her future husband, a much wiser part of Ty told him things needed to end. He'd had amicable fuck-buddy arrangements before and while he was always a little possessive of the women he slept with, this was different. He'd been thinking of Middleton as a refuge, a place where he could relax and be himself as he could nowhere else, but really she was a crutch. The smart thing to do would be to disentangle himself from her before either or both of them got hurt.

He pulled out his phone to suggest they get a 'this has been fun, but I need some space' coffee and found she'd sent him a picture text.

Last week he'd laid her on her living room rug, written 'Daddy's girl' on her tits with lipstick (a cheap, cherry-coloured one he'd bought from the chemist) and jacked off onto the letters. He hadn't realised she'd taken a picture of the damage and yet there it was, his words and his come glistening all over her perfect breasts. Her message was three words long—*punish me tonight?*

Ty groaned and decided the smart thing could always wait until tomorrow. *I'll be there at seven,* he wrote back. *Just you fucking wait, Middleton.*

"Yay," she wrote. *"See you soon."*

When Ty was with the MFB, one of the things he loved most had been coming in from a job and pulling off his uniform. The relief of being able to move without fifteen kilograms of damp, smoke-saturated gear was ecstasy. It was also the closest thing he had to describe how he felt knowing he had a date with Middleton.

Another bad sign.

Ty shoved his phone in his desk drawer and attempted to do some work. He was only just settling in when Johnno, the big boss, appeared in his doorway. "Got a minute, Hendo?"

"Sure thing."

Johnno swaggered into the room. He was an enormous man, even taller than Ty with a bald head and a big round middle which he seemed to deliberately emphasise with too-tight shirts. A week ago Middleton had said he reminded her of Humpty Dumpty and Ty hadn't been able to think of anything since. He cleared his throat. "What can I do for you, boss?"

"What can't you do for me, Hendo?"

Johnno stood in the centre of the room, rocking his bulk backward and forward.

Humpty Dumpty sat on the wall...

"S'pose you know about the Walker-Mills pitch tomorrow?"

Humpty Dumpty had a great fall...

Ty cursed Middleton's imagination. "Er, yeah, Stormy's on it, right?"

"He was until I found out WM are sending Daniel Warhurst to negotiate."

"Shit." Stormy and Warhurst had a long-standing feud over a bungled fibreglass order and could barely be in the same room together. "Who do we put up instead?"

"I'm thinking Middleton could take the wheel."

Ty felt the usual stab of panicky surprise at hearing his lover's nickname at work, then recovered when he realised the conversation wasn't about him doing unspeakable things to her. "Sounds good. I'm sure she'd appreciate the experience. You want me to have a word with her? I can move some stuff around, go into the presentation with her if you think she needs the support."

Johnno gave him the kind of shifty grin that usually precipitated a visit to a strip club. "Here's the thing, Hendo—actually, hang on a sec..."

He strode over to the door and pulled it shut with a snap. Ty's stomach roiled. "Is everything okay?"

"Of course." Johnno turned to face him, his smile shiftier than ever. "Just wanted to say, you know how Warhurst has a bit of an eye for the ladies?"

"Yeah," Ty said, though he'd have phrased it *'Warhurst can't confine his dick to places where it actually belongs, like his pants and his wife.'* "So

you do want me in the meeting with Middleton? Make sure he
doesn't pull any funny business?"

"Not exactly." Johnno continued rocking on his heels. Backward
and forward, backward and forward. Ty waited for him to keep talking. His guts were heavy again and not because of Middleton's imaginary spouse.

"Word on the street is Warhurst likes 'em young with brown hair,"
Johnno said, staring out of Ty's window.

"And?" Ty knew he was being rude but he couldn't handle the
suspense.

"And, we've been having a bit of trouble with WM lately, I reckon
having Middleton pitch will soften him up, metaphorically speaking.
What do you think?"

Ten years ago, Ty's crew had been assigned to a fire at a canning
factory. The situation had been contained and all the fireys and
cops were bantering back and forth, discussing who'd give state-
ments to the journalists hanging around. Then a grinding metallic
screech had cut through the air like a blade. Someone shouted
'backdraft' but before they'd gotten half of it out, the building
exploded. The force of it had been so strong it knocked Ty to the
ground, and when he got to his feet, all he could hear was the
whine of his inner ear cells dying. He could hear that ringing
again now.

His boss wanted to use Middleton as fuckbait. His boss wanted to
use Middleton as fuckbait and he was confiding in Ty as though he
was sure he would think it was a fantastic idea.

"Hendo?" Johnno raised a brow at him. "What do you think?"

Ty wondered what Johnno would do if he just stood up, walked
around his desk, and hit him dead in the stomach. What did *he* think?
He thought serving Middleton up like she was a fat juicy steak would
have gone against his moral code even if he *wasn't* attracted to her,
but the fact that he *was* attracted to her; had in fact slept with her,
bruised her skin, eaten her food and seen her hedgehog pajamas
made him so angry he thought he was going to fucking explode.

He opened his mouth to tell Johnno he was as big a pervert as

Warhurst—only stupider—when common sense tapped him on the shoulder.

Ty wasn't an engineer by trade. He'd studied law and political science at university, trained as a chef, then joined the MFB. When his body was wrung out from firefighting, and he desperately needed a job it had been Johnno who'd hired him despite his negligible qualifications. It had been Johnno who promoted him within six months and let him take all his yearly leave at once so he could travel. Ty had been to his house, had dinner with his wife and kids. He'd always considered him a solid acquaintance, if not a friend. He was in his late sixties. Maybe he didn't know what he was—

Inside his head, Georgie gave a high mocking laugh. *Of course, he doesn't know what he's doing is wrong! He's just a widdle business baby!*

Shut up George, Ty thought. *I need to concentrate.*

He mustered every ounce of his self-control and said, "I don't think that's a smart idea."

Johnno looked taken aback. "Why not?"

"If Warhurst says anything inappropriate, we could have a serious HR problem on our hands."

Johnno laughed. "Middleton's a good girl, she won't say anything."

Ty gripped his thigh under his desk and squeezed so hard it hurt. He didn't know what was worse, the blatant disregard for Middleton's well being or hearing Johnno call her what he himself had called her a roughly million times, *good girl*.

Ty took a deep breath. "Remember when Harry Telfer groped that waitress at the end-of-year Christmas party and she pressed charges?"

Johnno gave a sympathetic groan. "Had to sack him *and* we lost three major deals."

"Right. The last thing we need is that kind of shit happening again. If this Warhurst prick wants to see some T and A, have Dutchy take him to the strippers. We'll make the sale either way, Walker-Mills always buy with us. It's not worth alienating Middleton or sending her off on stress leave if the presentation goes sour."

His boss blinked at him, as though the pitfalls of encouraging sexual harassment in the workplace had never crossed his mind. "That's a fair point, Hendo."

The tension in Ty's chest eased a little. "So can Dutchy take the pitch? I think he's free."

"S'pose." Johnno made a noise like an irritable old elephant. "That's the problem with having females on staff, isn't it? They come with their own little set of problems."

The ringing in Ty's ears started up, louder and more urgent than before. He stood.

Johnno frowned at him. "Are you feeling okay?"

"Bit tired, I might go get a coffee," he improvised, his blood pumping hard in his ears.

"No worries," Johnno said easily. "One more thing, the Pinkleton job up in Queensland, looks like it might be a big one, two weeks or more. I know it's below your pay grade, but Kingsolver's wife's just about due and I know you've got family up that way. Would you think about going?"

"Sure," Ty said, his head too full to process any new information. "I'll let you know."

"No problem. If you do decide to go, book your flights and bill 'em to accounts. See you this arvo."

With that, his boss swanned out of the room, not a care in the world. As soon as he was gone Ty shoved his hands into his hair. "Fuck. Fuck. Fuck."

He wasn't stupid; he knew GGS was a bit blokey, a bit old fashioned, but he hadn't thought his boss would treat Middleton like she was a bikini-clad promotional model *'let us design your apartments and you might get a feel of our only female engineer's tits!'* And sure, he'd stopped Johnno from pimping her out but he'd also deprived Middleton of a chance to pitch to a big company solo; an opportunity he was sure she would have wanted.

Ty decided he would go and get himself a coffee, if only for the chance to stretch his legs and make some sense of this mess. He grabbed his coat and headed out to the street. The winter air went some way toward clearing his head.

He could fix this, he decided. He'd email a few clients and suggest Middleton could handle their orders. He'd set up some training courses for her and ask her to pitch to someone who wasn't a fuckin' perv. Or let her decide if she wanted to do it and then sit in the corner of the room and glare at every motherfucker who couldn't keep their eyes and mouths to them-fucking-selves. If anyone said it was favoritism they could go fuck themselves. Middleton was a solid engineer and she'd been at GGS for over two years. It was high time she moved up the greasy corporate totem pole. Feeling slightly better, Ty ordered a large latte and stood in the waiting area. He was scanning a discarded newspaper when his phone buzzed in his coat pocket. He pulled it out and when he saw the name flashing up on the screen, dropped it. The device hit his foot and bounced, skidding across the marble floors and between the legs of a woman in a pencil skirt.

"Shit, sorry!" Ty bent to retrieve it and the woman shrieked and backed away.

"Shit," he said again. "Shit! Fuck! Sorry!"

By the time Ty recaptured his phone, it had a chip in the screen and a brand new voicemail message. He shoved it deep into his pocket, collected his coffee, and headed back out into the cold. This time the icy wind barely even registered.

It had been Ty's experience that few exes stayed away for good. A supernatural force seemed to compel them to make contact months, or even years after the breakup, to dip a toe into the waters where passion had once flowed. It was always a stupid idea. As Victor Frankenstein could attest, reanimating a corpse was a fucking minefield. Failed relationships were better off dead, in Ty's opinion, and he'd thought Veronica had agreed. She'd given him his ring back and left him to his misery. Except now she'd decided to put electrodes to the rotting remains of their relationship and give it a small, tentative pulse. Swearing, he stepped into the doorway of an abandoned bookstore and dialed his voicemail service. The seconds it took to connect felt like an eternity and then,

"Hi Tyler, I was just ringing because...because I don't know why I'm ringing."

Veronica's voice was thick as marmalade, the way it always got when she'd been crying for hours. It was unnerving how he could still predict each little gasp and pant, how familiar she sounded.

"I'm so sorry. I was crazy to do this. Ignore me, forget about me, I'll never call you again."

The line disconnected.

She wanted him back. Ty wasn't egotistical; he knew her, knew the way her mind worked, and calling him and leaving this message was exactly what this was. Two and a half years they'd been separated. Twenty-eight months since she'd torn out his insides, stuffed them into the toilet, and hit flush. She was a wife now, a mother, and yet she was calling him, making her name flash up on his phone as 'Veronica Chapel' when they damn well knew it was Veronica Boyle.

Ty's fingers shook as he deleted the voicemail, pent-up anger tremoring out from his chest into his limbs. It was all too much. Georgie's saying Middleton's husband would thank him one day, Johnno's suggestion they use her looks to make a little money, and now this. The incomprehensible return of the woman who'd broken his heart.

Ty pulled off his coat, suddenly so hot it was stifling. He needed to blow off steam, needed a release. It was stupid. Reckless. It flew in the face of his promise to treat Middleton with the respect she deserved, but then there were times when she got off on disrespect. He hoped this would be one of them. He unlocked his phone and texted her to meet him in the GGS storeroom fifteen minutes from now.

13

M iddleton was dead on time. Her low heels clicked on the slate floor as she wove her way through the cramped space. Now that she was sleeping with him she'd mostly reverted back to her old wardrobe but even in a thick pink skirt and a woolly jumper, she couldn't hide the body he knew so well—long legs, apple-sized breasts and a flat velvet-skinned stomach. Her hair was pulled into its usual loose plait and lying across her right shoulder like a shining snake. She squinted in his direction. "Ty? Is that you?"

Her voice was hesitant in the way that said she'd still be a lot more comfortable calling him Mr Henderson. Why that made him ache, Ty had no idea. "Hey, Middleton. Did you take your lunch break?"

"Um, yes." She moved cautiously toward him, stepping over loose bricks and bits of broken glass. "Is this, er, workplace-related?"

Ty gestured around at the old printers, broken fax machines and stacks of building materials whose purpose had long since been forgotten. "What do you think?"

She shook her head, her plait swinging across her shoulder and settling down her back. "So this is a sex thing?"

Ty nodded.

"I, uh, thought you didn't want us to do anything at work? On account of suspicion?"

He eyed her over again, slowly. The predatory lust he felt whenever they played together pulsed through him like a second heartbeat. It wanted to flex, to sprint, to own her in ways that would distract him from everything that wasn't his body and hers. "Rules were made to be broken. Why don't you come on over here?"

She licked her lower lip. "Are you sure?"

"Would I have called you in here if I wasn't sure?"

In his mind Ty had imagined every minute of what was to come. He would grab Middleton around the waist, bend her over the desk he'd cleared off, spank her until she cried, then fuck her from behind. He was going to both hurt and pleasure her and in doing so it would release some of his tension. And yet when she came to him and laid a cautious palm on his chest, something else happened entirely. Ty folded her into his arms and kissed her full on the mouth.

They stood there for god knows how long, swaying from side to side, making out like a couple of teenage virgins. A voice in his head asked him what the fuck he was doing but he ignored it, ignored it and kept kissing Middleton as though all he'd ever intended to do to her in this storeroom was kiss. She was so fucking sweet, a balm on injuries he hadn't even known he had. In the end it was her who ended the kiss. She leaned back, puffy-lipped and dazed and said, "This is amazing but I'm so scared Collins or someone is going to come in looking for Xerox paper and we'll be screwed".

Ty chuckled. "Only two people have the passcode to the door and both of them are in this room. I changed it before you got here. You're safe with me, Middleton, I swear."

She smiled up at him. "I know."

A warm tender sensation, blazing between his ribs like fire. Ty pulled away, knowing if she kept her hands on him he would only want to kiss her some more. He tapped a hand on the desk. "Bend over and pull up your skirt."

She did what he asked, and when her skirt rose, Ty saw she was wearing thick black tights that went up to her waist.

"I'm sorry," Middleton said, clearly embarrassed. "I didn't wear garters or anything, I didn't think we would—"

Ty silenced her with a smack on her ass. "I don't care about your fucking tights. I care about you sending me slutty photos in the middle of the day, like you don't know what that does to me. Like you think you can control my dick. Can you control my dick?"

She looked over her shoulder, the yellowish light of the desk lamp turning her irises to ochre. "No."

"Apologise."

"I'm sorry, Daddy."

If he lived a million years, Ty was sure that word would still affect him the same way, like a pleasurable punch to the stomach. "Not as sorry as you're gonna be."

He yanked down her tights and panties, exposing the round swells of her ass to the musty air of storeroom. She said nothing, just waited with bated breath for him to continue, his perfect little doll. Ty raised a palm and then lowered it again. Something about this didn't feel right. He didn't want to be the bad man spanking his sweet, confused submissive for no reason. He wanted to be the righter of wrongs, to feel justified in punishing her. He seized the base of Middleton's plait. "Tell me something that'll piss me off. Something that'll make me want to spank you."

Most women would have said 'what the fuck?' Middleton didn't so much as blink before screwing up her brow, clearly thinking hard. "I used to put sand in my sister Claudia's lip balm?"

"I said, 'something that'll piss me off,' not 'something adorable.'"

"A guy at JB Hi-Fi once gave me five dollars' change instead of two and I didn't tell him, I just kept the money."

"Middleton, I'm fucking warning you..."

"But I feel really guilty about that! Okay, okay I...um, once spat in Dutchy's coffee."

Ty almost fell the fuck over. *"What?"*

Middleton turned and looked at him, her cheeks blazing with

mortification. "I spat in Dutchy's coffee, when I was getting him coffee from—"

"Yeah, I fucking got that, *why* did you spit in his coffee?"

"I didn't plan to do it," she said, chewing on her knuckle. "But he told the whole break room that women who go home with football players should expect to have sex with them 'one way or the other' and I felt so guilty about not saying something at the time. Then I was carrying his coffee and thinking 'what a stupid, horrible thing to say,' and then I just...spat in his caramel latte. I wasn't thinking about the consequences. I wanted to go back and get him a new one but I'd already been out of the office for twenty minutes... I Googled it and I don't think I could've, you know, *given him anything*, it was just kind of a gross thing to do."

Amazingly, ridiculously, Ty started to laugh. He couldn't help it; the idea of Middleton, sweet Katie McGrath, opening the lid on one of Dutchy's caramel lattes and spitting inside was just too fucking funny.

Middleton covered her face with her hands. "Please don't tell on me," she said through her fingers.

"I won't, but you are never getting me a coffee again."

"I wouldn't do it to you!" She said it with such earnestness, Ty cracked up all over again. He made a mental note to tell Georgie about this, then realised Georgie would see it as more proof that he and Middleton should make a proper go of things. The thought was instantly sobering.

"Are you mad at me?" Middleton asked, no doubt sensing his change of mood.

"No. If Dutchy wants to tell a room a girl can't say no to sex, he shouldn't be surprised to find his coffee full of spit."

Middleton smiled and for some reason it made his heart skip in his chest like he was a fucking milkmaid. Furious with himself and aware their time was running out, Ty re-gripped Middleton's hair. "You're a cute girl, I get that, but I don't want cute right now. I'm pissed off. Give me a reason to spank you like you've never been spanked before."

Middleton chewed her lower lip. "You were a firefighter, right?"

"Yeah."

"In high school me and these boys I used to hang out with lit bottle rockets in the middle of summer and accidentally set a paddock on fire. No one found out it was us. We got away with it."

Ty digested the story. That Middleton could have sparked a massive bush fire did piss him off, but not as much as knowing she'd been friends with the kinds of boys who lit bottle rockets. "Were you friends with a lot of boys, Katie?"

He expected her to say no, but she didn't.

"Yeah, I was."

Another ripple of jealousy flooded through him. He reached down and unbuckled his belt, taking immense satisfaction from the way Middleton's thighs clenched.

"Interesting, I thought you were shy," he said, pulling the leather from his belt-loops.

She mumbled something he couldn't hear.

"What was that?" Ty asked.

"I'm...I'm only really shy around girls.'"

"More and more interesting." Ty folded his belt over and shook out his hand, making sure she could see him doing it. Spanking wasn't just about pain, it was about building tension, making sure the periods before and between strikes were just as electric as the blows themselves. He'd never used a belt on her ass before but Middleton had a pain threshold unlike anything he'd ever seen. It wasn't that he couldn't hurt her, it was that she relished the hurt. The sessions which had reduced her to tears and marked up her ass had gotten her so wet, her inner thighs were slippery afterward. A belt would be well within her limits and would go a lot easier on his hand.

"These boys try to fuck you?" he asked, trailing the leather over her backside.

"Yes."

Ty felt his temper rise exponentially "Of course they did. The real question is, did you fuck any of those boys?"

"No."

"I don't believe you."

"But it's tr—"

He brought the belt down on her ass, the sharp crack like music to his ears. A pink stripe declared itself across Middleton's backside. *Mine,* it said, *she's all mine.* "When did you lose your virginity, Katie?"

"At uni," she said, her voice already quavering. "My first year."

Like me. A strange feeling swept over Ty, not quite nostalgia, but with a similar floating quality. He shoved it aside. "Lift up your arms so I can take off your top."

"Yes, Daddy."

She held up her arms, and he yanked off her heavy jumper, revealing a cream-coloured camisole. She wasn't wearing a bra, and her nipples were hard against the silk. Ty frowned. "Did you wear this for me?"

Middleton's cheeks went as pink as her ass. "No."

Of course she hadn't. *He* hadn't known they would be doing this until half an hour ago. But that didn't make sense; why wear such thick, unattractive tights and go topless? Then it dawned on him. "You like the way it feels, walking around, getting wound up by your clothes all day, don't you?"

She nodded, but he could see there was more. He clasped a gentle hand around her throat. "You pretend a man's doing it, don't you? Telling you that you need to stay turned on all day for him and you're not allowed to finish?"

Middleton whimpered. "Yes..."

"Yes and what else?"

She shook her head, breathing hard.

Ty cracked the belt across her ass, causing another rosy band to bloom across her cheeks. "Fight me and you'll only make it worse."

Middleton's eyes were glossy with tears. "I used to pretend it was for you," she whispered. "I used to pretend you were making me wait."

"Of course you did. I bet you went home and fucked yourself afterward, am I right?"

"No." She squealed as he spanked her again. "*Yes.*"

"You know what that makes you?"

"Yes."

He laid another fat stripe across her ass. "Tell me."

"A bad girl."

Ty huffed out a laugh. "Why does it make you a bad girl?"

He expected some throwaway line about her being dirty, more dialogue to keep the spanking going, keep both of them cranked up, but then she looked right at him and said, "Because I knew you didn't want me and I wanted you anyway. I made you a part of everything and now I don't know what to do."

A single tear fell from her right eye and lay glittering beside her nose.

Ty had never understood the expression 'took my breath away.' Inhaling air was the only thing humans did all day, every day, without fail, but in that moment it was like all the oxygen in his lungs had been sucked out. Like his body was caught in a backdraft.

"Ty? Was that too much?"

He inhaled. It made him feel as though his rib cage might burst through his flesh, but he did it. Then he brought the belt down so hard the sound reverberated around the room. "That's not what you call me when we play like this, is it?"

"Sorry, Daddy," Middleton said, fresh tears welling in her eyes.

"You think I didn't want you?" Ty demanded, bringing the belt down again. "You really think I wasn't panting after your ass, hating myself because I was your boss and old enough to be your..." he spanked her again "...fucking father?"

"I'm sorry," she cried. "I'm so sorry."

He spanked her again and again, telling himself it wasn't because what she said meant anything. It wasn't because he felt like he'd brought a ravenous demon to life and now he had no chance of ever getting rid of it. He used the belt and then his hand and then a discarded wooden ruler he found on an old photocopier. He spanked her until his hand grew numb and then he did it some more. Eventually, when her cries started to carry the faint edge of strain he stopped, his chest heaving, sweat budding all over his brow.

Middleton turned to look at him, her face shining with tears. "More? Please?"

He ignored her. Any more and she'd be limping back to her desk and besides, they were almost out of time. The folds of her cunt were gleaming, beckoning him to take his prize. It took all his willpower not to fuck her bare, slam into her soaked pussy and feel her freshly-spanked skin blistering against him. He unzipped his fly, pulling out the condom he'd stashed in his pocket. "You ready?"

Middleton arched her back. "So ready."

Ty sheathed himself and slid wordlessly into her cunt. She was hot and tight as a glove and moaning as sweetly as a man could hope for, but it didn't feel right. Or maybe it felt *too* right, like coming home or sinking into a warm bath. Somewhere in all the spanking he'd exorcised his anger and he wanted it back. Wanted to purge away the tenderness that was always brimming inside him when he was around her.

"Tell me something else," he said. "Something about other men getting to have what's mine."

"Wh-What do you mean?" For the first time, Middleton sounded confused by one of his requests. "You want me to talk about other guys?"

"I want you to make me jealous. Tell me something you know I don't want to hear so I can fucking punish you for it."

He was well aware he sounded insane but he couldn't stop. He'd been on edge all day, all month, all fucking year. He wanted to fuck hard and come angry, he wanted to hurt. Middleton understood that, he could see it in her eyes.

"Okay," she said in a small voice. "When I was at uni I used to sell my underwear to guys."

Ty was beginning to feel like he'd woken up on a particularly shitty roller coaster. He'd spent the whole day speeding up, dropping down, jolting back and forth until he had no idea what the fuck was happening. "You, *what?*"

Middleton's cunt squeezed tight around him and he knew it was out of fear. "I...never mind."

Ty smacked her ass, hard. Her skin was hot as the surface of an electric iron. "You explain yourself right now, or I will punish you in ways you never even dreamed of."

"Okay," she said into her fingertips. "I heard a girl in my psych class talking about doing it. Selling her underwear. She said it paid great and you didn't need to have sex with the guys you just needed to give them yesterday's underwear. I was so poor I could barely pay rent. I thought maybe I could do it, too."

"And why..." Ty barely recognised his own voice, it was so full of rage. "Did you think a thing like that?"

Middleton made a motion as though to pull away from his cock. Ty grabbed her milky hips and gave her a good hard fuck until she collapsed moaning onto the desk.

"Daddy, can't we talk about this—"

"No," he snarled. "You'll tell me why you used to sell your fucking panties with your tights around your ankles and your cunt creaming. I know how good you are at lying, and I want the fucking truth, now speak."

"I needed the money," she whispered. "I needed time to study and I thought it would be safe; all I had to do was go out for coffee, sometimes dinner."

It seemed impossible but Ty's temper rose. "You *met* these perverts? Why couldn't you have mailed them your underwear?"

"A-A lot of them won't pay for that, they like to see you..."

He spanked her ass, hard. "They like to see what, Katie?"

"They like to see you take it off."

Ty imagined a young Middleton heading out into the night to meet the kind of guy who'd not only pay a girl for her underwear, but insist she took it off in front of him. That dying ear-cell noise started ringing in his head again. "You didn't tell anyone, did you? You just went out on your own and met these arseholes without anyone knowing where you were?"

"I never slept with the guys." Middleton's tone was pleading. "I never went to their houses or a hotel. We would just meet in a public place and then I'd—"

Ty gave her another rough fuck, pounding his full length into her so hard his balls slapped into her tender flesh.

"Tell me," he said as he thrust. "Tell me why you would agree to do something so reckless? So fucking dangerous?"

When she didn't answer he pulled at her hair, turning her scalp so he could see her face. Her lips were trembling but there was a rare look of stubbornness in her eyes.

"Don't want to tell me, huh? I've got a cure for that."

He smacked her on her already blistered ass and she let out a whimper of pain. "Ty..."

"That's not my name right now, little girl."

"Daddy. *Daddy.*"

He spanked her again, even harder than before. Between this and the belt, he knew he was going to leave serious bruises, but he couldn't stop. "Why did you sell your underwear, Katie? Tell me."

"I thought I would like it," she sobbed into the wood. "I thought it would be fun."

Ty spread her thighs wider, the ripe scent of her wetness filled the air like perfume. He breathed it in. "Say 'I'm a lying little cocktease, who was sent to this earth to drive her Daddy crazy.'"

She repeated the phrase back to him as he fucked her, stammering and whimpering and begging him for mercy. When she was done he slapped her ass again. "You liked the idea, didn't you? An older man telling you what to do. You wanted a daddy, and you thought a sugar daddy would solve two problems in one, didn't you?"

Middleton nodded, her brown eyes brimming with fresh tears. "But it wasn't like that. The men...they were so not like anything I wanted."

"Of course they weren't, baby." Ty withdrew from her pussy then slammed himself back inside, making her gasp.

Middleton's right hand shifted, slipping under her hips to no-doubt toy with her throbbing clit. Ty slapped her hand away. "You won't come while I fuck you right now, understand? I'm using your pussy to get off, and that's all there is to it."

"Yes, Daddy."

Ty smiled, though he'd never felt so humourless in his life. "I am your Daddy, Middleton, your first Daddy. You'd never have found what you were looking for in those men, you know why?"

"Why?"

Leaning forward, he cupped her breasts through her camisole, using them as leverage as he began to work himself inside her, slowly, leisurely. She moaned against the wood, but he didn't worry she'd defy his orders and get off. She needed someone rubbing her clit to get there, something he intended to use to his full advantage.

"Daddy," Middleton pressed. "Why?"

"Because those sad cunts were paying you," Ty said. "You like power, sweetheart, and there's nothing powerful about paying girls who can barely make rent for their underwear. It's sad. It's lonely. I bet you had to make a game for yourself just to go through with it."

"Yes," she whispered, looking mortified.

Ty tugged her nipple through her camisole and felt her cunt flutter around him. "You've gotten good at playing those kinds of games with yourself, haven't you, Katie?"

She nodded. She was close, Ty could feel it, she was on edge from the spanking and the dirtiness of her confession, but she'd never make it without him rubbing her clit or angling his hips so that his balls ground up against her. She was trapped between need and satisfaction, and he planned on keeping her that way. He grasped her plait, winding it around his fist in a move that was now as familiar as donning motorcycle gloves before a ride. "Tonight you're gonna fuck yourself in front of me. You're gonna make yourself gush into your panties while I watch and when you're done, I'm gonna shove them in your mouth and make you taste them while I fuck your ass."

She moaned, her pussy tightening around him.

"Yeah, you like the idea of that, don't you? Giving Daddy your cherry. Well, it wouldn't matter if you didn't, I'd still make you give it to me. I'll make you give me everything you gave any of those perverts for free and have you thank me afterward. You know why?"

"Because...because you're my Daddy."

"That's right, sweetheart. I'm what you want and you'll do

anything to make me happy. Give me your used panties, suck my cock while I watch porn, let me fuck you in the ass even though you're scared it'll hurt."

She made a noise that was neither affirmation nor dissent, and he fucked her harder, thrusting so fast that their bodies clapped together. "I could make you pay me for what I do to you, Middleton, couldn't I? Bill you by the hour for the privilege of giving you my dick?"

"Yes," she breathed. "Yes."

Ty pulled her upward, plastering her warm body along his so he could watch her tits jiggle as he rammed himself home. Dimly, he realised when this was over he was going to smell like whatever strawberry scented lotion she used, but it was far too late to worry about that.

Kate's hand moved between her legs, and she began stroking her clit. Ty let her carry on for a few seconds then pulled her hands away.

She let out a moan of frustration. "Daddy, please?"

"No." Ty bundled her wrists in front of her and pinned them with one of his hands. "When I'm done with you, you're gonna go back to your desk, sit on your freshly slapped ass and think about how horny you are and how you're going to stay that way until I come by and fuck you again tonight."

He resumed pumping himself inside her and she let out a loud, piercing cry, more frustration than pleasure. Ty could feel her clenching around him, knew she was straining to get off, but it was too late. He thought about her squirming in her seat, her ass raw, her pussy needier than ever and came so deep and hard it was like diving into a bottomless, blood-warm river.

"No," Kate sobbed, humping back against him, trying to get more out of his already deflating cock.

"Sorry, baby, we're done here." Ty pulled out of her, folded a piece of paper around the condom and threw it into a nearby bin. He turned to find Middleton still slumped over the table, shaking from head to foot. He immediately registered wrongness and not the good 'I just had my mind blown' kind. Instinctively, he reached down and pulled her into his arms. She resisted for a second and then burrowed her face into his chest as though she was trying to disappear through his skin.

"I don't...know why...I'm crying," she sobbed into his torso. "What we just did was great. I don't know why I'm crying."

Ty smoothed a hand through her hair. "Hey, it doesn't matter. Everything's okay sweetheart, I'm here, everything's okay."

"I know," she said but she cried and cried and cried. They were both late now, their lunch hour pushing into the ninety-minute range, but Ty wouldn't have left her there for the world. He felt like he was expanding around her, his body growing larger and stronger so that he could protect her. It was that feeling, like he wanted to wrap her in a blanket and put her on a high shelf to the power of about a million. After several long minutes, she stepped back, mascara ringing her large brown eyes. "Are you, erm, are you still coming over tonight?"

"Of course."

She smiled then, and Ty felt something inside him tear loose, separating him into the man he'd been with her before and the man he'd have to be now. He cupped Middleton's cheek. "Here's what you're going to do. You're going to go back up to your desk, pack up your stuff, and say you've been sent to the Congreve site. Then you're going to go home, take a shower and get into bed. Wait for me, like we talked about."

"But I already took lunch and—"

"You've got about a million hours in lieu. Everyone cuts and runs sometimes, Middleton, today's your day."

"Okay," she whispered. "If you say so."

"I do, get out of here I'll make sure everyone knows where you are."

He watched as she pulled up her tights and donned her skirt and jumper. Her complexion, though pale, seemed to be adept at clearing up after crying. Aside from a slight puffiness around the eyelids, it was virtually undetectable. She looked fresh and lovely again, this girl who had so many secrets nestled inside her. His chest gave another throbbing pang. "Katie?"

She looked up at him, smiling brightly, probably thinking he was going to say something about sex. He opened his mouth to tell her she was beautiful and couldn't. "Keep your hands off yourself. That's my pussy, and I'll play with it when I get home."

She smiled at him, her expression both mischievous and excited. He'd done that to her just by holding her in his arms. When she left, Ty sat down at the desk where he'd spanked her and clutched his head. He was in trouble all right. Big, big trouble.

14

Kate didn't do exactly what Ty asked. Before she went home, she stopped in at Peter Alexander and bought a negligee. It wasn't a sexy negligee, at least not in the conventional silk and lace sense. It was made of pink cotton and patterned with cherries, symbolism that was almost too on the nose —yet as soon as she saw it, she knew it was the one she wanted to wear tonight. She felt like a pervert placing it on the counter, as though the sales assistant might know exactly what she was blushing about.

"We have a storewide sale on tomorrow," she told Kate as she shook out the bed-dress. "Do you want me to put this aside so you can buy it then?"

"No, I'm happy to pay full price."

The sales assistant gave her a funny look, but Kate just smiled. She wanted the negligee tonight, and she didn't mind paying what Peter Alexander (or someone) had deemed it worthy of. After growing up on a steady diet of thrift store jumpers, shop clothes still had a novelty for Kate. As a kid, the only new dress she'd ever gotten had been for her First Communion and that was because the white gown that had been Jessica, Molly, Grace, Hannah and Claudia's before hers was so battered it had torn like tissue paper the moment she tried to pull it over her head.

She thought about her First Communion as she showered and got ready for Ty. How she'd stood in the sunlight by the towering bluestone church, not understanding why she was there, but feeling pretty and new in her silk dress, her white veil held in place by the diamanté tiara Jessica wore at her wedding.

"Mum," she'd asked Brenda McGrath. "Am I getting married?"

Her mother had flicked her cigarette ash into the grass. "Yes. You're getting married to God."

Ah yes, getting married to God, the all-knowing father who punished and comforted and loved you better than anyone. The concept of god already intrigued Kate for reasons never encouraged by the Catholic Church but that comment had given her some weird day dreams. Maybe she was barking up the wrong tree with Mr Peterson being the root of her kink. Maybe her daddy/daughter obsession was born that day by St Michaels' when she was told she was getting married to the divine Father, and that was a perfectly respectable thing to do.

At the very least, it couldn't have helped.

Kate took extra care washing, shaving the hair in her underarms and on her legs and slathering her skin in strawberry lotion. She slid into her new negligee and white cotton panties and applied BB cream and clear mascara, hoping to avoid makeup stains on her pillows. Though it was only five thirty in the afternoon she climbed into bed the way Ty had asked.

Sooo... a snarky voice piped up. *What now? Lying motionless for hours on end until Ty shows up and performs the sacred rite of 'railing you?'*

Kate knew that voice. It was the one that encouraged her to sell her panties and spit in Dutchy's coffee, to buy sexy new clothes and write one sentence replies to Maria's increasingly demanding texts. It was speaking to her more and more lately, pointing out that the guys at work gave her the worst jobs on purpose and Aunty Rhonda's apartment looked like a mausoleum to the late nineties and how if Ty was any kind of gentlemen, he owed her oral sex.

Kate didn't know what was causing this upswing in angst, but she didn't like it. She felt like a previously calm lake upon which some dillhole on a jet-ski kept riding back and forth, chopping up the water. If she weren't so clear-headed, she'd have been worried something about her ADHD had changed. But the only thing that had significantly changed about her life was Ty, or more specifically, her relationship with Ty.

"He held me today," she said to her ceiling. "I was crying, and he held me."

It had blown her mind a little, how completely at ease he'd seemed with her tears and her need for comfort. He'd kept her close to his chest until she was calm and when he wiped away her tears, it had felt better than any orgasm he'd given her by far.

Please tell Ty that, the snarky voice advised. *He'll love it.*

But who knew what Ty loved? Kate didn't want to be That Girl but the way he'd grabbed her and kissed her today, it felt like things were getting more serious between them. Of course anytime she had those kinds of thoughts her pride told her she was delusional.

The other day, she'd had too much caffeine and asked Stormy about Ty's ex-fiancée. After rhapsodising about her beauty for almost five minutes, he'd given Kate a name. A quick Google search later and she was looking at the exceptionally beautiful woman who once owned Ty's heart. She was relieved to discover Veronica Boyle was married and had a baby son, but some internal need for punishment had driven her deep into her Facebook timeline looking for pictures of her and Ty. She found the lion's share—albums and albums of images documenting their time together.

They looked like the ultimate Aryan power couple—tall, blond and insanely chiseled. Their expressions were always warm but a little aloof, as though they shared hot blond person secrets they couldn't reveal to anyone, even a camera. They clearly had a very exciting relationship. There were snaps of them riding elephants in Africa, sitting by the pool with cocktails in Samoa, drinking Burgundy in ultra-cool Parisian wine bars. There were even pictures —horrible, horrible pictures—of their engagement. Veronica's parents had hosted a huge party at the Marriott Hotel with balloons and doves and the bride-to-be waving a fat diamond in the camera as Ty kissed her on the cheek.

"Why the heck would you leave these pictures up?" Kate asked Veronica's lovely, immobile face, as though it was her fault she had gone snooping and now wanted to spew.

Ty's Facebook profile was little more than a shell and yet here he was, tagged in all these pictures of a love that hadn't worked out. Stormy told her, amidst furtive glances around the office, that the engagement had ended because Veronica cheated on Ty, but Kate couldn't believe that. Anyone who cheated on Ty would surely have horns.

She wasn't sure what those old photos meant, only that it seemed very unlikely Tyler Henderson wanted to downgrade from a PR beauty queen to a girl who cried all over his shirts and had, like, two friends. Sex was what they had in common and sex was a world away from elephant rides and diamond rings.

Time ticked by slowly as Kate lay in her bed. She could have read a book or watched YouTube, but it felt wrong to do so, as though she was defying orders. With nothing to do but feel the fresh bruises pricking on her ass, she started getting turned on. She kept absent-mindedly pressing her hand against her underwear, pulling it away and chiding herself. The gaps between these incidents became smaller and smaller until, finally, when the sky was dark outside, she decided the right thing to do was to make herself come. It would take the edge off, and then she'd be more focused when Ty finally showed up. With the guilty relief of a dieter who finally caved to a packet of biscuits, Kate shoved her hands into her panties and began to rub. She had barely gotten things started when her front door slammed shut.

That man has impeccable fucking timing, the snarky voice said. This neo-version of herself didn't seem to have her fear of getting her mouth washed out with Pears soap.

Gently, Kate eased her hands out of her underwear and closed her eyes. Her pulse was high, her pussy throbbing.

She listened as Ty moved around her kitchen, the clink of glass indicating he'd poured himself a drink. She wondered if he might go into her living room to turn on the TV and string out her anticipation. It seemed like something he would do to torture her. But then, to her relief, his footsteps came pounding up the hall. They were different to the way they usually sounded, but why, she couldn't tell.

Her bedroom door creaked open. "Katie?" He slurred the word as though it were spelled 'Kaydeeeh.' "Are you awake, sweetheart?"

She said nothing, trying to keep her body still and her breathing steady. Ty strode into her room, bringing with him the familiar smell of cologne combined with cigarette smoke and alcohol. Had he been at a bar while she lay there, hungry and impatient? Surely not, surely this was Ty's way of ramping up the drama, adding extra touches of reality to the scene.

The evil stepfather has gone out, gotten drunk, and now he's come home looking for me.

She bit her lip in anticipation of what was to come. She was going to be taken advantage of.

Yeah, excellent, Neo-Kate said darkly. *Because that's not what happens every single time he puts his cock inside you.*

There were two loud clunks as Ty removed his shoes. Peering out from between her lashes, Kate saw he was still in the same suit he was wearing at the office. How had he gotten to her place? He couldn't have ridden his bike, had he walked? She decided to show a few signs of life, rolling onto her back and moaning softly.

"Shh," Ty whispered. "Shh, baby. Daddy's just come in for a cuddle. Stay quiet, stay asleep."

She heard a swish-whisper of clothes hitting the floor and wondered what he'd taken off. Ty was almost always fully dressed when they had sex. She had still never seen his bare chest.

The bed creaked as Ty climbed onto it, bringing with him the musty scent of debauchery. It wasn't pleasant, but it added an air of authenticity to the dirtbag stepfather. Kate could just imagine him at an upscale bar, his golden hair gleaming as he chatted up everything in a skirt, laughing and sucking back bourbon. Ty's weight settled on top of her, trapping her beneath the covers. He kissed her cheek. "Hey, baby girl."

She struggled a little beneath his weight, shifting slightly. "Daddy, no. Please?"

"Oh, honey." Ty pushed her hair aside and pressed his face into her neck. "Daddy needs pussy, you know that."

A violent spray of goose bumps prickled across Kate's skin as she acknowledged the wrongness, the rightness, and the feeling of being so vulnerable and innocent. She let herself sink deeper into that headspace. "I'm sleeping."

"Then stay asleep." He pulled back the blankets and smoothed his hands over her breasts, cupping them gently. "You feel so good, sweetheart."

His words were mushing in his mouth and his breath was still hot with liquor. Wherever Ty had gone between work and now, he'd definitely gotten cut. Kate wanted to ask why but then Ty tugged her nipple through her negligee and her brain went utterly blank. "Daddy."

"Yeah, that's me." Ty buried his face in her neck, his cold hair rubbing against her cheek. "You're eager tonight. Were you hoping I'd come home and play with you?"

"No."

"I don't believe you." Ty nuzzled her neck, his five o'clock shadow scraping over her skin. "Daddy went to a bar tonight 'n tried to find a woman to help him relax, but there was no one as pretty as you."

He moved up and kissed her on the mouth. His lips were firm and wonderful, but Kate couldn't relax into the kiss. He was still wearing his suit pants and shirt and she could smell cigarettes on his clothes and taste alcohol on his tongue.

"You love that," Ty muttered into her hair. "You love being kissed by me."

It was an observation Kate felt was more for her than the step-daughter. "Yes, I like kissing."

"No, you *love* kissing me," Ty corrected. "Gets you wet between the legs, doesn't it? Feeling like you're Daddy's special little girl?"

Kate closed her eyes. If Ty turned her secret wish to be cherished into ridicule, it would hurt. It would hurt so much. She kissed him hard, wrapping her hands around his neck, hoping to keep him from saying anything else. It seemed to work at least until Ty pulled back and glared at her from the darkness. "You been waiting for me here like I asked? You did exactly what you were told?"

"Yes."

He grabbed her right hand and inhaled. "Then why can I smell you on your fingers?"

Oh damn. "I didn't...I wasn't..."

He bent down and sucked her pointer finger into his mouth, biting down gently before releasing it. "You couldn't keep your hands to yourself, could you?"

Humiliation played the piano forte in Kate's belly. "I'm sorry."

Ty shoved himself between her legs, his erection pressing hard into her stomach. "You're always sorry, baby, but you never stop because you're a bad little girl. I could spank your ass every day and that would still be true. Did you make yourself come?"

"No, I promise."

"You just played with yourself a bit, huh? Stayed up past your bedtime thinking about me coming in here and making your pussy feel good?"

Here Kate gave a token struggle. "No."

"I don't believe you, but I can find out for myself."

His hand moved between them, and he rubbed at her swollen pussy through her panties.

"Wet," he said, vindication and amusement mingling in his voice. "I can feel it though your underwear. You're always wet between the legs these days, Katie. You can't get enough."

Kate, whose arousal had jackknifed, let out a pitiful moan. "I'm sorry, Daddy."

Ty chuckled. "Don't apologise for that. I wanted something sweet to put my dick into whenever I was home, and you're shaping up beautifully."

"I—"

Ty pressed a hand to her mouth. "No more talking, baby, it's time to give me what I want."

He laid on his side, one hand alternating between her breasts, the other between her legs, rubbing her with a lazy finesse that made her hurt for his cock. Kate still didn't understand how he was so good at this. Her first boyfriend, Rob, had been a slut of the highest order and he barely touched her pussy. Patrick, the red-headed Dom Maria set her up with, had bragged about how he made women all across the globe squirt and yet he'd pillaged her genitals with all the finesse of Edward freaking Scissorhands. Ty never bragged about sex, he let his skills speak for themselves.

A bad thought occurred to her—Ty in bed with his beautiful fiancée the woman who got to go to Samoa and Africa and wear his ring. Had she once felt everything Kate felt now?

Concentrate, woman. You need to enjoy this.

Why? She thought, but the voice didn't elaborate.

Ty brushed his thumb against her clit. "You okay, sweetheart?"

"Yes, Daddy."

"Good." He kissed her cheek and the smell of whiskey floated over her face, strong but not unpleasant. "I'm gonna fuck you now, Katie."

There was the crackle of plastic, and then he was there, inside her, sliding her walls apart and filling her as only Ty ever had. Rob's penis had been squat, Patrick's so long and bendy it resembled a peeled banana. Ty's was perfect—thick, long and curved in all the right ways. He might have been made just for her, though the very idea was ridiculous. He was a god and she was, at best, one of those priestesses with the robes and the flower crowns that were sacrificed to his glory.

He began to thrust inside her, and it occurred to Kate that Ty was her third sexual partner and that three was a lucky number. She wrapped her legs around him and to her astonishment felt the familiar ripples of orgasm billowing through her center. She'd never come from sex before, but in this position something about his weight and the grind of his hips and the comfortable bed was making it work for her.

"Daddy," Kate said in astonishment. "I think…I think I can come?"

A soft chuckle. "Go on then, sweetheart. Give it a try."

Kate closed her eyes and relaxed back into the bed. As he continued to roll his hips, she smiled. This was perfect. She reached up and buried a hand in Ty's thick curls and that was when he swatted her away, like a fly. "Focus on my cock, Middleton, concentrate."

And she tried, she really tried, but all she could feel was the hurt of being whacked like a bug. Pleasure continued to radiate from the place where their bodies were joined, but the rest of her was uncomfortable. Ty's pants were scratchy, and the buttons of his shirt were pressing into her chest, no doubt leaving little red circles on her skin. Kate looked up and saw Ty's eyes were closed and it occurred to her that she was alone. He was inside her and she was alone. She tapped his shoulder. "Ty, please get off me?"

He was on his knees at once. "Are you alright?"

"I'm fine," she lied. "Can you just take off your pants and maybe your shirt? They're digging into me."

Ty hesitated, then got up. For a brief, painful moment she thought he was leaving, then she heard the sound of his clothes being pulled away. She couldn't see him very well in the dimly lit room but she tried to take him in, the stretch of his shoulders, the shape of his back. When he returned to bed, his skin was hot and hairy against her own. "Better?"

"Yes," she whispered, fighting the stupid urge to cry again and cement his opinion of her as a basket case.

Ty's palm brushed over her cheek. "Anything else?"

Neo-Kate gave her a nudge. "When I erm, tried to touch your hair, you kind of smacked my hand away."

Ty kissed her neck, soft as bird wings. "I'm sorry. I wasn't expecting it. You can do it now if you want." He took her palm and pressed it into his hair. "Better?"

"Yes, but I feel kind of silly grabbing your hair while you're not having sex with me."

He laughed. "In that case, can I keep having sex with you, Katie?"

"Did you know that's my real name?" Kate said, apropos of nothing. "Actually, it's Katie May. Katie May McGrath."

She felt rather than saw Ty smile. "It's pretty. It suits you."

"It's a dumb name. I started calling myself Kate when I was ten. I always meant to change it properly but I never have."

"Kate suits you, too," Ty said. "Both names suit you."

Kate wove her fingers through his longish gold hair, and they kissed again. It felt so different, she realised, with his long hot body lying atop of hers. She could feel the hair and skin of his legs and chest. He seemed both bigger and smaller at once. More human. She wished she could see him, but her room was pitch dark now. Ty's cock naturally slipped between her legs, and she began working her hips against him in silent confirmation of what she wanted. Ty nipped her lower lip. "I asked you a question before, Katie May McGrath. I asked 'do you want me to keep having sex with you?'"

"Oh," Kate said, surprised. "I thought I was telling you without words; yes, please."

Ty shook his head and once again asked, "What am I going to do with you, girl?"

This time the answer seemed to be 'give you a slow, comfortable screw until you're begging me to let you come.' He worked away at her with lazy languid thrusts, as though he knew he had all night, as though this was his favourite thing in the world. When she was close —she still couldn't believe she was so close—he wound his fingers through hers, and pressed her hands back into the bed. "Go on baby, come on me."

Pinned down and luxuriously aroused, Kate let go, her body shuddering, her mouth sucking on the salty skin of his shoulder.

"That's it," Ty muttered. "That's it, beautiful girl."

Had he ever called her beautiful before? Kate didn't know. She let the word wash over her along with her orgasm, revelling in the newness of both. When she was done, Ty's motions sped up, and he began taking her with a sleek force that had her jolting with orgasmic aftershocks. He pressed his mouth to her ear. "Say what I wanna hear while I ride you, baby. Say it."

Kate moaned as he drove deeper inside her. "Daddy."

"Who owns your pussy, honey?"

"You do, Daddy."

Ty came then, his whole body stiff and his jaw so tight not a sound escaped him. There was latex between them, but Kate swore she could feel the fluid filling up the condom. She wished there was nothing between them, not her nightie or the latex. Ty exhaled and rolled off her. Kate, unsure of what to do, stayed quiet. Despite the release, there was a tight tingling feeling in her belly. It wasn't fear. It was like when she had to give a big presentation at school. Something, her body told her, was going to happen.

"I'm turning your lamp on, okay?"

Kate wanted to ask how Ty knew it was there but didn't. "Okay."

The switch to her salt lamp was flicked, and there was Ty standing by her bed. Seeing him without a shirt on was odd. He had a gorgeous body but Kate had never pictured the golden-brown skin of his shoulders, the heft of the muscle and bone. She'd given him countless blow jobs but the sight of his jutting collarbones seemed almost obscene, wrong somehow.

That feeling intensified when he turned to pull the condom from his cock and wrap it in a tissue. He had thick, muscular thighs and a round peachy ass covered in golden brown hair. Kate couldn't help staring at it, wondering why men had hair on their butts and women didn't.

Be grateful. If they did, you'd have to wax that shit, too. Neo-Kate told her. *You know something is about to happen, right?*

Ty caught her eye as he returned from throwing the condom in her wastepaper bin. "Help you with something, Middleton?"

"I've um, never seen you naked before."

Ty picked up his briefs and tugged them on. "True. How are you feeling? It felt like something went wrong halfway through."

"It wasn't anything serious. I just kind of freaked out. It felt different having you here in my bed."

"That's understandable. You sleep here, and you need to feel safe where you sleep."

"Sure," Kate said, unnerved by the fact that he was dressing so quickly, that he'd yet to come back to bed. He never cuddled, but that seemed less obvious when they hadn't been in a bed.

"I wonder if that's why kids see monsters in their cupboards," she said to fill the slightly chilly silence. "Because they're meant to feel like they're safe and they don't?"

Ty shrugged. "Maybe. Did you see monsters when you were a kid?"

"No, but I shared a bedroom with two of my sisters, and they were kind of like monsters if monsters were really into hair extensions and guarana-based energy drinks."

He chuckled, but Kate sensed it was more out of obligation than anything else. "Fair enough."

"What about you? Did you see monsters in your cupboard?"

Ty went rigid and she knew she shouldn't have asked but it was already too late.

"Once or twice," he said, without meeting her gaze. "Most kids do I guess."

Kate tried to imagine a young Ty hiding in his bed, afraid of monsters, and came up with nothing. Children were vulnerable and a vulnerable Ty was an impossible image. She watched as he tugged up his suit pants, cutting off the V-shaped muscle lines that forked his groin.

"Why don't you like taking your clothes off when we have sex?"

Ty fastened the top button on his pants. "Just don't. It's nothing personal."

"Like you not wanting to go down on me?"

Ty sighed. Not in the satisfying way he had after they were done fucking, like a basketball with a puncture. "You know I used to be a firey, right?"

"Yes," Kate said, deciding now wasn't the right time to ask for a picture of him in his uniform.

"I know everyone at work gossips. Do you know why I was retired from the MFB?"

"You saved a baby and got a medal."

A ghost of a smile flashed over Ty's face. "That doesn't explain why I had to give up the job."

"Oh. Then I don't know."

"Because of this." He twisted his body to the side and at first, she was too distracted by the flex of his muscles to see what he was showing her, then she gasped. A mottled burn was melted into his golden-brown skin. It was the size of a car tire, spanning his rib cage and half his back. She felt instantly, impossibly, stupid for not seeing it sooner. "Oh my gosh..."

Ty's lips twisted into an ugly smile. "Nasty, huh?"

"How did you get it?"

"My last job. The one with the baby."

"You got hurt bringing it out?"

"No. We had the family in the clear but the house was coming down either way. We were trying to work out what to do when I found out one of my guys was still inside. Emmett Poletti." Ty picked up his shirt and slung it over his shoulders. Even in the dim apricot light of her salt lamp, Kate could see the spots where she'd stained it with her mascara in the storeroom.

"He'd just gotten married, the silly prick," Ty said, buttoning his shirt. "But he was always a loose cunt, always putting himself in danger even when he didn't need to."

"Did you...did you go back in for him?"

Ty met her gaze, his brow was furrowed and his eyes were cold, no, not cold as they could sometimes be when he dominated her. Dead. His eyes were dead.

"I tried to go back in for him," he said. "Got about a meter inside when a load-bearing beam came down on me."

"Oh my gosh," she said, feeling woefully inadequate.

Ty did up the last button on his shirt and straightened his collar. "Yeah, it was shit. Em died, burned up in the house. I had to be dragged out myself, third-degree burns all over my back. Once I recovered, there was an inquiry. I got told I shouldn't have gone back inside for him. Went against standard procedure."

"But you were trying to save him!"

"And I couldn't," Ty said flatly. "No one wants a hero who can't do the thing he broke the rules to do. I was retired two months later."

There was a bitterness in his voice she'd never heard before. A pain that was far more disturbing than the marks on his skin. Her feeling of inadequacy surged even higher. "You were an amazing fire-fighter. The fact that you were in the MFB at all is incredible."

Ty shook his head. "You don't understand. That fire was the last one I ever fought, and it won. It was hard enough leaving my dream job, but knowing that..." he shook his head again.

Without any solid idea of what she was doing, Kate moved across the bed. When she was as close to him as she could get, she reached out and lightly touched the place where his scars began. "I'm so sorry this happened to you. I wish it hadn't."

"You still want me to take my shirt off when we fuck?"

Kate knew he was aiming for a joke but the uncertainty in his voice was heartbreaking. "You got those scars trying to save some-one's life. When I look at them they'll remind me you're a hero."

A quiet huff of laugher and then, "I feel beat up around you, Middleton. I'm like this..." he gestured to his scars "...and you're so fucking smooth and pretty."

Kate thought of all the times he'd had sex with his clothes on and her heart throbbed. "You don't need to hide anything from me, Daddy."

They both froze.

It was a slip-up like no other. They were talking as equals, as Kate and Ty; referring to him as that unholy word, especially after he'd told her something so personal, was ridiculous. She pulled her hand away. "I'm so sorry, that was weird."

"Don't worry about it."

"I won't but you should know—"

He bent his head and kissed her. It was a lovely kiss, full of easy affection, but Kate felt her pulse spike. Something was about to happen.

"I got you a present," Ty said, when he pulled away. "I'll go get it now."

"Okay?"

"Hang on a second."

He was gone a few minutes and though she heard him in the bathroom, then clinking around the kitchen, part of her kept saying he was gone. Her palms kept prickling with sweat. Something was going to happen.

Ty returned with two glasses of water and a silver parcel under his arm. He held out a drinking glass. "Water first, then present."

Kate drank quickly. Her tongue was prickly and though she wanted to drag out the moment, the glass was soon empty. Ty took it from her and placed it on the bedside table. He gave her the silver package.

"You shouldn't have done this," Kate said, peeling at the paper.

"You have to open it before you say that."

Kate was already pretty sure she knew what it was; nothing much felt like a dildo except a dildo.

She opened the bag, determined to act pleased no matter what it looked like then gasped. It *was* a dildo, but it was the prettiest one she'd ever seen; clear glass with a heart-shaped handle. A violet ribbon ran through the length of the toy, immobilized beneath the crystal. It looked more like modern art than something you should use inside yourself.

"You like it?"

Again Kate fought the ridiculous urge to cry. "I...yeah, it's beautiful."

Ty's smile didn't touch his eyes. "I want this to be the only toy you use when you think of me. I'd say the only toy full-stop, but I don't want to be a prick."

"You're not," Kate whispered. "Thank you."

"Not a problem." He gave her a swift kiss, then took a long swallow of water from his glass and put it down on her dresser. "Middleton, work's sending me away for a couple of weeks."

This is it. "Oh, uh, where are you going?"

"Queensland. I fly out early tomorrow morning." Ty paced to the other side of the room and inspected the small painting Aunt Rhonda had hung there when this was her bedroom. "Is this a Delaney?"

"I have no idea. So you'll be gone for two weeks?"

"Yeah. They need someone to look over the Pinkleton project."

"Oh." Kate knew she sounded like an idiot, so she forced herself to add, "Are you going to see your family while you're up there?"

"Might do."

The air between them thickened with everything they weren't saying and after a few tense seconds, Kate couldn't take it anymore. She held up her dildo. "So is this a substitute for a while you're away?"

"Of course." He gave her a small smile. "You didn't think I'd leave you all alone, did you?"

Yes, I did. Because you are. You're leaving, and when you get back, you'll never get back to me. That's why you went out and got drunk tonight, that's why you're giving me a present. Maybe it's why you let me see your scars because tonight was the last time.

She was surprised, but she was also utterly unsurprised. She had felt this coming the moment she cried all over him in the stockroom, the moment she opened herself wide and he allowed her, however briefly, to take comfort from him. She wanted to ask why. Instead, she smiled and said, "I hope you have a great trip."

"I will." He knelt down on the bed and kissed her again. It was soft and sweet, but she could feel the distance between them. Space seemed so relative to her at that moment; their bodies were close, but Tyler Henderson and Katie May McGrath were as far as far could be.

Ty picked up his suit jacket and left. Kate wasn't sure where he was going but she suspected it wasn't home. Back to the bar, maybe, or to see a friend. They were over. Kate could feel it in her bones. So much of what she and Ty had was ignited without a word, and this was no different. She looked down at the severance package dildo and a line from church came to her, blasphemous given the context, but so incredibly apt—*take this, in memory of me.*

15

The next day Kate got up, took Ritalin, and went to work. She signed off on three projects, ate something with chicken in it, came home and went to sleep. The next day, she did the same things except she ate something with lamb in it. The day after that was a Saturday, so she went for a five kilometre run, cleaned Aunty Rhonda's apartment, organised her wardrobe according to the KonMari method, and caught up on all of her emails.

By Sunday, she was standing at her bathroom sink, Ritalin between her fingers, wondering for the first time since she was eighteen, if she should drop it down the sink. She wanted to let all the sharp edges dull, let the clear radio transmission return to static. She wouldn't be able to function as well, but surely she wouldn't feel this acute, painful emptiness. She let the pill slip towards the end of her fingers, then caught sight of herself in the mirror.

No, the sober brown of her eyes told her. *If you do this you'll let Ty be responsible for wreaking your head and breaking your heart.*

She took her pill.

That night she tried to touch herself. After an incredibly frustrating fifty minutes, she discovered she couldn't come. She tried every toy and technique in her arsenal—except the severance package dildo—and nothing worked. For a moment she considered the glass wand, then she got up, dressed herself and went for another run.

Now that Ty had left, her lack of a social life was even more apparent. She accepted an invitation to Sunday night dinner at Maria's out of sheer desperation. Maria insisted on hearing the full story, and though it felt like pulling a string of razor blades out of her stomach, Kate told her. It didn't sound that dramatic out loud; she and Ty had been having casual sex, and now it was over in the way casual things were over.

"How did you know it was over if he never said it?" Maria asked.

"I just knew."

The naked relief on Maria's face was irritating, but Kate could understand it. She had known this was coming, was probably relieved the ending hadn't been messier. Kate had been the one in denial.

Five days after Ty's departure, she deleted all his texts. She was so sick of reading them over and over, searching for meaning in messages like 'be at your place in thirty minutes, take off your panties.'

She went into Kinkworld to delete their correspondence and found a direct message from someone called '@BadBastard1995.' The subject line was 'You're a slut,' and the content read, 'No man will ever love you.'

It was just mean-spirited trolling, but reading the words was a slap in the face, especially since she was spending so much time dwelling on the fact that no man, specifically Tyler Henderson, loved her. She screen-shotted the message, reported the account to moderators and deleted it. She wanted to cry but the sadness wouldn't come; instead she found herself furious. How dare someone send her that message? How dare Maria smile when she told her the man she'd fallen for had left? How dare Ty give her a stupid dildo and then leave without explicitly stating he was leaving?

"Fuck this," she whispered. "Fuck all of this."

She stormed to her bedroom and pulled on the cherry nightie

she'd bought for Tyler. She then went to the bathroom, put on as much makeup as she would wear to a wedding and snapped a few pictures of herself in the mirror in various sexy poses.

She knew it was narcissistic and borderline irresponsible, but she didn't stop. She was alone in every sense of the word and she wanted to do something reckless, rip off her skin and expose what lay beneath. She chose the best picture, applied a flattering filter, then posted it to her Kinkworld profile. She thought about making the caption '*suck a big fat penis, Tyler Henderson and also BadBastard1995,*' but wrote '*new nightie, what do you think?*' instead.

The response was instantaneous. Her phone pinged with notifications about likes and 'Phwoar!' comments and she started getting messages from guys wanting to meet up and couples seeking a unicorn (they never read her goddamn profile properly). She read through everything, wanting to feel flattered, and instead feeling emptier than ever. Sycophancy from strangers, it turned out, was no cure for heartache. It was barely even a Band-Aid.

Kate looked across the room at Aunt Rhonda's painting of Grecian goddesses. They were cavorting under a mountain spring, not a single problem between them. What would Aunt Rhonda have said if she was there?

Nothing, Kate realised. She'd have gone to the nearest ATM, withdrawn a bunch of cash, and told her to pack her bags because she was driving her to the airport for an adventure. Kate considered finally doing it, just packing a bag and going overseas the way Aunt Rhonda had always wanted her to. Then she remembered her job and the apartment and how she was so, so afraid of getting on a plane by herself.

"Sorry, Aunty," she said to the painting. "You were a lot braver than me."

Ty GOT up and swam laps in the hotel pool. He drank coffee and ate bacon and eggs. He attended meetings. In the afternoons, he drove out to work sites and inspected the progress of the eco-motels GGS were building. He ignored Middleton's name whenever it cropped up on the blueprints, the same way he ignored the workmen who muttered he was a Melbournian asshole who didn't know shit. He could have told the guys he was a born and bred Queenslander, but what was the point? At night, he drank alone at the hotel bar. There was a Women in Business conference on and he received offers of nightcaps from pencil skirted executives whose husbands were far, far away. He turned them down. Even if he'd wanted to be complicit in their deception he couldn't muster the energy. He hadn't gotten hard once since leaving Middleton's apartment. It was as though someone had flicked the switch on his sex drive to '*off*.'

"Are you alright?" Johnno asked him via Skype. "You look a bit rough."

"I'm fine. How're the troops?"

Johnno rattled off what the boys were up to, but didn't mention the only person Ty wanted to hear about. What was Katie May McGrath working on, what was she doing? Did she miss him? Was he the biggest prick in the world for *hoping* she missed him?

On the first weekend of his trip, Ty drove his rented Audi four hours out of the city to visit his family. The Gold Coast, with its web of skyscrapers and fried chicken chain stores, looked different from how he remembered it as a kid, but the roads that led to his hometown was so familiar it hurt—the faded general stores and potholes and fields of bananas and pineapples. As he wound down the window and inhaled the scent of baking asphalt, Ty felt with perfect clarity how it had been to be eighteen-years-old, driving for the sake of driving, dreaming about the life that lay ahead.

As the kilometres passed, a doomed little fantasy entered his mind. Katie May McGrath, born twenty years earlier, attending university at the same time as him. She was Georgie's friend and why wouldn't she be? Georgie had collected shy girls trying to break into male-dominated industries the way other people collected stamps.

They'd meet at one of Georgie's punch parties. Katie would look exactly the same as she did now, but he would be the man he was back then—shaggy gold curls, unlined forehead, some glimmer of hope in his eyes. He'd be a virgin, just like her, and still a gun-shy around women. When their eyes met he'd make himself a promise—he wouldn't leave until he talked to her.

It might have taken a few hours, but eventually he'd muster up the courage to introduce himself. They'd talk about school and home and living in Melbourne. They'd get drunk on Georgie's near-poisonous white-wine punch and kiss in some quiet corner of the house. Ty would ask her out and she'd blush and say yes and write down her number. They'd go out for cheap Chinese and walk through Fitzroy gardens because that was the most romantic date a broke eighteen-year-old could think of. Then they'd go on more dates, to the movies, to the beach. He'd have brought her flowers a lot because he assumed that's what men did for women they were falling in love with.

He'd be scared of rushing her, but unable to keep his hands off her, either. Within a few weeks, they'd have started getting each other off in his dorm room until finally he made love to her under his Pearl Jam poster. From the start, it would be clear she liked him being rough. Once they grew comfortable with each other, they'd have started pushing the boundaries.

"I want to call you..."

"I like it when..."

He'd have flexed his dominant muscles against her. He'd have been clumsy, but she wouldn't have cared. Her calling him 'Daddy' would have always had a theatrical, laughable quality because they were the same age, the same age, the same age.

A deep and treacherous pothole startled Ty back into the present. He swore and pulled over. The underside of the rental was okay, his morale not so much.

When he arrived at his old house his mum and dad rushed out to the car to see him. His brothers and their wives hung back, smiling stiffly. They resented the fuss his parents made whenever he came home, marveling at every little detail of his life in Melbourne. They sat down to a long, uncomfortable meal, and by the time Pavlova was served, the familiar barbs were offered alongside them—when was he going to bring a girl home? Was he *sure* he didn't want kids? Did he ever get lonely living by himself?

When Rhys' wife, Minnie, brought up Veronica's new baby, Ty said he needed the bathroom and went and stood on the veranda by himself. He stared up at the crescent moon and thought about Middleton. What would his family say if he ever brought her home to dinner? Where was she tonight? Curled up on her couch watching TV or out at a bar auditioning his replacement?

"How's it going, Tyso?"

He turned to see his oldest brother Rhys holding out a can of Four X. "Sorry 'bout Minnie. She's a bit drunk."

Ty took the beer and cracked it open. "S'fine."

"She's worried about you. We all were after the job and Veronica, she and Minnie got along so well y'know?"

Ty wished he didn't know. "Yeah."

"You're not...I mean, you're not seeing anyone, are you?" Rhys asked with palpable desperation. "That would go a long way toward everyone worrying less."

Ty took a long swallow from his beer. He was a successful businessman with his own house and plenty of money and friends and yet in the eyes of his family he was suffering a fate worse than cancer —being single. He sighed. "I had a thing going with a girl from work, but that's over now."

"Shit..." Rhys said, sounding surprised. "Was it serious? What happened?"

"She's twenty-five."

There was a short pause.

"Twenty-five?"

Rhys' tone was neutral, but Ty could hear the envy throbbing beneath it. Inwardly, he groaned. He shouldn't have told him about this. He wouldn't listen, wouldn't give good advice, he'd just mark it down as another way in which his younger brother had one-upped him, the list starting from the moment Ty made the first string senior rugby team before he did. "Forget it," he told Rhys.

"I can't just forget it, are you really rooting a twenty-five-year-old?"

"I *was*. Now it's over."

"Fucking hell." His brother shifted on the veranda as though grinding out an invisible cigarette. "You know, it's probably for the best. You're almost forty-six. You can't be running around with a girl half your age. You're not DiCaprio."

"I know I'm not."

Rhys shook his head. "Twenty-five...with that generation she might as well be seventeen. You don't need that in your life."

"Well, I don't *have* that in my life. Look, can we drop this?"

"I get it. You're by yourself, you're getting old, and fucking a girl that young's an ego boost—"

"It wasn't like that!"

His brother raised his hands. "Okay, look, have you heard from Veronica lately?"

"No."

It was a lie. She was still calling him. Every few days, her name flashed up on his phone along with another teary voicemail begging him to call her back. He didn't, but he didn't block her number, either. He wasn't entirely sure why.

"You need to find another woman like her," Rhys said. "She was a diamond, pretty, smart, put up with all your moody shit. If you'd just...but it's too late now, eh?"

Ty didn't answer. He'd learned long ago that his family wouldn't —couldn't—understand why he refused to give Veronica a baby.

"Mate." Rhys glanced cautiously at the porch door. "Mate, no bloke wants kids. You just have 'em and get used to 'em. It's part of getting older."

Rhys always talked like that, as though social expectations were carved in stone and you got no say in any of it. Marry the girl you're dating when you're twenty-eight, have as many kids as she decides she wants, buy a four-bedroom house in the suburbs and pay it off until you're sixty-nine and a half.

"Are you listening to me?" Rhys pressed. "There's still enough time to do things properly. You can still meet someone else and have a family."

Ty thought about dinner, his nieces and nephews running around the table screaming, Robbie downing about nine glasses of wine and sighing whenever his wife spoke. Rhys' personal anecdotes about how Minnie nagged him and that their kids were always in his way. His brothers had both gained weight since Ty saw them last, both looked about ten years older than they were, and that was the life they wanted for him? Ty crushed his empty can of Four X against his palm and wondered if he still had the number for the vasectomy place.

IF KATE WASN'T SO desperate for company, she wouldn't have gone to Lorena's baby shower, but seeing as she was desperate for company and the former Barbie Troll had promised copious amounts of champagne, she was there at eleven on the dot.

She'd expected the party to be sweet but boring. As it turned out she'd severely underestimated Lorena's ability to party with an almost fully-formed baby inside her. Five hours into the shower, Kate was drunk—really, really drunk—and she and the rest of the Barbie Trolls (minus Maria who was at a family barbecue) were drawing on Lorena's swollen stomach like it was the cast on a broken arm, ignoring the dire warnings of her Italian aunts who swore it would poison the baby in utero.

Kate had just finished her picture of a lion cub (Lorena's derby name was Lion Maiden) when the older women in the room steered the conversation toward kids—namely grilling the baby-less about their plans to become baby-full. Kate was on the verge of running to the toilet and hiding for an hour when Rapunzel saved the day.

"Why the fuck would I?" she said to Lorena's great aunt when she asked if she wanted to have kids. "I'm a dyke. I love vaginas. I'm all about vaginas. Why would I want to shove a watermelon-sized shit-factory out of one? Especially *my vagina*, the nicest, most relevant vagina of all?"

The look of horror on the old woman's face, Lorena's screech of laughter, and the fact that Rapunzel followed her pronouncement with a casual 'too much?'—Kate couldn't help herself, she burst into hysterical champagne giggles and had to leave the room.

When she finally calmed down she went into the kitchen and found Rapunzel sitting on the counter, nursing a cup of tea. "Not doing so hot at this party, am I?"

"Well, you did say the word 'vagina,' like, fifty times. But you also almost made me break a rib from laughing. And you saved me from being grilled."

Rapunzel raised a pale brow. "You don't want kids, either, huh?"

"I don't know," Kate said honestly. "I get why people have kids, but I get why people don't. I don't have the most normal role models. My Aunt Rhonda had no kids, and she was the happiest, nicest person I knew and my mum has nine kids and she, like, hates us. Swings and roundabouts you know?"

"Sure," Rapunzel said with a smile. "You've got eight brothers and sisters?"

"Yeah. For the record, we are Catholic."

Rapunzel laughed. "How's your man, by the way? Treating you well?"

For a moment Kate was confused, then she remembered that she'd told the derby girls about Ty because she was a stupid, fool-hardy fool. "He um...it's over. It's no big deal though, it was never meant to be serious."

To her surprise, Rapunzel leapt off the counter and pulled her into a bone-crushing hug. "I'm sorry, Peach. You wanna talk about it?"

"If I start, I might cry," she said, her eyes already burning. "Thanks though."

"Anytime. Wanna go out on the balcony and smoke weed?"

"Erm, no thanks."

"Well, come keep me company. I need a lookout in case any more of Lorena's aunts show up and judge my lifestyle."

Kate laughed.

They stood outside in the cold for half an hour, talking without the slightest awkward pause. When Kate got so cold her fingers went numb, she ordered an Uber. To her surprise, Rapunzel insisted they swap numbers so Kate could text her when she was safely home. When she did, Rapunzel replied with '*Glad to hear it. It was good to see you, Peach. You should come out with us more often.*'

Kate smiled. She was still miserable about Ty, but unless she was mistaken she and the hardest girl on her derby team were kind of becoming friends and that was pretty cool. She only wished it had happened a few months ago. Rapunzel seemed like someone who'd know exactly how to talk you out of embarking on a doomed fling with your boss that left you questioning the very foundations of your life.

Ty's flight back to Melbourne was delayed, first by two hours, then five. He sat in the executive bar getting progressively drunker and more introspective. Airports always did that to him, it was something about the floaty timelessness of a place dictated by non-stop arrivals and departures.

His delay was inconvenient, but as he sat on his cushy bar stool, being served by a friendly, non-judgmental bartender, he had to admit that no one was expecting him. He would have to be delayed by another twenty hours before it mattered that he was getting drunk in the airport instead of at home.

He pulled out his notepad with the vague idea of doing some writing and instead found himself sketching big disjointed words: *golden boy, bachelor, pervert, alcoholic* and *Middleton*. He circled the last word, then crossed it out. Then he drew it again in wide bubble letters. *Middleton.*

"You're almost forty-six," Rhys had said. "You can't be running around with a girl half your age. You're not DiCaprio."

He wasn't. But he wasn't like Rhys, either, not married or mortgaged to the hilt. He'd chosen his life for himself and already endured all the slights that came along with it. Family dinners were already painful, would it really be so bad if he and Middleton made a proper go of things? If his brothers and their wives had to accept that, in addition to being a childless weirdo, he was the kind of tacky middle-aged asshole who had a twenty-something girlfriend? Did it matter?

Not really, he decided. It mattered that he'd left her, ending things without a word, though. It mattered what she was doing now. Ty drained his pint and decided to investigate. He pulled out his laptop, and logged into Kinkworld. His pulse spiked when he saw messages in his inbox, but they turned out to be from some dickhead called '@BadBastard1995' who felt the need to tell him he was a pervert. He deleted the messages and typed Middleton's pseudonym into the search box.

She had a new profile picture. She was posing in front of her bathroom mirror in the cherry patterned nightdress she'd worn when they were last together. Unlike her other photos, you could see her face, all wide brown eyes, and pink lips. She'd angled herself so that her legs looked a mile long, her body flawless. She looked young and beautiful. So sexy she was almost a stranger.

"Why would she do this?" Ty muttered. From the way that nightie had smelled when he'd been fucking her, it was new. Why would she take something she bought especially for him and show it to every goddamn perv on this website?

Because she's in the market for a Daddy, asshole. Don't act like you're surprised.

"You okay man?" The bartender asked.

"Fine," Ty lied. "Makers on the rocks, thanks."

As he waited for his drink he scrolled through the comments listed below Middleton's picture. Again, most of them were moronic, but one by a man called RedRight was irritatingly eloquent. *"Very pretty but you look like you need a hug, gorgeous girl. Dinner this Friday? (I just DM'd you.)"*

Ty googled the term and was unimpressed to learn that it meant 'direct message.' Had Middleton responded? He clicked on RedRight's profile and learned the guy was a twenty-nine-year-old property developer. He was irritatingly good-looking, heavily muscled, and well-hung—something Ty learned against his will when he accidentally clicked on a video of RedRight doing a woman in the ass. He'd never back-clicked out of something so fast in his life.

Surely Middleton wouldn't be interested in dating someone who put their homemade porn on the internet? Surely? The question did nothing to help Ty's growing unease. He went back to Middleton's profile and looked at her posing in her cherry night dress. She looked gorgeous, but as RedRight had pointed out, there was something sad about the look in her eyes. It wasn't too much of a stretch to imagine why. Yet Ty knew better than he'd ever known it before that she'd find someone else, eventually. Maybe not a handsome buttfucker with sex tapes all over the internet, but someone. She was too precious for another man like him not to want to keep her.

Ty closed his laptop and considered the glass of Makers the bartender had left at his elbow. Another drink would have gone down like water, but it wasn't going to help him make the decision he knew he needed to make. He gave the drink to the bored-looking guy next to him, paid his tab, and wandered over to the food court. He ordered a custard tart and ate it, savouring the sweetness he normally detested. He'd always made his own choices, regardless of what other people thought. Maybe it was time to man up and make another one.

16

"We're. Dying out here. Ladies." Maria was breathing so hard her words were coming out in bursts. "If we don't. Catch up. We're going. To lose."

Kate and the rest of the team moaned their agreement, sinking on their designated seats. It was only halftime, but the stench of failure permeated their bench. The A-Bombs had a ten point lead, and if the Barbie Trolls didn't earn it back early in the next half, they'd lose and lose hard.

The crowd was in high spirits, browsing at the mini market that had sprung up on the other side of the stadium, filling their bellies with crepes, fairy floss, burritos, and craft beer. Derby wasn't huge in Australia, but there were enough interested hipsters, goths, indie rockers and pervs that the finals always drew a decent audience. Kate wished she was among them now, nodding her head to the pop-rock that was blaring through the sound system and eating jam doughnuts. She rubbed her spasming thigh, trying to keep the muscles from locking up. Thunderbox, The A-Bombs largest defender, seemed to have taken a particular disliking to her. Kate had no idea why, but she'd still been knocked to the ground a dozen or so times. She was going to have bruises tomorrow and not fun butt ones. Ugly limb ones.

Maria finished emptying a small bottle of water into her mouth and rounded on her teammates once more. "Where are your heads tonight, girls?"

"Getting mashed into the track." Tam shot The A-Bombs sitting on the opposite side of the track a filthy look. "Those molls are playing dirty, even by their usual bullshit standards."

"Don't blame them for the fact we're losing—"

"She's not," Casey interrupted. "Look at this!" She lifted her ice-pack to reveal a swollen eyelid. "This wasn't even the worst one. Daisy twisted her ankle when number forty-four pushed her over and that big bitch has it in for Macca—"

Maria scoffed. "She hasn't 'got it in for Katie.' She's just being unfocused and sloppy."

Kate felt her cheeks burn and was glad she was wearing so much novelty makeup. It wasn't like Maria to call her out in front of the rest of the team, but then again, it *was* a final. Tensions were understandably high.

"Hey." Tam nudged Kate's side. "Don't worry about it. You're doing great."

"You don't have to lie."

"Well, you're not skating any worse than the rest of us. Besides, there's no need for Maria to be so pissy. We can still win this back."

"I hope so." Something across the track caught Kate's eye. Thunderbox, her purple Mohawk freshly spiked into stegosaurus spines, was giving her the finger.

"Oh geez," she muttered.

"What?" Tam spotted Thunderbox. "Wow, you've made yourself a friend, haven't you, Mac? Go on then, bird her back."

Kate gave Thunderbox a half-hearted finger. The larger woman flashed her a grin that could only be described as 'ominous' and slashed a finger across her throat.

"God, that's a bit full on." Tam patted Kate on the shoulder. "Just ignore her, Mac."

Kate tried, but in her mind the big defender was dragging her to the ground and taking a bite out of her face. She wished she hadn't given her the bird. She'd never been any good at on-track razzing. She had a fundamental fear of confrontation, particularly toward people who looked like they might curb-stomp her.

As she listened to Maria's proposed plays, Kate wondered, not for the first time, if she'd made the right choice joining the team. She loved skating, but she was one of the weaker members of the Barbie Trolls, and everyone knew it. Bigger players could knock her down with the effort it took to extinguish a birthday candle. She'd joined to make friends, but the only friend she really had was Maria and Maria was pissed off with her more often than she wasn't. Come to think of it, she was probably depriving a much cooler girl of her rightful place on the team. Maybe when the sign-on forms for next year were passed around, she'd forget to add her name, let her insurance run out, and sell her six-hundred dollar skates on Gumtree. Maybe she should stop pretending she belonged in the ultra-cool derby world and adopt a cat and join a poetry reading circle. Embrace the void.

Maria dismissed her team for the rest of the break. Kate was skating back and forth, trying to stretch out her hamstrings when Rapunzel came skidding up to her side. "Hey, Peach."

"Hey," Kate said, her new nickname making her feel slightly better. "Where have you been?"

"Around. You're having a rough game, eh?"

"I...yeah."

Rapunzel patted her on the back. "Don't stress. I've got something that'll make you feel better."

Her shifty expression reminded Kate that her income was propped up by selling substances of dubious legality. "I can't take anything, I'm already on Ritalin. Besides, isn't that like, sports doping?"

"That only counts in the AFL and when you do it to greyhounds and stuff. Hang on, why are you on Ritalin?"

Kate found she didn't have the energy to lie. "I have ADHD."

"*Really?*"

"Yeah, I was diagnosed when I was seventeen."

Rapunzel eyed her up and down as though looking for some physical demonstration of her behavioural disorder. "Well, there you go. You know there's decent money in Ritalin. If you've got a scrip, I could—"

"Not a chance."

"Fine. Well, setting the topic of prescription medication aside, I've got a non-pharmaceutical gift for you."

"What is it?" Kate asked nervously. It would be like Rapunzel to yell 'refreshment!' and dump Powerade on her head.

"Oh, nothing." Rapunzel polished her fingernails on the front of her pink and white t-shirt.

"But you just said it *was* something."

"Maybe it is and maybe it isn't..."

"Rapunzel," Kate said desperately. "What are you doing?"

"Okay, okay. I was skating through the crowd when I came across a tall blond gentleman who seems genuinely incapable of smiling."

Kate blinked at her. Clearly, there was some kind of punchline coming, but Rapunzel didn't say anything, just grinned and blew on her unvarnished fingernails. "Impressed?"

"What are you talking about?"

"I spotted a tall, blond gentleman in the crowd," Rapunzel explained. "Are you surprised, Peach? A little turned on, perhaps?"

"Please don't tease me," Kate begged. "I'm already skating like crap, if I have another half like the last one, Maria's going to kill me."

"I'm not fucking with you!" Rapunzel grabbed her shoulders and steered her around so she was facing the entrance. "Cast your eyes to the Pepsi machine yonder. You'll see."

Kate did what she was told, though she was sure Rapunzel was wrong. She and Ty were over, and even if they weren't, he'd made it clear he'd rather self-immolate than go to a roller derby game. She located the bright blue and black Pepsi machine, and began scanning for Ty's doppelgänger. She spotted a tall blond man who definitely wasn't—

All the air rushed out of Kate's lungs. "What the...? It's him!"

"Pretty cool, ay?" Rapunzel said happily. "Thought it must have been."

Surrounded by goths, hipsters, and weirdos, Ty looked completely out of place in his suit and beautiful checked coat. He looked like a visiting prince prepared to witness, if not join in, with the natives' reverie. His expression was tense.

"He's been skulking around the back of the stadium all game," Rapunzel said. "I spotted him when we were lining up for the first play."

"How did you know he was the guy I was seeing?"

"I didn't but he kept staring at your arse. He wasn't even pretending not to. It was like, single-minded perving. I thought we might have a Dexter situation on our hands."

Kate stopped staring at Ty and turned to look at Rapunzel. "What?"

"Dexter. You know, the serial killer? Kind of looks like old mate."

"I don't think Ty looks like Dexter."

"Yeah, but how often do you get good looking guys in suits coming to derby games by themselves? I figured it was worth checking him out and when I got closer, I realised he was probably your man having a bit of a regret-lurk on a Thursday night."

Kate's heart raced. "He came," she said to herself. "Wait, what do you mean, 'when I got closer?'"

"I went over and asked him what he was doing, staring at my friend's arse with the laser-like focus of that laser that almost slices off James Bond's dick," Rapunzel said matter-of-factly.

"You...what did he say?"

"Well, first of all, the guy's got a glare on him that could straight-up *peel paint*. I'm not convinced he'd smile if he was getting sucked off in a money tornado."

Kate winced. "Sorry."

"What are you apologising for?"

"I don't know, I'm sorry."

Rapunzel gave her a look.

"Sorry." Kate clapped her hands over her mouth. "Sorry."

"Okay, you're clearly stuck in a loop." Rapunzel yanked her hands off her mouth. "Listen to me. I went over to Dexter and said 'kind of you to show up, but Kate's new boyfriend won't be happy you're here.'"

Kate's hands flew back to her mouth.

"I know." Rapunzel said, with a smug smile. "It was ingenious shit. Your man straight up turned *maroon*. Jealous doesn't even begin to cover it. He was glancing around, all angry, saying 'Who is he? Point him out' like he was going to initiate some kind of duel for your pussy and I was all, 'new boyfriend doesn't exist, but fair warning, Peach is a sexy girl, and if you don't want someone else tapping her, stop being such a shitheel.'"

Kate shoved a knuckle between her lips and bit down so hard she tasted blood. "Are you *serious?*"

"Oh yeah. And then Dexter glared at me and asked if I could send you over to talk to him, which pretty much brings us to now." For the second time, Rapunzel reached up and pulled Kate's hands out of her mouth. "Stop it, you'll fuck ya teeth. Now, do you want to see him or not?"

Kate glanced over at Ty who appeared to be buying himself a doughnut from a nearby vendor. After weeks of misery and confusion, he'd come back and she was wearing a blonde wig, roller skates and enough makeup to paint a deck. "I don't know."

"That's fine. I'll go tell him to piss off, shall I?"

For a brief moment, Kate considered it. There would be something satisfying in blowing Ty off without even seeing him, making him feel powerless the way he had when he'd told her he was leaving for Queensland minutes after they had sex.

"Righto," Rapunzel said. "I'll tell him to fuck off. You want me to say anything in particular? Like, maybe he should bring some fucking flowers next time instead of showing up empty-handed like a slack piece of shit?"

Kate grabbed Rapunzel's arm. "No, um, I think I should go talk to him. He came here for me. I shouldn't be a coward."

Rapunzel looked a little disappointed. "Fair enough. Get over there quick, though, only seven minutes until half time's over."

"I'll be fast. Thanks so much."

"Anytime, Peach. Hope it goes down the way you want it to."

So did she, though she had no idea what that would look like.

As Kate made her way toward Ty, the crowd parted around her like the proverbial red sea. At first she had no idea why, then she remembered she was in a skimpy uniform and skates with crazy makeup all over her face. She wished she was wearing something else but she needed to speak to him now or she'd go insane waiting for the game to finish. Why the hell had he come here? Surely it couldn't be a coincidence, although knowing her luck...

As she drew closer, Ty turned toward her, balling up his brown paper doughnut bag and sucking cinnamon sugar from his fingers.

"Ty?"

He looked at her and when their gaze met, everything went very slow and soft. It was tacky to feel this way about someone who'd hurt her so badly, but Kate felt warm with relief. It had been sixteen days, sixteen miserable days but now her handsome, blue-eyed Daddy was back.

"Hi, Middleton," he said in his deep, rough voice. "Come over here?"

Funny how his orders never failed to provoke the same reaction in her, a weakening in the back of the knees, as though he were a king and she was literally about to genuflect to him. Kate was aware of all the women staring at them, no doubt trying to weigh up her relationship to this beautiful, well-dressed man.

She straightened her spine, making herself as tall as possible. "You came to my derby final."

The corners of Ty's mouth kicked up. "I did."

He moved toward her, his arms slightly raised, and Kate automatically took a step back.

Ty winced. "I guess I deserve that."

He'd wanted to hug her. Why had she reacted as though he'd pulled a knife? Again, she was glad she was wearing so much greasepaint and pink glitter, it might be concealing some of her shame. "No, sorry, I was just..." She extended a hand. "How are you?"

Ty stared at her outstretched fingers. "I'm not going to shake your hand, Middleton."

She only had a second of extreme mortification before Ty stepped forward and kissed her on the cheek, numbing half of her face. "Hi again. You make a cute blonde."

"My name's Princess Bleach," Kate whispered. "If I'm not blonde, it doesn't work as a name."

"Makes sense." Ty's hands slid around her back. "You look beautiful."

"Th-Thank you?"

"You're a great player, too," he added, as though all of this was very normal. "You're quick. Seeing you get knocked to the ground was hard, though."

Kate swallowed, trying to think of something to say that wasn't 'what the hell is happening?' "I thought you liked seeing me in pain."

Ty pulled her body closer to his, apparently unconcerned about getting glitter all over his fancy coat. "Only pain I put you in, sweetheart."

Warmth spread through Kate's belly like lava. She wanted to give into it, wanted to sink deep into the familiar gratitude of his presence, but she couldn't. "Ty, what are you doing here?"

"Apologising to you." He took her hand and pressed it flat against his chest to where his heart lay. "I couldn't stay away. I know I left things unsaid before Queensland, but I fucking miss you. I want things to go back to the way they were."

Kate had pictured this a hundred times, a thousand, and though it was better than she imagined; Ty coming to her derby final and holding her like this in front of all these indie nerds, she couldn't help but question his motives. His motives and her heart's capacity for forgiveness.

"Katie?" he said softly. "Please look at me."

"I can't. If I do, I'll want to say yes, and I shouldn't say yes."

"Why?"

"Because the way things were was weird. I liked being with you, but there were so many times when I felt like I was a doll that got put in a cupboard whenever you were done playing with me. We never went anywhere except my place. I thought you were just a really private person but you were engaged once, you must have known how to...you must have wanted..." Kate stopped short of mentioning all the parties and special dates on Veronica's Facebook page but she could see from Ty's expression that he understood.

"I *am* a private person, Middleton but I never meant to make you feel like a toy."

Kate's chest tightened. "But you did. I didn't want the world from you, I just wanted proper dates and a bit of romance and..." she fell silent, unable to keep listing the many tiny, silly things she needed from Tyler Henderson.

There was a short, painful silence.

Kate removed her hand from Ty's chest. Part of her wished she'd been born without vocal cords and Ty didn't know sign language but she was proud she'd said what she said all the same. "I should go. Half-time's almost over."

"Katie." Ty cupped her jaw and brought their faces close again. In her skates she was almost as tall as he was.

"Yes?"

"Look at me."

It was an order, like the velvety ones he used to issue in Aunt Rhonda's lounge room. Kate met his gaze and when she did, everything changed. Without words, without any real explanation, she understood why he'd left, and why he'd come back. He was the dominant one but he hadn't planned for this any more than she had. He'd jumped in feet first for the sex and then a tide of feelings had swept them both away. He hadn't been ready, but he was ready now.

"I know," she whispered. "I know you didn't want to hurt me."

"Never." Ty's eyes were hard as blue diamonds. "Never, Katie."

They stared at each other until she had to ask, "So what now?"

Ty smiled, soft as a summer sky. "You want proper dates? I'll give you proper dates. You want romance?"

He kissed her then, in full view of everyone. Kate had never experienced enough PDA to form an opinion on it, but as soon as Ty's lips met hers she melted into his arms, ceasing to resist any element of his crusade to win her back. She had missed this, she had missed him so much. They were saying hello with their bodies and her body was so, so happy to be back near Ty's.

A wolf-whistle sliced through the air, and she turned to see her teammates pointing and laughing. Their attention drew the crowd's attention, and suddenly dozens of people had turned to look at her and Ty.

She stepped away from him, her skin blistering under her makeup. "Sorry."

"Don't be," Ty said and to her amazement, turned and waved at her teammates, smiling the ten-megawatt smile she associated with the end of blow jobs.

The Barbie Trolls' reactions were mixed—some girls flushed, others laughed, Rapunzel made her hand a cylinder and wanked the air. The only person who didn't look at all amused was Maria. Her beautiful face was contorted into an expression Kate had only ever seen once, when her brother Mick bought fake Linkin Park tickets from a scam website—horror tinged with fury. Her stomach squirmed. "I should go."

"Not just yet." Ty pulled her in for another hug and his palms dipped to her ass. "I hope you know you'll be wearing this uniform to bed tonight?"

Despite Maria's expression and the very real possibility Thunderbox would smash her into the ground like a fence-post, Kate smiled. "I do know that, yes."

Ty leaned in close. "Yes, what?"

Excitement throbbed from the tips of her fingers to her toes. "Yes, Daddy."

Ty released her behind. "Get going, then. Good luck."

"Do you want to come up closer? They have special spots for people who know players."

Ty shoved his hands back into his coat pockets. "I'm okay."

Kate kept smiling, but her giddiness deflated a little. She knew she should be amazed and grateful he was here, not already wanting more, but her hurt at being left in her bed hadn't entirely faded. How could it? It would take more than a soulful kiss at a derby game to fix weeks of heartache and uncertainty.

There was no time for the Barbie Trolls to heckle her about Ty. As soon as she was near them, Kate was dragged into a team huddle.

"We can still win this." Maria told them. "We just need to play fast and tight. No mercy."

Kate remembered Thunderbox's finger sliding across her throat. Was she just razzing her or was she in actual danger? Girls broke bones playing derby, it happened all the time.

"Kate," Maria snapped. "Are you thinking about how we're going to win this game or are you thinking about kissing?"

The rest of the team looked at her and Kate was sure, in spite of the greasepaint on her face, they could see exactly how embarrassed she was. "Sorry."

"Concentrate," Maria hissed. "That goes for all of you. Now hands in!"

Kate placed her hand on the sweaty multi-coloured pile and shouted 'Trolls!' along with her teammates. The siren wailed through the stadium and The A-Bombs shouted "Kill!" and broke their own huddle. The battle cry did nothing to ease Kate's nerves, still, knowing Ty was watching her, she clenched her jaw. She would show him what she was made of tonight, make him look at her in a way he never had before. She moved toward the starting line, but Maria gripped her wrist. "You're not jamming, Gilly is."

"But—"

"Bench," Maria said to her eyebrows. "Now."

The second half kicked off. The A-Bombs were determined to maintain their lead, and the play was bloodier than any Kate had ever seen. Elbows connected with faces, knees with thighs and feet stuck out to send unsuspecting players crashing to the ground. Gilly managed to steal three points before Thunderbox shoved her so hard she went spinning into the crowd.

"Fuck," Maria muttered, but she didn't tell Kate to go on. Rapunzel helped Gilly to her feet, and she returned to the jamming line.

The A-Bombs scored two points and their fans, who seemed as rough as the players, cheered and heckled loudly. They were forced to go quiet, however, when Gilly broke through The A-Bomb ranks to steal six points. The gap was closing; there were only three points between the teams. Excitement thickened the air, the possibility of a comeback alive and electric.

Kate's knees jiggled as she watched the plays. She wished she could help but knew she was probably doing more by keeping her butt on the bench.

It seemed impossible, but the game became even rougher, long minutes passing without either team scoring. Girls kept going down like ninepins, Thunderbox and Rapunzel the only two whose height and strength kept them upright. Rapunzel was gunning for the defender, but Thunderbox didn't seem keen to confront her, she kept moving away or dropping back to avoid a collision.

Yeah, don't pick on someone your own size or anything, Kate thought and shouted, "Come on, Rapunzel, knock her over!"

As the timer dwindled down to ten minutes and the Barbie Trolls remained four points behind, Kate felt nauseous. They were so close, all they needed was one good run, but morale was dwindling and with it, their chances of winning. There was a scrimmage in the middle of the pack, and a sharp scream split the air. Jumping to her feet, Kate saw Gilly lying on the ground holding her forearm.

"I think I sprained my wrist," she said as Rapunzel helped her onto the team bench.

Maria swore. "Can you keep playing?"

"Of course she fucking can't." Rapunzel extended Kate a hand. "Up you get Peach, it's showtime."

"She's not jamming!" Maria whirled around to look at Casey. "Can you go back on?"

"No, she can't. She's injured too," Rapunzel snapped. "And don't you think about going up there, either. Peach is the obvious fucking choice."

Maria jabbed a finger into Rapunzel's clavicle. "Don't you tell me how to run my plays."

"Rapunzel," Kate said, feeling sick. "It's fine—"

"It's not fine," Rapunzel didn't take her eyes from Maria's. "You need to sort out your Sapphic fucking feelings, Mama Bear, and you need to do it when we're not on the cusp of winning a fucking final. Now, *let Peach jam.*"

It was a mark of how serious Rapunzel was that she didn't laugh at her unintentional condiment pun.

Maria glared at first Rapunzel then Kate. "She can't go up there. Look at her. She's not strong enough to push through the pack. Do you want to win? Or do you want to spend the last ten minutes of this game trying to keep Katie from killing herself?"

Rapunzel said something, but Kate didn't hear it. Rage, genuine rage, was boiling up inside her. She couldn't remember ever being so angry, it was wonderful—hot and sharp as a needlepoint. It made her fingers tingle and her heart race. It told her what to do. She stood up. "Gilly, can I have the jammer's cap, please?"

"Sure." Gilly gingerly removed the pink and white cover and handed it to her. "Good luck. Watch out for Thunderbox, she's rabid."

"Sure." Kate pulled on the cap and without another word to anyone skated to the jamming line.

"And the Barbie Trolls have substituted Shrilly Temple with Princess Bleach," the announcer, a chubby man in his fifties, shouted. *"A risky choice this late in a high-contact game. Bleach is quick, but as you can see from those baby giraffe legs of hers, not very strong. One would guess it's the last possible option."*

"Cunt," Rapunzel growled, sliding up alongside her. "I'll give *him* the last possible option. You ready for this, Peach?"

Kate thought about Ty, Maria, her parents, the guys at work, all the people who saw her as sad, helpless, baby Kate. She bared her teeth. "I'm ready."

"Good. Go hard, no mercy." Rapunzel clapped her on the back and sped off to the defenders line.

The skating official's whistle blew, and Kate pushed herself forward with all her strength. The announcer was right—she was quick. Within seconds, she was attempting to shove her way around The A-Bombs as Rapunzel, Tam, Nikki, and Jenna tried to help her. It was like throwing herself into a sea of hot tangled bodies, no one accomplished much of anything and then the play was over and they all had to return to their starting lines.

Though Kate had well and truly thought the game couldn't get more aggressive, it did. Jenna was sent off with a bloody lip, and Kate collected more elbows than she ever had in any previous games. She barely felt the places where they connected, though—all she could feel was the track moving beneath her feet like buttered marble and her clear bright anger. Three points, all she had to do was score three points in eight minutes.

Then the A-Bomb jammer broke through their defences and secured an extra point. They were now five points down. The crowd cheered and booed, and Kate felt defeat lay a soft hand on her shoulder. She skated back to the starter's line and found Rapunzel waiting for her. "You feeling brave?" she asked.

"I'm feeling angry."

Rapunzel grinned. "That'll work. I'm gonna J Thunderbox. It's the only way you'll be able to get past her."

Kate recoiled slightly. "Are you sure?"

"Course I am, I was born to J."

J-blocking meant bending down and arching your body back in a J shape, using almost all your body weight to knock a player off her feet. There was a strong chance you'd go with them, and the fact that you needed to drop your weight backward, like a trust fall in which no one was going to catch you, deterred most players from attempting it.

"What about a cross block?" Kate asked. "We can try—"

"No time. There's less than two minutes on the clock, we need to go big before we go home. The question is can you back me up?"

"Yes," Kate said, not knowing if it was true.

Rapunzel grabbed her wrist and shook it. "You're stronger than anyone thinks you are. Let's fucking show them."

Again she thought of Ty and Maria. "Yeah," Kate said. "Let's."

The ref's whistle sounded, and Kate and the A-Bomb's redhead jammer burst forward like bullets from a gun. As they circled the track, Rapunzel surged ahead, positioning her Viking berserker body in front of Thunderbox's. She bent low, so low the crowd gasped but as she arched back into her, Kate saw Rapunzel's aim was too far to the right. Thunderbox wobbled but pulled up straight again and with a flick of her hip sent Rapunzel crashing to the floor.

The crowd gasped and so did Kate, partially because she was scared for Rapunzel, mostly because Thunderbox had just met her gaze and her grin said that she was finally going for the kill. Kate skated faster toward the scrimmage. The crowd, perhaps sensing that blood was about to spill, seemed to swell around her like arteries.

"Get her," a woman screamed and Kate had no idea if she was the 'her.' It felt like she was the 'her.' She remembered that Ty was out there watching her and so was Maria. If she got knocked down, she'd lose the game and any chance of them seeing her as anything other than a helpless baby. It wasn't fair.

Like something in a movie she remembered what Rapunzel had said, *you're stronger than anyone thinks you are.* Her expression had been completely serious, she hadn't been lying or flattering or trying to pump her up for the game. She'd seen something in her that Kate had only ever seen in herself—a drive to persist even when everything screamed not to. She'd kept her aunt's apartment even though it made her family hate her, she spat in Dutchy's latte for saying football groupies deserved to be raped, and she went into Tyler Henderson's office and gave him a sex note. She *could* be strong and Rapunzel had seen that and Kate had promised to back her up.

Thunderbox loomed large as a dinosaur in front of her. Ordinarily, Kate would have tried to skate out of her path, but not this time. She picked up her pace.

"Mac," someone—it sounded like Casey—shouted. "No!"

She ignored them. As her and Thunderbox's bodies drew closer, Kate swerved sharply right. The crowd gasped, but Kate knew she was okay, knew she'd stay on her feet. She could have easily passed Thunderbox then, but instead, she slammed her hip into the defender's side.

The big woman was going to fall, Kate felt it the instant she struck Thunderbox's stomach. She felt her weight shift against hers like a planet tipping on its axis, a pool ball tapped in exactly the right place so that it went spinning into the corner pocket. Kate didn't have time to inspect the damage; she pulled ahead as Thunderbox collapsed, the weight of her body shaking the stadium floor. From the cries that emanated from behind her, it sounded like she'd collected a few other players on her way down. Kate barely had time to hope one of them was the A-Bombs jammer before she swerved around another blocker in neon green fishnets and a girl in gold booty shorts. The announcer shouted something, but Kate didn't hear him. She'd passed three players. That meant she was two points down. She raced in front of a dark haired A-Bomb, and the crowd bellowed their excitement, expanding and contracting like Kate's lungs. The Trolls only needed one more point to draw, two points to win.

The last two A-Bombs were in front of her, a round blonde and a tall brunette. They were skating shoulder-to-shoulder with their hands joined and Kate knew they'd do anything—legal or not—to stop her passing. It was time to do or die. She skated faster, recklessly fast, unsustainably fast. As the track turned, she swung wide and grabbed the brunette by the hips. The woman shrieked and tried to elbow Kate in the face but as the joint descended, Kate leveraged her weight against the brunette and whipped herself forward. The brunette yelped and Kate turned back and watched her flop onto the ground, taking her teammate with her. She was still looking the other way when she crossed the finish line.

The buzzer sounded. Kate barely had time to register her amazement before the A-Bomb jammer slammed into her, wrapping her hands around her neck and pulling her to the floor.

As she struggled to fight the girl off, she heard Rapunzel bellow, "It's fucking *on!*"

Kate had witnessed a few derby brawls, but she'd never been in one. It was similar to a scrimmage, but with a lot more hair pulling. Thankfully, it didn't last long. A few staff members intervened and Kate found herself being hoisted onto her feet and hugged by her teammates in a manner that wasn't so different from being choke-slammed.

"We did it!" Rapunzel shouted from somewhere behind her. "Peach did it! We did it! Suck my dick, A-Bombs! Suck it hard!"

"Rapunzel!" Tam scolded from somewhere to Kate's left. "There are kids here!"

"I don't give a fuck, we won!"

Kate suspected it was Rapunzel who flung herself on top of the hug pile, causing them all to collapse in a tangle of fishnet-covered limbs, but she didn't care. Somewhere in her brain, it was starting to dawn on her that she'd led her derby team to victory right in front of Tyler Henderson.

After several exhilarating, sweaty minutes the hug ended and Kate scanned the crowd for Ty. He was leaning against a taco stand applauding and when she caught his eye, he smiled in a way that said she'd surprised him, maybe even impressed him, and it was like winning a second time. She was moving toward him when Maria tapped her on the shoulder. "Wait a minute Katie, the presentations are about to start."

Her colour was still high but she looked calmer and maybe even a little embarrassed.

"I hope everything's okay between us?" Kate asked, too happy to engage in any lasting animosity.

Maria smiled and patted her cheek. "Of course. I'm sorry for not putting you on earlier. You played beautifully."

Kate smiled. "Thanks."

The Barbie Trolls lined up to shake the losing team's hands. Some of the A-Bombs were friendly, some sulky, but Thunderbox was the real surprise—she gave Kate a smile, albeit a strained one. "Nice work, even if it was a lucky shove."

Kate shrugged and moved to shake the next girl's hand when Thunderbox put out a hand to stop her. "I saw you kissing that guy at half time," she said.

"So?"

Thunderbox stared down at her massive boobs. "So, I thought the tall blonde chick was your girlfriend."

Several things occurred to Kate at once. "She's not," she said, trying not to smile. "I'm not gay or bi. Rapunzel is though, gay I mean, and she's single. Want me to give her your number?"

Thunderbox's eyes lit up, then she shrugged, feigning disinterest. "She wants it, she can come find me."

The presentation went for much longer than anyone wanted, with speeches from the league president, then a stadium official, then a sponsor and then the medals were handed out.

Kate used the time to unpin her wig and wipe away the worst of her makeup, cheering loudly as Casey was announced as the league Best and Fairest. When the presentation was over, she was just about to attempt to duck into the crowd when Tam seized her collar. "I don't think so, Macca. We just won the fucking grand final. We're going out for a drink."

"I'll come out for a drink, I just need to find Ty!" Kate protested.

"So you can run off and canoodle? I don't think so. This so-called Ty will come with us."

"Tam!" Rapunzel shouted as she whizzed past. "Have you got her? Is she coming?"

Tam shook Kate by her collar as though she were a poacher with a successfully snared ocelot. "I got her!"

Rapunzel shot them both a thumbs up. "I'm gonna find Dexter and bring him with us," she told Kate. "Meet you at the bar!"

17

Kate was frog-marched—frog-rolled—out of the stadium by Tam who refused to let go of her until they were inside Rumba. The bar staff had put up streamers and balloons in honour of the final and Kate had barely pulled off her jacket before someone forced a bright red shot into her hands. She downed it, wincing at the cherry cough syrup flavour and looked around the bar. She couldn't see Ty anywhere. Tam squeezed her arm. "He'll be here. No one gets the better of Rapunzel. Let's get another round."

Turned out that meant another round of shots, and not a soft option like Cowboys or Skittle Bombs—straight tequila. Tam gleefully ordered chasers and Kate made a mental note to sip it slowly. Rumba had that tangible kamikaze feel of a party about to go off. She couldn't get too drunk tonight. If Ty had to carry her out of a bar again, he might think she had a problem.

Ten minutes passed without a glimpse of him and Kate's vodka sunrise vanished. People kept pounding her on the back, telling her how amazing her last play had been, but she could barely concentrate. She ordered another vodka sunrise.

Twenty minutes later and she was drunk. She was just about to tell Tam she was leaving and stagger out into the night to find Ty, when everyone in the bar cheered. Rapunzel appeared in the doorway beaming from ear-to-ear. Propping her up was a red-faced Ty.

"What the hell?" Tam shrieked. "Where have you two been?"

"I fell over on the road and did my ankle," Rapunzel said gleefully. "If this cunt hadn't picked me up, I'd have been run over!"

Everyone within earshot started laughing and Tam nudged Kate's side. "That's good he's helping her. I was worried Rapunzel brought him here as part of a hostage situation. Let's go give them a hand."

It took the combined strength of Kate, Tam, and Casey to ease Rapunzel off Ty and into a booth. She refused to take off her roller skates ("We just won the fucking final!") and instead propped up her leg and started icing her ankle with a bag of frozen cherries.

"I'm fine," she kept shouting. "Someone get me a drink!"

Kate dutifully headed for the bar and Ty came with her. She was relieved to see that he was grinning.

"How are you feeling?" he asked, once he'd ordered a beer and a cranberry martini.

"A bit out of it," Kate said. "Thanks for coming."

"Glad I could make it, you were incredible. Here, this is for you." He handed her the purplish martini. "The beer's for...what's her real name?"

Kate laughed. "Jacinta. Jacinta Smith-Bentley. But she gets angry if you call her that."

"But I feel stupid calling a grown woman Rapunzel."

"You get used to it."

"Right." Ty looked her up and down, his gaze suddenly hungry. "Drink your drink, Middleton."

Kate took a sip of the martini. It was strong, tart and sweet. "It's nice."

"Good." He kissed her right on the mouth, his tongue sliding between her lips to flirt with hers. When she moaned he pulled away. "Wanted to taste that on you."

Kate was dizzy, drunk on his lips—and about six standard drinks in the space of an hour. "Was it nice?"

Ty rubbed a thumb over his lips. "Yeah."

She decided to throw caution to the wind and tell him how insanely happy she was that he had come to see her tonight. "I'm so glad you—" Her skate connected with something squishy and she tipped backwards. "Whoa!"

"Katie!" Ty pulled her tight against him, breaking her fall.

Kate exhaled. "Thanks for saving me."

"I seem to be doing a lot of saving at the moment. Can you please take off your bloody roller skates? It was hard enough watching you roll around in them when you hadn't been drinking."

Emboldened by the alcohol in her blood and the fact he'd been worried for her, Kate pressed her body against his, rubbing her hips along his suit pants. "I thought you said my roller skates were sexy?"

Ty's smile was feral, a starving dog pacing behind a chain mail fence. "You need to be careful about what you say to me, Little Miss Middleton. I've gone too long without your body and I'm in no mood to be a gentleman."

The implicit threat in his words made Kate's heart skip a beat. "I wouldn't mind if you weren't a gentleman."

Ty smoothed his hands down her back, resting them on her hips. To anyone else, it might have looked like a sweet gesture, but his grip was hard and his cock was now flush against her stomach.

"Feel that? The way you're going, you're going to spend the night sucking it until your jaw aches."

Kate shivered. "Is that a promise?"

"Disrespectful little thing tonight, aren't you?" Ty bit her earlobe, sending shivers down her spine. "Let's get out of here and find out."

She was just about to agree when one of her nicknames was shouted across the bar. She turned to see Rapunzel pointing at her. "Don't even think about running off with Dexter until we've had a drink! Bring my beer over!"

"Princess Rapunzel has spoken," Ty said drily, and Kate was sure he was going to suggest he leave and meet her at her place. Then he wrapped his arm around her shoulder and walked with her toward the booth where her teammates were sitting.

"One drink with your friends," he muttered into her ear. "Then we're getting out of here so I can pound sixteen days' worth of frustration into you while you beg me for mercy."

Kate was so full of conflicting emotions she could only stare. "You don't have to do this. Meet my teammates like this. Right now."

He smiled. "I want to, Middleton. I promised things would be different and I meant it."

"Okay, well you should know the girls can be a bit full on. They're nice but, um, a bit intense."

Ty smiled in a way that said she was being silly, that he'd never felt out of place anywhere, never had any trouble getting anyone to like him. Yet for all his confidence Kate's stomach wouldn't unclench.

Please let this go well, she prayed. *Please let everyone like everyone.*

When they reached the crimson faux-leather booth around which most of the team was packed, Ty placed Rapunzel's pint in front of her. "How are you doing, girls?"

"Good," her teammates said in a flirtatious chorus.

"Glad to hear it." Ty squeezed Kate's shoulder. "Have you got enough room for us to join you?"

"Hell yeah," Tam said. "Everyone bunch up. And someone go get some more tequila."

And so, against all Kate's expectations, she and Ty settled into the booth, his hand clasped around hers. The next forty minutes passed in a blur of conversation and alcohol. Ty laughed and told jokes and listened attentively when anyone talked. He asked thoughtful questions about derby and whatever jobs the person he was talking to worked. It was a full-scale charm attack, so all-encompassing Kate was sure the devil would have been left starry-eyed and woozy. Her teammates were easy fodder, compared to that. Soon they were hanging on his every word. Casey, in particular, kept tossing her hair and laughing a strange laugh Kate had never heard before. It sounded like helicopter blades shredding through a bowl of lipstick.

Rapunzel, who for obvious reasons was completely unaffected by Ty's charisma, shoved herself closer to Kate. "How are you doing, Peach?"

"Good," Kate said, swirling a straw around in her martini. "You?"

"I'm all right." Rapunzel jerked her head at Ty. "He's a bit charming, isn't he?"

"Yeah," Kate said, her belly tightening for some reason. "You should see him at work."

"I can imagine. He's a good choice for you, though. You make a good match."

Kate nodded, then the vodka made her ask, "You don't think it's weird he's older than me?"

Rapunzel snorted. "No, why the fuck would that matter?"

"Maria thinks it's weird."

"Look, Peach, about Maria..." Rapunzel broke off and stared up at the ceiling. She'd been drinking steadily since she arrived at the bar, but Kate had a feeling something else was putting the glassy look in her eyes, something that probably wasn't legal in the state of Victoria.

"Are you okay?"

"Oh fuck yeah." Rapunzel yawned. "What was I saying? Oh that's right, old or not anyone can see why you'd wanna hump that breeder. He's a good looking bloke, charming like we said. Casey's beyond moist just breathing his air."

"I know. She keeps laughing weird."

Rapunzel's brow furrowed. "You're not pissed at her, are you? She doesn't mean anything by it. She just hasn't had sex in ages."

"Oh no, I totally get it! Everyone stares at Ty like that. *I* stare at Ty like that."

"Cool." Rapunzel put an arm around Kate's shoulders. "You're a good partner for a beautiful person, Peach. Sometimes people can't handle it. Or they like it at first, but then they get jealous and take it out on their girl—or man, or whatever."

Rapunzel let out a long, low sigh.

"Do you want to talk about it?" Kate asked.

"Nah, it's all good, I've made my peace with it now. Older and wiser, you know? But I wish I'd had a little more self-respect back then. Understood that Amy couldn't help people falling in love with her left, right and center. She was beautiful, that's just what happens."

Rapunzel tapped Kate's sternum. "You won't do that. You know it's not personal just because his light shines a little brighter than yours."

Kate thought about Ty's ex-fiancée. She had been miles prettier than her but it still hadn't worked out. "I'll try."

"Shit!" Rapunzel shouted. "Not that you're not hot! Sorry if it sounded like I was saying you're not hot! You're *such* a sexy nun, I just mean your boy's got that Jason Statham charisma thing happening—"

"It's okay, I totally understand," Kate said loudly, because Gilly and Jenna had turned to look at them.

Rapunzel nodded, relaxing back into the booth. "Good. That's very good. And don't worry about the age gap either. When you're gay..." She stared up at the ceiling again, as though something fascinating was happening up there.

Kate nudged her side. "Um, you were saying something about age gaps and being gay?"

Rapunzel gave a little start. "Oh yeah, I was trying to say that when you're gay, those things don't matter the same way. I've dated nineteen-year-olds, and I've dated fifty-three-year-olds, and there are differences, sure, but there isn't this shame or power shit because there isn't a history of old women forcing hot chicks to marry them and lick their wrinkly old balls."

"Ergh."

"I know, but you need to listen to me, Peach." Rapunzel gripped Kate's chin, her water-blue eyes boring into hers. "I don't get called a cougar because I date young chicks and people don't say I've been taken advantage of when I screw older women. Why should it be different for you?"

"I don't know," Kate admitted. "I guess there's a history of older men dating young women without any social kickbacks. Like they're allowed to upgrade, but women only get grosser with time. Maybe I feel like I'm a part of that, especially, because I like it when Ty—"

Kate clamped her mouth shut. Discussing her and Ty's age difference was hard enough without bringing up their daedalean labyrinth of a sex life.

Rapunzel hiccoughed. "Okay, so men have been shitty and used their power to attract women who'd never fuck them normally. But does that mean old men and young women can't fall in love, get married and go down on each other forever?"

Kate felt like this would be a bad time to tell Rapunzel that Ty didn't go down on her. "No?"

"Right. You're not helping the cause by telling your fancy little man that he can't be your fancy little man. Just be with him and be happy, I say."

Kate smiled. "Thanks, Rapunzel."

"Anytime. Now, are you sure you don't wanna sell me some of your Ritalin?"

"No."

"Fair enough."

Despite Ty's claim they'd stay for one drink, they ordered another round, then another. As it neared midnight Kate felt totally justified in 'accidentally' brushing her hand across his thigh. She had barely touched him, when he gripped her wrist. "Middleton," he said in her ear. "We're done here. Finish your drink."

Kate obliged, then realised she desperately needed to pee. She extracted herself from the booth with some difficulty and stood, wobbling slightly, but refusing all offers to accompany her to the bathroom. "I'm fine you guys, really."

"Be careful, Middleton," Ty said. "If you fall I won't be there to catch you this time."

"Why'd you call her Middleton?" Casey demanded.

"Because…"

Kate skated away before she could hear him explain. She felt like a semi-badass tonight with her derby win and her hot date, and Middleton was the girly girl from work.

She was a foot from the Rumba bathroom when someone called her name. She turned to see Maria sitting with a group of women Kate had never seen before. "Katie," she said. "Come over here!"

Kate was desperate to pee but figured a quick hello wouldn't hurt. She skated closer. "Hi. How's it going?"

Everyone at the table said some variation on the word 'good.' Their mouths were red with wine and from the empty bottles in front of them, Kate guessed they were as drunk as she was. "Okay, well nice to meet you guys but I've gotta..." she gestured to the bathroom.

"Just a second." Maria said, her accent even thicker than usual. "I wanted to ask if your boyfriend wanted to come sit with us? He might feel a bit more comfortable here with people his own age."

Everyone laughed, which meant everyone knew. Kate's cheeks burned. "I think he's okay."

"I bet he is," Maria slurred and Kate decided to leave. Maria said something and the women burst into laughter behind her.

It was only once she'd peed that Kate noticed the walls of her cubicle were careening from side to side as though she were on the deck of a heavily graffitied pirate ship. She needed to leave, go home, take some pre-emptive ibuprofen and have a cuddle with Ty.

Except Ty doesn't cuddle. You'll be giving him a nice blowjob without any reciprocal downtown action. Doesn't that sound fun?

"Shut up," she mumbled, pressing her hands to her ears as though that might stop the unremitting thoughts. "Shut up, shut up."

Someone pounded hard on her cubicle door. "Katie?"

She frowned. "Maria?"

"Yes, please come out. I want to talk to you."

Kate glared at the door. Drunk as she was, she knew she shouldn't be getting into any arguments, but she couldn't help herself. She burst out of the stall and almost knocked Maria over. "What the actual hell?"

"Katie, be careful!"

"No!" Kate said pointing a petulant finger at her. "You were super mean to me just now!"

Maria's expression was pained. Her usually flawless eyeliner wings were smeared and she had lipstick on her teeth. "I know, I'm so sorry."

"I don't care! Why did you do that?"

Maria took her hand, her skin was very hot. "Because of him. I don't like him, Katie."

"Too bad." Kate shook off Maria's hand and skated over to the sinks.

Maria followed her. "That man is using you."

"Oh my gosh, not this rubbish again!" Kate pounded the soap dispenser so hard it jizzed pink detergent all over the sinks and the mirror. "Shoot!"

She tried to wipe it off as best she could with her vision still swaying from side to side.

"You don't understand." Maria grabbed her hips from behind and pulled Kate into her chest. "You think because he came to your game and met all the girls, he's changed, but it takes nothing for him to come here and buy you a drink. *Nothing*. He ignores you for weeks and with just one kiss you're his again!"

Kate shouldered her friend's body away from hers. "God, Maria, what's gotten into you?"

"I'm sorry," she moaned, still holding Kate's hips. "Please just forgive me and tell me you won't see him anymore?"

"I can't do that! I don't *want* to do that! I have no idea why you hate Ty so much but I can have sex with him if I want to."

Maria glared at her in the soapy mirror. Unlike her teammates, she'd changed out of her uniform into jeans and knee high boots. She looked tall and powerful, an Amazon in action.

"Katie, this man is not what you've been fantasising about. You want someone to love you and what you have is an old man using you for sex. Unless you make it clear what you deserve, Tyler Henderson will never commit himself to you."

"You don't know that!" Kate's voice bounced off the mirrors and sinks, echoed against the graffitied ceiling. "You don't know anything about him!"

"Maybe, but I know everything about you. I helped you when you didn't have anyone else, and I'm not going to see you get hurt again. I'm the only one who cares about you!"

It was a good thing Maria had changed out of her skates. At her words, Kate became so full of bright, white rage, she shoved Maria's shoulder and sent her staggering backward.

"Katie!" Maria looked shocked. "What are you doing?"

"Why would you say that to me? Why did you hurt me then follow me in here and try to hug me better and say it was Ty's fault?"

Maria shot a panicky look at the door. "You don't need to yell, I just—"

"You really think you're the only person I can trust?"

"What I meant was—"

"No!" Kate had never been so angry in her life. Her whole body was shaking from head to toe. "I know you meant it. You really think you're the only person who knows me or likes me and you want it to stay that way."

Tears welled up in Maria's eyes. "Katie, I'm sorry, I shouldn't have come in here. I'm sorry. Let's just forget this for now. We can talk about this tomorrow or—"

"No." Kate skated toward the door. "No. I'm done."

She wrenched the door open, the noise and heat of the bar hitting her right in the face. She turned and looked over her shoulder at her mentor, who stood wiping sooty tears out of her eyes. "We're over," she told Maria. "We're not friends anymore."

Without waiting to hear what she would say, Kate skated forward, letting the door close between them.

It was as if the booth with her teammates had been frozen in time when she left and quickly defrosted upon her return. Everyone was still drinking the same drinks and listening to Ty explain why they called her 'Middleton.' How could so little time have passed when a huge bombshell had fallen and detonated upon her? Maria wasn't really her friend. Maria didn't have any of her best interests at heart.

"Macca!" Tam cried. "Sit down, we'll get more shots!"

Kate shook her head, making deliberate eye contact with Ty. He got the message at once, finishing his glass of water and rising to his feet. "Goodnight girls, thanks for having me."

There was a chorus of boos. Gilly threw a straw at him.

"Hang on! It's not even..." Casey grabbed Ty's arm and turned his Seamaster toward her. "It's not even midnight. You can't just leave!"

"Yes, they can, Sabrina." Rapunzel pried Casey's fingers away from Ty's wrist. "Give Peach and her boytoy credit for staying this long."

Kate knew she was calling Ty her boytoy to reassure her about their age gap. It was so sweet she almost started crying. "I'll see you later, guys. Amazing game all of you."

"You too."

"Later, Mac."

"Yeah, enjoy the sex."

A loud burst of laughter followed them from the booth and Ty chuckled as he led her toward the door. It was freezing outside, minus one at least. Ty bundled her into his arms and wrapped his coat around her back.

"Are you okay?" he asked. "You looked a bit dazed when you came back from the bathroom."

Kate thought about telling him what Maria said, unloading the whole dirty story, then she shook her head. "I'm fine, just a bit drunk, maybe."

Ty gave her a wry look. "I don't think it's a maybe, Middleton, and the wheels aren't helping. Did you bring a change of clothes?"

Kate slapped a hand to her forehead. "Yeah, but Casey put my sports bag in her car. I should go back inside and—"

"No, we'll only get stuck talking to everyone for another hour." Ty peeled off his coat and placed it around her shoulders. "Button it up, it should do you until we get to the car."

Kate stared at him, running a hand over the thick Ty-smelling fabric. Who would have ever thought she'd be wearing this coat? "What about you?"

"Queenslanders are tougher than southerners. Besides," Ty smirked at her. "I've got something better to keep me warm."

He bent down and picked her up, wrapping her legs around his waist. "That should do me until we get to the parking tower."

"I can walk," Kate protested. "Or roll."

"Not a chance. You're drunk and in roller skates. I'm not spending the rest of the night in the emergency room when I could spend it in your bed."

The thought of them having sex in her bed again made Kate bite her tongue. When they reached the parking tower, Ty stopped in front of a glossy black Toyota Hilux.

"Is that yours?" Kate said, surprised.

Ty pulled a set of keys from his suit pocket. "Course. You didn't think I was gonna take you home on my bike, did you? You'd freeze to death."

Ty opened the passenger side door and eased her in. As he walked around the cab, Kate glanced around and tried to absorb any and all of the car's details. It was a manual, of course, because Ty was butch and butch guys drove big manual cars, even in the city where you were at risk of dinging someone at every turn. It also smelled new and was very tidy. Only a few crumpled receipts on the floor indicated it was in use. Kate wondered if his house was the same, clean and butch and barely used.

Ty jumped in the driver's seat and shut the door. "Seat belt."

Kate dutifully tugged the safety device across her chest and clicked it into the holder. "I haven't been in a non-Uber car for ages."

"You have one, right? Red Hyundai?"

"Yeah, but I hardly use it. I keep thinking I should sell it and rent out my parking space."

Her voice was as husky as if she were telling him all the ways she planned to screw him tonight. Ty caught the scent at once. "What are you thinking about, little girl?"

The truth was Kate's mind was pinwheeling across a hundred different topics. So much had just happened, so much to absorb and process. She knew she and Ty should talk about why he left and why he came back, but all she really wanted to do was something that required no words whatsoever.

"I'm thinking you have tinted windows," she told him. "And there's no one around."

The interior light had gone off now Ty had shut the door. All Kate could see when she looked across at him were the sharp planes of his face, hard, unforgiving angles. Air hissed between Ty's teeth and then her seat belt unclicked itself, the strap sliding across her chest.

"Is that a yes?"

His hand closed over her breast, massaging it softly. "You take something now, you'll pay for it later."

Kate smiled, remembering she still owed him thirty or so blow jobs from when she 'stole' from his wallet. "Put it on my tab."

Ty made a soft tutting noise, as though she had no idea what kind of trouble she was in. "You wanna sit on my cock, little girl? You wanna get fucked in a parking garage?"

Kate pictured it, her back against the wheel, riding him up and down. Her pussy clenched excitedly, but she shook her head. "I want to go down on you."

Ty stopped massaging her breast. "You sure? You must be tired from your game."

She was, but it didn't matter. Serving him was exactly what her submissive self-required—to be nothing but a cog in someone else's machine for a while.

"I want to be a good girl," she said and even though it was dark, she knew Ty smiled.

"If that's what you want, it's yours. But if you suck it now, you'll ride it as soon as we get home, understood?"

Kate gave a nod that was pointless in the dim light, then she said, "Yes, Daddy."

Ty's cock was as beautiful as she remembered. When she opened wide and brought her lips around it, he groaned.

"Stay low," he said, weaving a hand through her hair. "We get caught, both of us'll have some job-searching to do."

Kate knew she should have been worried about that, but she had no thoughts to spare for anything that wasn't Ty's cock. She gave herself over to the act of sucking him, ignoring the tricky angle and her sore neck, ignoring everything that wasn't her job.

Ty's hand rose and fell with her head. "Fuck, I missed you," he groaned. "I missed your greedy fucking mouth."

"I missed you, too," Kate moaned around his shaft and because she knew all he could hear was garbled nonsense, she added, "I think I'm in love with you."

When he was done, Ty wiped a thumb over her damp lips.

"You were perfect," he said. "Now, let's go home."

Kate nodded, feeling as though he'd poured warm, glowing liquid into a place that had been empty for far too long—not his semen, obviously—the fact that he'd called Aunt Rhonda's apartment home. The fact that they were going there together, after a social outing that was almost, maybe a date.

They made out in the elevator, Kate not giving a damn about Stephen who was surely watching them at the security deck downstairs. Kate had barely closed her front door before Ty pressed her up against it, tearing off her underwear and fucking her with a ruthlessness she hadn't felt since their first night together.

She came within minutes, screaming his name as the wheels of her roller skates bashed against the wood. One of Aunty Rhonda's daguerreotypes fell off the wall and splintered, but Ty didn't stop, and Kate didn't care. He came a few minutes later, groaning about what a good whore she was, his lovely girl, his beautiful little slut.

"You want a shower?" he asked when they'd both caught their breath.

"You mean, me and then you, or you and then me?"

Ty huffed out a laugh. "I mean, together."

Kate tugged at her ear, unable to fully believe what she'd heard. "Ah, yeah, if you're having one? Maybe? I guess?"

And so for the first time in their brief, unusual history she and Ty showered together. Initially, Kate stood away from him, shyly admiring his body, but Ty tugged her close, laying her head against his chest. "How are you feeling? Are you warm enough?"

I think I'm in love with you. "I'm great."

They stood under the hot waterfall together for a very long time, until everything felt floaty and safe and surreal.

Aftercare, Kate thought, *is fucking sweet.*

No sooner had she thought that than Ty grabbed her body wash and loofah. He applied one to the other then gave her a big cheeky smile. "That's the fucking smell!"

"Huh?"

"The strawberry fruit smell you've been carrying around since February. This is where it comes from, right?"

Kate frowned at him. "You noticed when I switched my lotion?"

To her delight, Ty's cheeks went red. He scowled at the body wash as though it had just called him an ignorant asshole. Kate giggled. "Do you know what flavour it was before?"

He didn't answer.

"Please tell me?" she begged. "If you say it, I'll give you a million blow jobs."

"You'd give me that anyway."

"I know, but please tell me? Please, please, please? Please?"

His scowl intensified. "Mango. It was mango, okay? Mango. Now turn around and let me wash your ass."

Kate couldn't help it, she laughed. She laughed until she had to press a palm to the shower stall to keep herself upright. She laughed until Ty threatened to spank her into submission, which she took seriously and shut up. The last thing she wanted on top of her evening was a spanking. What she needed, and got, was Ty washing her, his big rough hands rubbing strawberry body wash into her skin with such tenderness it made her stomach twist and flutter like a cut kite. When they got out he wrapped her in a towel. "Better?"

Yes, Kate thought. *And no.*

The need to ask, to define, was almost overwhelming—*do you like me? Will it be different now? Can you be my boyfriend? What will we tell the people at work? Is there a chance you could be in love with me, too?* But there was no way to ask those things without sounding insane, even in her own head. So she just said yes and watched as he dressed himself in his suit again.

"I'll stay the night soon," he promised. "But this is new for me, and I don't want to rush things."

"I understand," Kate lied, because after sixteen days all she wanted was to stay with him. "I'll see you soon?"

He kissed her cheek. "Of course. I'm so fucking glad we could do this, Middleton."

Kate, she thought. *My name is Kate.*

Once he left, Kate couldn't sleep. She sat on her couch and stared at the TV without absorbing a single pixel. Ty had come back and things would be different, she'd won a grand final and cemented her friendship with one of the coolest people she'd ever met, so why couldn't she be happy?

She thought back to Rumba Bar, to Ty smiling and laughing, drawing in her teammates as easily as a fish breathed water. As impressed as she'd been at the time, something about it had felt strange, and as she lay aching on her couch, Kate knew what it was.

For someone praised as an Errol-Flynn-meets-Casanova-meets-James-Bond charmer, Ty had never actually charmed her. From the moment they'd met, she'd only seen him wield his allure from afar while he gave her first indifference, then resistance, then a kind of amused acceptance with occasional flashes of heart-stopping tenderness. When he laughed at her jokes or took her in his arms, it was always felt a little, well, *grudging*. As though he wished he could stop himself, but couldn't. What did that say about her and him and their possible future?

Maria's words came back to her. *What you have is an old man using you for sex. Unless you make it clear what you deserve, Tyler Henderson will never commit himself to you.*

"She's wrong," she told the apartment. "I don't have to make anything clear, this is just the start of a normal relationship. Everything is gonna be okay."

18

K ate's phone buzzed. She flipped it over and found a green-apple message waiting for her.

I'll be there at nine, Ty had written. *When I come through the door, you'll be bent over your dining table, naked. To your left will be a wooden spoon and to your right a glass of scotch. If you're lucky, and everything's laid out perfectly, you might be able to sit down tomorrow.*

They had been dating for over a month and yet the very idea got Kate so worked up it might as well have been the first time. She closed her eyes and imagined it—the sound of Ty's motorcycle boots thudding toward her, his mind intent on nothing but punishing her for her transgressions, his rough palm sliding down her lower back before he—

"Middleton?"

Kate jolted upright. "Huh?"

"Look alive, will you?" Dutchy sniggered at his own joke and dropped a heavy leather-bound folder onto her desk.

"What's this?" Kate asked, with all the politeness she could muster.

"Sloane brief," he said flicking the edge of the folder. "You need to take it down to The Breton Club. There's documents inside that need to be signed."

Kate looked out of the nearby window. It was raining so heavily it was like god was emptying a Jupiter-sized bucket of water on the city. "So, maybe we could get a courier to do it?"

"Too expensive."

And sending an engineer in the final stages of a six week project isn't? Kate inhaled deeply. "What about the interns? Why can't they go?"

"They're busy."

"With what? The last I saw they were making a nip-slip pinboard."

Dutchy chuckled. "Johnno asked them to do that, it's for his mate's birthday. You're not jealous, are you, Middleton?"

In her mind's eye, Kate picked up the leather folder and swung it square into Dutchy's face, spraying bone and brain-meat everywhere. These comments, which had never come her way when she wore pelican shirts and baked lamingtons, were happening more and more. Especially since the bro-town interns—Johnno's nephews—had arrived on the scene, ramping up the office douche-vibe with their polo shirts and constant references to pussy. Ty thought they were idiots, but everyone else acted like they were some unholy combination of Bill Hicks and Tyler the Creator. It didn't help that she'd stopped bringing cake to work. It had been Ty's idea.

"You were hired to be a fucking engineer, not cater morning teas," he said. "You wanna bake for someone, bake for me, at least you'll get laid afterward. Otherwise don't bother. It just makes them all think less of you."

He had a point, but he also didn't realise apple-cinnamon scrolls went a long way toward keeping her colleagues friendly. Kate took another deep breath. "Look, Jake, I'm crazy busy right now. Can we please find someone else to take the folder?"

Dutchy pointed upstairs. "He wants you to do it."

"Who, god?"

He didn't smile. "Johnno. He says it'll be nice for you to get out of the office and stretch your legs."

Again, Kate looked out of the window. A woman's umbrella was blown clean out of her hand and onto the road where it was struck by a passing taxi. "But it's pouring out, I'll ruin my clothes."

Dutchy rolled his eyes. "You're such a girl. Fine, if you don't want to do it then you can go upstairs and tell Johnno that yourself. I'm not telling him for you."

"Fine," Kate said through gritted teeth. "I'll take the folder."

"Cheers, Middleton. Don't be too long."

Dutchy strode off and Kate glared after him, loathing as sour as month-old milk in her heart. What the hell was his problem? She thought about Ty. If he suggested she do something pointless and uncomfortable just to please him, she got wet, and yet other people treating her that way just made her angry.

Maybe it was like the cake, she decided as she pulled on her jacket. When she baked for Ty, she got laid afterward; when she baked for Dutchy, all she got was the dumb expectation that she'd do it again and again and again.

Fighting through the water-blasted streets toward The Breton Club was every bit as miserable as it had looked from her window. The sky was black, and the wind whipped the rain sideways, making her jacket and umbrella pointless. Still, Kate marched grimly forward, the leather folder tucked into her chest, determined that when she got back to the office she was going to give Johnno a piece of her mind. Or at least send him a strongly-worded email.

The Breton Club doorman wasn't keen on letting her inside, but once Kate explained who she was, he reluctantly took her sopping coat and ushered her in.

"Hello there, can I help you?" A crimson-lipped hostess called from behind a wood podium.

"Yeh-hehehehs," Kate said, her teeth rattling like Yahtzee dice. "I need to give some documents to my boss, Mr Henderson. I think he's having a meeting right now?"

The hostess consulted a guestbook. "He's on the third floor. Would you like me to take the folder to him?"

Kate considered it, seeing Ty when she looked like a drowned rat wasn't appealing, but at the end of the day, confidentiality was confidentiality. "Could I please bring it to him myself?"

"Sure thing. Take the stairs over there."

Kate climbed the stairs slowly, trying to give herself time to dry out. Unsurprisingly, it didn't work. When she reached the top of the stairs, she ducked into a small service alcove by the door, applied a fresh coat of cranberry lip-gloss and attempted to wipe any and all water droplets from her face. She was steadying herself to enter the dining room when she heard a familiar voice. "Does anyone have the time?"

Through the gaps in the wood panels, Kate could see Ty sitting at a nearby dining table. His golden hair was mussed with what she now knew was surf wax and his grey suit was impeccable. To his right was Stormy who looked a lot less put together. He had gravy down his front and his cheeks were as blotchy as Kate's uncles' on Christmas. The third man at their table had his back to her. He was balding and his suit looked expensive. He must be the investor who needed to sign the documents. She watched as he raised a wrist to look at a Panerai watch that Kate knew cost upward of thirty-thousand bucks.

"It's almost three," he told Ty. "But it's still pissing down. Let's have another drink."

Stormy slapped the table. "Excellent!"

"I should head off in a minute." Ty's voice was as neutral as his expression, but Kate could tell he was bored. Bored and tipsy. He was holding it better than Stormy, but she'd spent the past few weeks drinking with him, first in her home and now in dimly lit Lebanese cafés and tiny wine bars. Whenever he had too much, his eyes grew sharper and his expression more carnivorous, as though his darker desires were wending their way to the surface.

She thought about the spanking she had coming and grinned. Ty had probably texted her during this lunch meeting, plotting the ways he was going to punish her, even as he pretended to listen to Stormy talk. There was something deliciously perverse about that. Almost as perverse as it would be to appear out of nowhere and hand him a folder, knowing he wouldn't be able to do anything but smile and say 'thanks, Middleton,' while his eyes promised to turn her ass black and blue. She brushed the hair from her eyes and prepared to make her big advance.

"You're no fun, Hendo," the investor said with what sounded like an old-man pout.

"I know, but I've got shit to do back at the office."

"The day's as good as done! If you don't want to stay here, we can always go to Tommy's."

Kate stopped in her tracks. She knew about Tommy's. She'd unearthed a navy blue business card in one of her briefing folders last year and googled the name to discover it was an upmarket strip club. She'd hoped it had been a one off, that the guys she worked with didn't actually go there to bond in front of naked tits as a part of their freaking jobs. That hope wasn't holding a lot of water right now. Was this why she was never invited to lunch meetings? Why she had to stay in the office instead of getting smashed and eating pork medallions on the company dime?

"Tommy's sounds great." Stormy glanced across the table at Ty. "Can we go to Tommy's, Hendo?"

Ty picked up his phone and twiddled with it. "I can't. I need to get back to the office. I have plans tonight."

"Really?" The investor straightened in his chair. "Business plans or something else?"

"Business plans."

"I don't believe you. Word is you've been in a very good mood these last few weeks. I know what that means. Who's been priming your pump, Henderson? And don't bother denying it."

As terrified as Kate was by the timing of this conversational shift, she had to wonder how businessmen were so effortlessly sleazy. Did they take seminars? Or did sleazy people just gravitate toward the corporate world like sleazy stars and form sleazy constellations shaped like dick jokes and daytime visits to strip clubs?

Ty shot Stormy a sharp look. "Who told you I was getting laid?"

The investor chuckled "Oh, don't blame him. We were having a drink, before you arrived and Mr Merriweather revealed you'd been seen laughing, something no one has witnessed since the summer of 2015. I joined the rest of the dots myself."

Ty gave him a rueful smile. "Clever, but once the talk turns to my sex life, the meal is officially over." He glanced around, presumably for the wait staff, but there was no one in the room except other diners. He rolled his eyes and tapped at his phone some more. To her horror, Kate felt her pocket vibrate. She pulled it out to see yes, yes, he had texted her from the table she was less than three meters from.

Daddy's going to make you scream tonight baby, you'll be begging for mercy by the end.

"Oh sugar," she whispered. "Oh my gosh, what am I going to do?"

Kate knew she should just hand Ty the folder and leave. Or better yet, creep downstairs, give it to the hostess and leave, but she did neither.

The investor let out a loud, wine soaked laugh. "Stop being coy and admit you're fucking someone."

"I might be. Does that make you happy?"

"Not quite." The investor picked up his wine glass and swirled the crimson liquid like it was brandy. "What's her name?"

"Never you mind."

Stormy made a noise like a dog desperate to go outside. "Oh, but Hendo, everyone at the office's dying to know."

"Then everyone at the office needs a little more excitement in their lives."

The investor tapped the table. "I think Henderson's hiding something. I think he's fucking someone he shouldn't be."

Kate bit the insides of her cheeks. How the hell could Pervy McPerverson have known that? Was he some kind of sex bloodhound?

"That's no one's business but mine." Ty's smile was easy, but there was a fire flickering in his eyes, the kind that preceded a particularly brutal spanking. "Are we done?"

"Not quite." McPerverson's tone was light but Kate sensed irritation beneath it. He was surely the kind of man who got what he wanted when he wanted it and he wanted to know who Ty was sleeping with. The taste of coppery blood spread across her tongue.

"What do you want to know?" Ty said.

"I want to hear you admit you're playing around with a lovely little thing you shouldn't be." McPerverson might as well have come out and said 'or else,' it was clear that's what he meant.

There was a short silence. Ty's jaw hardened and Kate was sure he was going to tell him to go fuck himself. She was just wondering what she should do if McPerverson threw his wine in Ty's face like a Real Housewife of Wherever, when Ty's expression changed. He smiled a smile she knew well, but seemed bizarre in this well-lit restaurant; the slow, hungry grin of her sleazy stepfather. "I'm playing around with a lovely little thing I shouldn't be, happy?"

Kate's stomach tightened.

"Marginally. Was that so hard?" McPerverson's sounded like he was wearing a very satisfied smile. "Now, *why* shouldn't you be playing with her, is she married?"

Ty's lupine smile grew wider. "Young. Very young."

Stormy moaned. "How young?"

Twenty-five. Say twenty-five, or they'll think I'm jailbait. Twenty-five isn't that young.

"Legal."

McPerverson laughed as though he'd told a hilarious joke and Stormy looked sick with envy. "Fuck me, how do you do it, Hendo?"

"Do you need to ask that?" McPerverson raised his beer glass to Ty. "Look at him, he's a perfect specimen of masculinity."

"You need to stop drinking." Ty glanced back at his phone. Dimly, Kate wondered if he was expecting a reply and wondered what he'd do if she texted him the word 'legal' followed by a billion question marks.

McPerverson nudged Stormy's side. "My wife *swoons* whenever this one comes over for dinner. Fifty-one and she blushes like a schoolgirl. When he leaves, it's nothing but 'Tyler, Tyler, Tyler' for days on end. Why can't you have hair like Tyler? Why can't you be in shape like Tyler? Puts us all to shame, he does."

Stormy's fat mouth puckered. "I was in shape before I got married."

It took everything Kate had to not shout, "As if, dickhead!" She'd met Stormy's wife at last year's Christmas party and somehow between working and raising two kids she'd managed to run four marathons. Blaming her for the fact he shoved crème éclairs in his face twice a day was like blaming the sun for the rain. Kate had heard enough. She turned to walk back down the stairs, confidentiality be damned, when a waiter moved toward with a plate of beef Wellington. Not wanting to be caught coming out of the service alcove, she shrank back into the shadows.

"So your young *amour*," McPerverson was saying. "How long have you been seeing one another?"

Ty shrugged. "Few weeks."

"And when are we going to meet her?"

Kate felt the warning then, it twanged deep within her body. *Leave.* Nothing else, just *leave.* She took a step toward the stairs, but it was already too late.

"You're not gonna meet this girl. She's got one place in my life and that's it."

McPerverson laughed. "On her back?"

"All fours."

There was another chorus of male chortling, though Kate barely took it in. Her head was throbbing, her grip loosened on the leather binder and it went tumbling to the ground. No one noticed.

"Some of the best relationships start on all fours," McPerverson said. "Be careful though, or you'll find yourself tied down again."

Ty scoffed, scoffed like someone said the Beatles were a bunch of hacks. "No chance. I've done the love thing. Never again."

Stormy's smile bordered on bashful. "Oh yeah, you were engaged once, weren't you?"

Ty picked up his previously untouched glass of wine and took a deep swallow. "For my sins."

McPerverson laughed, and Kate felt sick, actually physically ill.

"So it's not serious? With you and this mystery girl?"

Another scoff. "No."

"You know how women are," Stormy said. "Aren't you worried she's gonna get the wrong idea?"

"An excellent point," McPerverson chipped in. "What *does* this girl think about your stance on love and romance, Henderson?"

Another horrible stepfather smile. "We don't talk about that shit. She knows the score."

McPerverson pounded his fist on the table. "I want to meet this girl!"

"Well, you can't. What's the point of having a dirty little secret if you share it?"

Kate thought about last week when Ty had come to her door with a fresh bottle of Sailor Jerry and a small bunch of gardenias. They'd had sex, then watched *Hot Fuzz* and when Nick Frost and Simon Pegg were chasing the swan around the countryside, Ty had taken her hand and kissed it.

"What?" she'd said.

"You."

"What about me?"

The skin around Ty's eyes had crinkled. "You're cute when you smile, you're sexy when you're naked, but when you laugh..." he shook his head.

It had taken her two hours to pry out the rest—nipping him with her teeth, tickling his sides and threatening him with endless memes he wouldn't find funny, until finally he said, "You're beautiful when you laugh. That's what I was going to tell you. You look beautiful when you laugh."

What part of that was meant to encourage her to not think it was serious? What part of going out to dinner and sleeping in her bed and telling her she was beautiful was making sure she knew the score? She wanted to rush out there and confront him, confront all three of these seedy asshole men. She wanted to see the fear in their eyes when they looked up and realised she'd heard every single word. She inhaled, like a diver preparing to plunge and then the chemical message pulsed again: *leave.*

This time, Kate obeyed. She scooped up the folder and walked toward the stairs, her feet squishing in her wet Mary Janes.

"Is everything okay?" the hostess asked when she returned to the lobby.

"Totally wonderful," Kate heard herself say. "My boss seemed busy so I couldn't give him the forms. Can you please give this folder to him when he leaves?"

The hostess agreed, and Kate headed back out into the typhoon, barely noticing the watery wind as it thrashed against her body. She was thinking of the hole-in-the-wall restaurants, dark bars, and half-empty cafes where she and Ty had been going on 'real dates.' She was thinking about the fact that she'd yet to meet any of his friends or see his house or have one conversation about declaring their relationship to Johnno.

What's the point of having a dirty little secret if you share it?

That's what she was, a dirty little secret. She had a place in his life, and that place was on all fours. He'd been engaged once, for his sins, but his interest in love was over. He'd thrown her scraps from his table and she was dumb enough to think she'd been invited to the meal. Tears welled in her eyes, hot and thick like silicone.

She walked on for a minute or so, then decided she couldn't go back to work looking like a mermaid whose parents had just died. She staggered to a nearby café.

"What can I get you?" a waiter asked, looking even more alarmed by her bedraggled appearance that the doorman at The Breton Club. Thinking caffeine and sugar might help with the shock, Kate ordered a latte and a custard tart then sat at a corner table and tried to stop crying. After ten minutes of hiccupping and snuffling and ruining serviettes with mascara-water, she managed it. But that only left her free to address other problems—like what she was going to do next.

More than anything she wanted to go back to work, finish her day, then head home and prepare for Ty's spanking. She didn't want it to be over. She didn't want to have to look him in the face and say *'I heard what you said about me and you're every bit the asshole Maria told me you were, so screw you Tyler Henderson, we're done.'*

She couldn't imagine what Ty would do if she said that, if he'd try to defend himself or simply put on his coat and leave, but she knew she couldn't do anything without discussing this through with a more neutral party first. The question was, who?

Aunty Rhonda would have been perfect but she'd gone where no call would reach her. Her sisters would answer, so would her mum, so would Maria. But Kate didn't want to be lectured, or sneered at, or made to feel guilty. She didn't want to be told to see a shrink or a new Dom, or to date only mildly attractive men her own age. She wanted someone who understood and who would listen without judgement. A silly thought occurred to her—messaging Deirdre Peterson on Facebook and asking her for Mr Peterson's mobile number. Another daddy figure to rescue her from the first. Fresh tears welled in her eyes. "I am such a fucking idiot."

The waiter delivered her tart and coffee, and she ate with single-minded numbness. As the caffeine and sugar absorbed into her blood, Kate did feel a little better, and by the time her plate was clean and her cup was empty, she realised there was another number she could call. She hadn't spoken to Rapunzel since derby season ended, but if anyone would be able to help, it would be her. Her hand hovered over her phone and then she reached up and slapped her cheek, just a little. "Come on bitch," she whispered. "Do it."

Rapunzel answered after the second ring. "'Sup, Peach! How you been?"

"Rapunzel..." Kate hadn't realised how terrible she sounded. Her voice, which alternately got her called a man and a porn star at school, was even throatier than usual, clogged with tears and tart. She swallowed thickly and tried again. "Rapunzel..."

"What's up? What's wrong?"

The concern in Rapunzel's voice took her from tears to all-out weeping. "Something bad's happened, and I have no idea what to do..."

"Talk to me. Tell me everything."

Somehow, between gasps and napkin dabs, Kate managed to tell her Ty was her boss, they'd been dating in secret, and that she'd been sent to The Breton Club where she'd overheard him talking about her like she was a piece of ass.

When she was done Rapunzel cleared her throat. "You free tonight?"

"Yes. Well, Ty was meant to come over—"

"Fuck him off."

"I don't know if I can talk to him…"

"*Don't* talk to him, text and say you're on your rag. Guys hate that, or so I'm led to believe."

"But I had my period two weeks ago…"

"He's a fuckin' man, Peach. He doesn't know shit about periods. Just say you're cramping and have no need for his dick. Then text me your address, and I'll come over. I'll invite Tam and Casey. We can have some drinks. It'll be fun."

"Are you sure? What about work?"

"No stress, I've sold all I needed to sell today, I'm golden."

"I meant me, I'm supposed to go back to work."

"Ditch," Rapunzel said without hesitation. "Say you've got diarrhoea. Or use the period story, two birds, one stone, that whole thing."

"I do have some time in lieu…"

"Use it." Rapunzel gave a soft groan, as though she was getting up from somewhere. "I'll catch the train in and meet you at yours. Text me your address, yeah? Also, do you like Southern Comfort?"

"I'm…not sure."

"Well I'll bring a bottle anyway. If old mate shows I can use it to knock his head in. I'm taller than he is, you know?"

When Kate left The Breton Club she was sure she'd never smile again and yet hearing that, she did.

19

Rapunzel prodded one of Aunt Rhonda's bronze statues of Eros. "Peach, what the fuck?"

"I'm sorry," Kate said nervously. "I know it's a bit fancy."

"No, it's beyond a bit fucking fancy." Rapunzel brandished her bottle of Southern Comfort at her. "Here. Although, I feel like I should have brought caviar or quince paste or something."

"It's great, thank you so much. Do you guys, um, want to come in?" Kate gestured down the hall where her immaculately clean lounge room was waiting, the coffee table loaded down with sweet potato brownies, fairy cakes, veggie sticks, homemade hummus, and sandwiches—the result of a slightly manic cooking outburst when she got home from work.

None of the girls moved. They looked at her, she looked at them. It was strange to see Tam, Casey and Rapunzel in non-wheeled shoes. They all looked shorter than usual, even Rapunzel, who had to duck to get in the doorway. Both Tam and Rapunzel were in jeans and hoodies, but Casey was wearing a long-sleeved amethyst coloured maxi dress and—Kate had to admire the way she made it look utterly natural—a white rose flower crown. "Macca," she said in a conversational tone, "Do you seriously live here?"

"Yes."

"Alone?"

Kate tugged at the hem of her A-line skirt. "Yes."

"No, seriously? Do you live here?"

"Yes."

"Really?"

"I think she's made it abundantly clear that she lives here, Case." Rapunzel set off down the hall toward the lounge room. "Fuck," she called behind her. "You guys have to check it out. This room's even fancier."

Tam and Casey followed Rapunzel, wearing dubious looks, as though this might be a practical joke. Kate walked behind them and when she entered the lounge she found Rapunzel lying across her couch, a sandwich in each hand.

"Thanks for all this food, Peach. You didn't need to make anything, we coulda just ordered pizza."

"Its fine, I really needed something to do while I waited for you guys."

Casey was gaping at her again. "Do you...?"

"I promise I do live here."

"Right..." Casey's indigo-blue eyes narrowed. She turned to Tam who was toeing off her pink Cons. "Where did you picture Macca living?"

"On one of those red mushrooms with white spots?" Tam glanced at Kate. "I'm saying you look like a fairy, no offence."

"None taken. Would either of you like a drink? I have red wine, white wine, orange juice, apple juice, tea, coffee, or—"

"Macca," Casey said. "You live here? By yourself?"

"The next person who says that is going to collect a bottle to the head," Rapunzel said through a mouthful of chicken and cheese.

Casey walked over to the window and looked out at the city. "I'm sorry, I don't mean to be a dick, but this is the nicest apartment I've ever been inside. I thought you were an office drone like me."

"I am," Kate said at once. "Or you know, a civil engineer."

"So you're like...wealthy?" Tam asked.

"No, she isn't," Casey said before Kate could reply. "She grew up poor, with heaps of brothers and sisters, like me, Maria told me."

Rapunzel pounded a fist on the coffee table. "Stop talking about Peach like she isn't here and sit down and eat some fucking sandwiches."

Perhaps she was a Domme, because Tam and Casey instantly grabbed food and dropped their asses onto Aunt Rhonda's couches. Kate hovered, wondering if she should offer drinks again. She'd never had friends in the apartment before. It was stressful.

"Mac," Rapunzel said. "Sit down."

"What about drinks?"

"Got any glasses? We'll crack open the Comfort."

Kate pulled four of Aunty Rhonda's crystal tumblers from the bar and set them on the coffee table. Rapunzel poured large quantities of peach-coloured liquid into them as Tam stood and wandered toward the window.

"What a view," she said. "This place would be excellent for parties."

Kate almost said she didn't have enough friends for parties, but stopped herself just in time. "You guys can always crash here if you're in the city. I have heaps of space."

"Don't say that in front of Rapunzel, unless you want a room-mate," Casey warned. "She's on the prowl for new digs."

"I wouldn't mind a roommate."

Rapunzel looked up from her bottle work. "Seriously?"

"Yeah, I thought about putting up an ad on flatmate finder, but I'm worried I'll get stuck with someone insane and then I'll have to evict them and they'll kill me."

Casey made sympathetic noises. "I get it. My last roommate used to wash her pet chickens in our shower."

"Seriously?"

"Yeah, seriously. And I've learned there are two responses to that statement: 'what the fuck' and 'why would you wash a chicken?'"

"Here, this one's yours." Rapunzel handed Kate a tumbler full almost to the brim with peach liquor.

"Do you think it's big enough?" Casey asked.

Rapunzel poured a thimbleful of Southern Comfort into a tumbler. "That one's yours, Case."

Kate laughed and took a small sip of her drink. It was sweet, spicy and strong. "Thanks. It's good."

Tam wandered back toward them and picked up her glass of Southern Comfort. "Kate," she said in her red-velvet voice. "I don't want to be rude, but I have to know, how do you afford to live here with no roommates? The rent must be insane."

Kate looked down at her drink. "I..."

Tam put a hand on her shoulder. "We're not bitches. I promise we won't judge, it's just...this is like when the regular kids go and visit Richie Rich, and he has a McDonald's inside his fucking house."

Kate couldn't help but smile at that. "I'm not Richie Rich, I only have this apartment because..."

"Go on, Peach." Rapunzel was reclining on the couch again, big and butch and calm.

Seeing her there, blatantly not giving a shit about anything, gave Kate the strength to say it. "My Aunt Rhonda was kind of rich because she took photos of Patti Smith, and when she died, she left this place to me. I like living here, but I can't get my head around living here. Having this much money and space after being so poor freaks me out. I know it's ungrateful, but sometimes I wish Aunt Rhonda never left her stuff to me. If she didn't, things could just be how they were before, which was shit, but at least it made sense and my family didn't hate me as much."

She said all of this very fast. So fast that in the silence that followed, she wondered if they'd understood a single word. Then Rapunzel reached across and patted her leg. "I get it," she said, as though she heard stories about blood feuds and excessive wealth every day. "It's a cool place though; your aunt must have been awesome."

Kate started to cry. She couldn't help it. "She *was* awesome. She was my best friend."

"Oh, Mac." Casey stood and pulled Kate into her arms. She smelled of patchouli and lavender oil and was as warm as a puppy. Kate hugged her for all she was worth, sobbing a big wine-coloured stain into the amethyst dress. When she finally pulled away, she expected to see the other girls staring at her in disgust. They weren't. Both Tam and Rapunzel wore looks of concern so sincere Kate almost started crying again.

"Sorry about that," she said wiping her nose on her sleeve. "I know you shouldn't cry because someone left you a nice place to live."

"It's cool," Tam said. "Still, if everyone I loved died, none of them would leave me with shit."

"Tam," Casey scolded. "Don't say stuff like that!"

"Why? Will I curse them or something? Ooh, look, records." Tam ran over to the shelf and scanned the rows of vinyl. She tugged out a record. "Can I put this on?"

"Of course."

Tam let out an excited squeal, and a few seconds later Billie Holiday began to croon from her aunt's record player.

Rapunzel gestured to the couch. "Sit back down and drink up, Peach. You've had a shitty day, and this is the Janis Joplin cure for sadness."

Casey frowned. "Didn't Janis Joplin kill herself?"

"She OD'd on heroin," Rapunzel said defensively.

"So, should we be following her advice?"

"Shut up and drink, moll."

So they sat down and drank and talked about the derby league and a conservative politician's gaffe and the fact that Thunderbox and Rapunzel went on a date.

"Pillow queen," Rapunzel said with a mournful sigh. "Funny how they come out of nowhere. I'd have thought a girl like that would have been a tiger in the sack..."

As the Southern Comfort bottle emptied and the sandwiches and brownies disappeared, Kate began to feel a hot, internal glow. Most of that was alcohol, but part was knowing she had guests in her home. The girls were enjoying themselves, she could tell by the way they kept talking and laughing, the way they accepted glasses of wine once the Southern Comfort was gone. She decided she wouldn't bring up Ty. This was her first ever get-together, she didn't need to freak Tam, Casey and Rapunzel out by divulging all of her secrets. Unwittingly, her thoughts wandered to Ty. He'd accepted her period lie instantly, but she had no idea where he was now. Was he at home or trawling a bar for another dirty little secret? Her chest clenched.

It doesn't matter. It's over, it doesn't matter.

Rapunzel slapped her hands to her knees. "So, we all know why we're here, to suss out where our mysterious teammate lives, get drunk and help her with her life-woes. Now, I think we can all agree Macca's apartment is the tits."

Casey nodded. "Oh yeah."

"No question," Tam said.

"And we're pretty drunk?"

"Oh yeah."

"No question."

"So we need to get a move on before we're too wankered to give good advice." Rapunzel nodded toward her. "Mac, I hope you don't mind, but I already filled Tam and Case in about how Ty's your boss and a prick, hope that's okay?"

Kate blinked at her. "Erm sure, but hang on...*mysterious*? I'm not mysterious?"

"You are," Rapunzel and Casey said at the same time.

"We've been teammates for three years, and we barely know anything about you," Tam pointed out. "And now we *do* know things about you, they're things like 'you're sleeping with your boss' and 'you live in a rich person apartment.'"

"When you say it like that, it sounds impressive, but I'm seriously not interesting."

"Then why does Maria like, worship you?"

Kate gaped at her. "She doesn't worship—"

"She does."

This time all three girls spoke at once.

"Put it this way," Tam said. "Rapunzel thought you might be gay, Maria was that into you."

Rapunzel yawned. "Yep. Then we talked, and I realised you're about as queer as this." She tapped a foot on Aunt Rhonda's coffee table.

Kate stared at her. "But...Maria and I have been friends for ages. She never made a move and I promise I'm not one of those self-pitying people who think no one finds them attractive. If she did like me like that, don't you think I'd have noticed?"

Rapunzel shrugged. "Not if she didn't want you to. She's pretty devious. Great coach, amazing hair, devious as fuck."

Casey drained her glass of Cabernet. "Let's talk about Maria later. I want to know Ty's deal."

"What about Ty's deal?" Kate asked.

"How'd you start screwing him? You look so whole-wheat, I bet the story's really sleazy."

And just like that, Kate was crying again.

"Good one, Hindley. Ten out of ten for tact." Tam got up and rubbed Kate's back. "I don't blame you, Mac. The man is insanely buff. Especially for an old guy."

"He's not that old," Rapunzel interrupted. "He's forty-five. Only twelve years on me."

"Yeah, but Macca's, what, twenty-three?"

"I'm twenty-five."

Tam raised her eyebrows. "Shit, I was aiming high. I thought you were twenty-two."

"I have a baby face. If you want to know the whole story, me having a baby face is probably a good place to start."

Tam raised her dark eyebrows. "Go on, then."

"I should warn you, it might get weird."

"I love weird." Tam settled back into her place on the couch. "Let's do this."

Kate tried to start with the pub in Bendigo and Ty carrying her to his hotel room, but that demanded an explanation of her ADHD, and she couldn't talk about her ADHD without talking about getting diagnosed, something Tam, who was doing a Master's in psychology, found particularly interesting. By the time they returned to Bendigo, it was almost midnight. Explaining the daddy situation and Ty's trip to Queensland and her eavesdropping session in The Breton Club took so long they needed two separate bathroom breaks. They also killed the two bottles of red Kate had dug out of Aunt Rhonda's wine rack, hence the bathroom breaks. When she was finally done all of them were lying on the floor, their finger-stained wine glasses balanced precariously on the carpet in front of them.

"So..." Tam said slowly. "That's one intense story."

"Yeah," Kate and Rapunzel said at the same time.

Casey stared at Kate, her large eyes slightly unfocused. "So...you and Ty pretend like he's your daddy while he fucks you?"

Kate squirmed against the carpet. "Not my actual father, neither of us likes the incest thing but, yeah."

"And he spanked you?"

"Yeah it, erm, felt nice, though."

"And Ty's into that?"

She said his name as though she was savouring a delicious cocktail. Kate remembered the hungry way Casey had studied Ty's face, his body and his expensive clothes. She'd pressed him to talk about himself and laughed at his least funny jokes. *Beyond moist just from breathing his air,* as Rapunzel said. Kate hadn't been jealous that night, and she wasn't jealous now, only aware that she must have looked just as obvious in her own lust for Ty, probably even more so. "Yeah, he's into that."

"God." Casey closed her eyes. "God, that's so hot."

"Seriously?" Tam said, looking surprised. "I didn't think you were into kink."

"I'm not, but the way Mac described everything, and knowing

what Ty looks like..." Casey let out a long, luxurious sigh. "Shame he's turned out to be such a cunt."

"Agreed," Tam said. "About it not working out, not that he's a cunt. Cunts are good things. I should tell Tim about this daddy stuff. Maybe we could give it a try."

"I used to do daddy stuff with my ex," Rapunzel said, crunching a leftover carrot stick.

Tam wrinkled her brow. "But, you're a woman."

"Oh, fuck. Really?" Rapunzel grabbed her tits. "What the hell? What are these? Tambara, I'm a woman—"

"Don't—"

Rapunzel threw her head back. "Noooooooooooooo!"

Kate and Casey laughed.

"Yeah, lol," Tam said, rolling her eyes. "I just mean, well...you don't have a dick."

"They have invented this thing called a strap-on Tam, look it up."

"No thanks. Hang on, why would you pretend to be your ex's *dad*? Why not her mum?"

"I dunno, it's a taboo thing, I guess. Ask Kate."

"Don't ask me!" Kate said. "I only know my own weird head. I know nothing of lesbian BDSM."

Rapunzel muttered something under her breath.

"What was that?" Kate asked, feeling uneasy for the first time since they'd started drinking.

Rapunzel exchanged a meaningful look with Tam, then sighed. "Sorry, I was being a shithead. I said 'Maybe Maria can help you with that?'"

Kate winced. "Is this the part of the night where we talk about Maria?"

Rapunzel looked at Tam who donned a serene expression Kate was sure would form the cornerstone of her psychologist's practise. "Yes. Although, there isn't that much to say, besides Maria's in love with you."

"But she's never even made a move on me! I was at her house all the time, she never even tried to kiss me!"

Tam raised a palm. "Let me explain. We don't want to bitch about Maria, but we all feel weird about how she treats you. She's possessive, she doesn't like you being friends with anyone else, and whenever you're alone with us, she muscles in. Remember the after-practise drinks?"

"That *was* kind of a weird night," she admitted.

"Yeah, because of her," Casey said. "How did she feel about you dating Ty?"

"She didn't like him."

"I bet she didn't."

"Yeah, but it was him specifically! She doesn't, like, want me for herself. She's always tried to set me up with guys in the past. They weren't the best choices for me, but—"

"She knows you're straight," Rapunzel interrupted. "She knew she was never gonna get to fuck you, deep down. But if you want my dyke opinion, she tried to set you up with nerds so she could always be your number one. Your mama bear. Ty's different. He's older and you're so obviously in love with him—"

"I'm not!"

"Peach," Rapunzel said gently. "No judgment, but you are, and I'm sure Maria knew that and was fucking terrified about it. I'm sure she thought he was going to take you away from her."

The four of them fell silent. Kate thought about the coffee she and Maria had all those weeks ago, how she'd seemed disturbed, not by her attraction to Ty, but by the fact she was trying to seduce him at work.

"It's more than jealousy," she said. "Maria doesn't want me to change. When she met me, I was so shy I was basically a lobster-person—"

"I remember," Casey chirped. "I asked if you were new and you were so surprised you screamed a bit."

"Yeah," Kate said, her cheeks blazing. "Well, it's like even though Maria helped me open up, she only wants me to go so far."

"Because she's scared she'll lose you," Tam said. "She helped you learn to walk, but when it looked like you were going to run away, she tried to hobble you."

Kate nodded, tears budding in her eyes again. "She wants me to stay the way I am, but I can't. Ever since Ty and I started hooking up, it's like I'm going through second puberty or something. All I want is for things to change."

"Like what?" Tam asked gently.

"Everything. I want a job where people take me seriously. I want to wear clothes that make me feel good. I want to talk to people without worrying they hate me. I want to not be trapped inside my aunt's house and trapped inside my own head. I just always thought..."

"What?" Tam pressed.

"I...I always thought I'd have a guy to protect me when I was older."

She looked around the circle. "I know that sounds pathetic and unfeminist and sad, it's just what I thought. I wanted to meet someone who'd show me how to be who I really am. You know, love me so much I understood everything about the world?"

"It's understandable," Tam said. "It's what girls get told to want, the prince who rescues you. But men are just people, they're flawed, they change their minds. You don't want them to hold ultimate power over you."

"I know," Kate admitted. "And I don't want that really. It was just a nice idea, y'know?"

All the girls nodded.

"So," Kate said, wiping her eyes. "Does anyone have any ideas about how to change yourself in every single way?"

It was a weak joke and she didn't expect anyone to respond, let alone shoot to her feet the way Casey did. "Do you have candles, a bowl of water, notepaper, and a pen?" she asked.

"Erm...yes?"

"Excellent." Casey picked up her handbag and pulled out a thick wand of what looked like weed.

"Whoa, what's that?" Kate asked, alarmed by the sheer volume of contraband now in Aunt Rhonda's apartment.

"Don't worry, it's a sage bundle. Can you please go get the other things?"

Rapunzel pressed a hand to her eyes. "It's about to get fucking Wiccan in here, isn't it?"

"Yes, it is," Casey said, pulling several shiny rocks out of her bag. "Yes it is."

She named the ceremony the *'healing and reinvigorating ritual for Katie May McGrath's vagina, heart, and other areas that may need cleansing.'*

Kate hadn't wanted to use her real name but Casey said it was important. "Names have power. If the name's wrong, the spell could go bad. But at least the moon's waxing, which means—"

Rapunzel pressed a hand over her friend's face. "Please hurry up before my disbelief turns this witch circle into a black hole?"

The ritual took almost an hour, but the time passed quickly. Kate wasn't sure if that was the novelty of watching Casey chant and wave sage and utter incantations, or if it was actually doing something.

It didn't matter, she realised, as Casey tried to bully Rapunzel into holding a chunk of rose quartz. The real charm was that someone cared enough about her to wave burning herbs all over her body to break the ties that bound her to people and things that no longer served her. When the ritual was done, Kate was holding three pieces of paper—a list and two letters.

"Take those and do with them what you must," Casey said, waving the sage over herself and then Tam and Rapunzel. "You're officially purified."

Rapunzel raised a pierced brow. "Officially?"

Casey shot her a dirty look. "I think you should choose a new name, Mac."

"I will. Births, Deaths and Marriages is on the list—"

"No, not that. I mean a new *derby* name."

"Why?" Rapunzel howled. "Princess Bleach is awesome."

"'Princess' is a word Kate's brothers and sisters used to pick on her because she had undiagnosed ADHD. It's not exactly associated with happy memories."

Kate thought about it. "If I change my name, can I still like baking and pink jumpers?"

"No," Rapunzel said. "Also, you need to shave your head and join the navy."

Casey rolled her eyes. "Ignore her. Of course, you can like all that stuff, but you can be a more authentic version of that person. Embrace the other aspects of your womanhood besides sweetness."

Tam patted her arm. "You're so granola."

"Thank you. So Kate, new derby name. Any ideas?"

"What about *The Inferno*?" Rapunzel suggested.

They all pulled faces.

Tam poured herself another glass of wine. "I think we can do better than that. You like cooking, Mac. What about...Julia Wild?"

Rapunzel made a fake gagging noise and Tam glared at her. "Oh, I'm sorry, *The Inferno*."

Kate looked at her hands and, like a key slipping into a lock, it came to her. "Sylvia Wrath."

The girls stared at her.

"Who?"

"Sylvia Plath was a poet," Kate told them. "I like poetry."

"Cool," Rapunzel said. "I hate it. All that fucking rhyming and sentences that don't make sense. But Sylvia Wrath is a boss name."

"Agreed." Casey picked up the box of matches. "Write it down, and we'll sage it."

Rapunzel groaned. "Not more fucking sage."

But they did sage her new name and then—because Casey thought it was a good idea—they saged her old derby uniform and then—because Rapunzel thought it was a good idea—they lit Aunt Rhonda's coal barbecue on the balcony and cooked a t-shirt Ty had left at her place. As Casey and Tam argued about the influences of the moon on civilisation, Rapunzel slung an arm around Kate's neck. "Miss him, don't you?"

Kate nodded.

"I can tell. You're having fun, but part of you wishes he was here. Wishes you'd ignored what you'd heard today, and he was with you instead of us."

Kate looked up at the velvet black sky, too numb and drunk and happy and sad to cry. "Yeah. I'm sorry."

"Don't beat yourself up. It'll fade with time. I know hearing that makes everyone feel like shit, but it's the truth. You'll get there."

Kate thought about Rapunzel in Rumba talking about how beautiful people needed respectful partners. "Do you want to talk about—"

"No." Her tone was friendly but firm. "You know when we were doing all that sage crap, I thought of a line. I think I jacked it from *Game of Thrones,* but you should listen to it, anyway. Here we go; set fire to the princess, let the woman rise from the ashes."

Kate thought about it and found it made a surprising amount of sense. "I like that."

"Cheers. I feel like I'm combining a bunch of different metaphors with some phoenix shit, but you get the gist." Rapunzel took a long swallow of wine. "Peach?"

"Yeah?"

She cleared her throat. "Are you, uh, really looking for a roommate?"

Kate could hardly believe her ears. "No, but I seriously wouldn't mind one! Do you really want to live with me?"

Rapunzel's face lit up in a way Kate had never seen before. "Hell yeah, I want to live with you! How soon can I move in? How much rent do you want a month? Can I bring my cat?"

"Lesbian cat!" Casey shouted from the balcony's edge. "She's a cat with a lesbian. What a cliché!"

Rapunzel shook her head. "Munted," she said. "Absolutely munted. You should be careful, Peach, she probably fuckin' cursed you during that ritual."

"I don't mind. Anyway, I don't know anything about having a roommate, but I'll look it up and get back to you with rent prices and—"

Rapunzel gripped her shoulders. "You mean it? You'd let me live here?"

"Gosh yeah! I really like you, Rapunzel."

"Oh, Peach." Rapunzel pulled her into her chest and hugged her so tightly Kate felt her eyes pop. "I like you, too, you adorable bug-person. You won't regret this."

Kate smiled into her jumper. "I know. Plus, having you here means I won't be tempted to invite Ty around."

"Accountability," Rapunzel agreed. "Plus, if he shows up here like he did at derby I can punch him in self-defense. Y'know, for invading my home."

"Yeah, I don't think that's how self-defense works, but—"

"Katie!"

Kate looked over to see Mr Petkovic from next door leaning out of his living room window. He didn't looked very happy. "Hey Mr Petkovic, what's up?"

"What in the hell are you doing?" he shouted back. "It's three in the fucking morning, and you're having a barbecue! Why are you having a barbecue?"

"We're, um, cooking the t-shirt of a guy who was a jerk to me?"

Mr Petkovic didn't seem to think that was an adequate explanation. "Go inside, you silly girls!"

"Hey!" Tam yelled. "We're doing witch stuff out here!"

"Yeah, we're allowed to burn shit on coals if we want to!" Casey screamed. "You can't tell us what to do! You're not our dads!"

Tam and Casey were debating Mr Petkovic on what was and wasn't a violation of city burning laws, when Kate realised something. She nudged Rapunzel, "This is my first ever noise complaint! That means this was my first party! I mean there are only four of us..."

"Hey, two's a party, three's a crowd, four's a fucking blowout. Nice work, Sylvia Wrath."

They smiled at one another and listened to the debate until Mr Petkovic gave up and slammed his window shut. Then they heard Casey ask, "On a scale of one to inevitable, how likely is it that you're gonna throw up right now?"

"Eleven," Tam moaned. "Eleven."

Rapunzel let go of Kate. "Shit. Do you have any buckets, or can she just do it over the side?"

Hosting a party, Kate learned, made you responsible for those kind of decisions.

20

Ty was disappointed when Middleton cancelled—okay, he was pissed off, but he understood where she was coming from. He'd never had a period, but he could imagine they were painful enough without adding a spanked ass. Still, he was morose as he rounded off his last few projects for the day, a hangover throbbing in his temples. He promised himself he'd never drink like that at lunch again, no matter how hard Roger McMillian was to be around sober.

He'd intended to go home that night; he had a rib-eye thawing on his kitchen counter. Instead, for the first time since he and Middleton began their affair, he spent the night on the couch at GGS.

The next day Middleton called in sick, something she'd never done before. He texted asking if she was okay, but no response came. At four o'clock he made the monumental mistake of closing the door to his office and calling her. The call rang out, and when her husky voice told him to leave a message, he opened his mouth, and made an even bigger mistake.

"Middleton, it's me. Ty. Just checking in to, uh, make sure you're alright. Do you wanna go out tonight? We don't have to fuck or anything, especially if you've still got your period, but we can if you want to. Look, I just wanna see you and make sure you're okay, please call me back—"

The dial tone beeped, cutting off the worst voicemail message in the history of voicemail messages, including some of the batshit ones Veronica had left him. Only the hope that Middleton would return his call kept him from dropping his phone off the roof. He went out that night with a few guys from a rival conservation firm, got drunk, booked a hotel room at two in the morning, and slept there.

On Friday he came in late and found her desk empty again. A wave of nausea that had nothing to do with alcohol swept over him. He'd just pulled out his phone to call her again when Stormy told him he needed to speak with Johnno.

"Shut the door and sit down," the CEO barked as soon as Ty showed up at his office.

He obliged. "What's up?"

"Middleton."

Instantly his mouth was ash-dry. He'd been outed. Less than forty-eight hours had passed since he told Roger McMillian he was fucking someone and the slippery prick had already found out it was Middleton. He was going to be fired and so was she, maybe she was already fired. He sat, teetering on the edge of panic. He'd help Middleton find a new job—he had the contacts— but what would he do for himself? He'd deal with that later. He had to call her and—

"Middleton quit."

Ty paused amid his frenzied planning. "Huh?"

Johnno slammed his fist on the desk so hard a cup of pens upended. "She quit. Quit this morning by registered fucking post."

It took several seconds for Ty to unglue himself from thoughts of a year-long sabbatical and absorb what Johnno was saying. "Middleton. She quit...?"

"Get with the fucking program, Henderson." Johnno held up a letter. "She quit. Reckons she got another job at Demonte and Decker. Isn't even giving notice because she called the union, and they told her we owe her a shitload of overtime. Now she's gone and the business'll be down an engineer for weeks."

"Right," Ty said, trying not to ask if Middleton had quit for the third time. "She say why she left?"

"No, and who gives a shit? That girl fucked over everyone in this office. Now I've got the union breathing down my neck, asking me about gender quotas and why I wasn't letting my only female employee take RDOs, acting like I've done something wrong when we spent years training her."

And she spent years getting coffee and being boxed out of management opportunities and offered as fuck-bait, Ty thought. *So you got a new job, huh Middleton? Good for you.*

He would call her again once this was over. He'd tell her he knew about D&D and offer to take her somewhere fancy to celebrate. Their situation was still a clusterfuck, but it had just been downgraded from a clusterfuck that could also get them fired.

Johnno let out a loud, petulant sigh. He began to pick up his spilt pens and place them back in the cup. "I think something happened to her on Wednesday."

"What do you mean?"

"I mean, I wouldn't be surprised if something happened with her after she took that file down to The Breton. She came back here in a right state and asked to take the afternoon off. Dutchy told her no, and she damn near told him to go fuck himself. Said she never got to take leave like everyone else."

Ty, who'd been rifling through his mental restaurant Rolodex, snapped to attention. "Middleton brought that file to The Breton Club? I thought that was one of the interns?"

Johnno's meaty forehead creased. "No, I sent her. You telling me she didn't hand it over herself? Fucking hell, those files were confidential!"

It was convenient that Johnno went off on another tirade because Ty was trapped in an acidic whirl of panic. There had been a moment during lunch when he'd seen a face peering at him through the panels of the serving alcove. He'd told himself it was a waitress, but something about it had made him edgy. Now he knew—it had been Middleton. She'd been there, and she'd heard him say—what? What had they been discussing when he saw her? The possibility of going to Tommy's? No, it had been worse than that...

Ty's guts churned as he remembered his comment about 'all fours.' He shot to his feet. "I should go speak to the rest of the crew. See who can take on Middleton's projects."

Johnno made a grumpy noise of agreement. "Tell Franco to mock up an ad for her position while you're at it. I want it advertised by midday."

"Sure. Right. Whatever you want."

Ty power walked back to his office, dialing Middleton's number along the way. Surely she hadn't quit because of him? She would have called, she would have asked him about it. She wasn't the kind of girl to end things without saying anything. Was she?

Something else he'd said to Roger came back to him—*what's the point of having a dirty little secret if you share it?*

His stomach contracted so violently for a second he thought he might throw up. Middleton's phone rang out and he didn't leave a message. He shut himself in his office and called Georgie. She answered on the third ring. "Hey, how'd you know my surgery got cancelled?"

"I didn't. You got a copy of *The Feminine Mystique* handy?"

There was a brief pause. "What have you done?"

"You're not gonna like this. I don't like this. I think I might be scum for doing this. I think it might be over."

"Tyler." His best friend's voice was hard. "Talk."

And so he talked. When he was done there was a long silence.

"You understand why I did it, don't you?" he pressed. "Roger's a bloodhound. If he thought Middleton was a girl I cared about, he'd have made it his life's mission to find out who she was. I had to act like she was nothing special."

"Is she?"

Ty frowned. "What?"

"Is. She. Special? Because it seems to me you didn't have to say any of that garbage about her. You could have just shut your mouth and told them it was none of their business."

Ty slumped back in his desk chair. "I know. I panicked."

"Bullshit excuse."

"I know." He pressed a palm to his sweaty forehead. "What are the chances I've fucked this and she's never going to speak to me again?"

"Realistically? I'd say between seventy-five to eighty percent."

"Fuck."

"You should be glad to be getting the silent treatment. If I heard you saying that about me..."

Ty's left eye-socket tingled. "Yeah, I know, so what do I—" he saw something that made him yelp.

"Is everything okay?"

"Yeah, I think..." He pulled on the corner of the pale yellow envelope and recognised Kate's loopy handwriting at once. "Fucking hell, she wrote me a letter. I've gotta—"

"Read it. Call me back."

The line disconnected.

As he looked at the envelope, Ty could taste his pulse. He knew the chances of it being filled with positive feedback was rare. Letters like these were never a good thing, except maybe in that movie Veronica liked, *The Notebook*. Why had it been called that, anyway? Fucking movie was all about letters. It should have been called *The Letters*. Ty slid the slim sheaf of paper out of the envelope, noting with a lurch that it had a buttercup border.

Dear Ty,

I guess you've heard by now I'm leaving GGS. I'm sure Johnno's pissed. And Dutchy, though that probably has more to do with getting his own caramel lattes than anything. I'm excited to work for D&D. They pay less, but I think I can grow there, become the engineer I know I can be. I'm also excited to work in a place with more than one woman and where no one will call me Middleton. You were the only person I ever liked calling me that.

Someone knocked on his door.

"Come back in ten," Ty called.

"But—"

"Do it."

The person—it sounded like Collins—walked away, no doubt cursing him under his breath.

So with D&D out of the way, I guess it's time to write about us. It's funny how hard it is for me to say 'us,' because I know it's not a word you wanted me to use in the context of whatever we were doing—sleeping together, fucking, exploring our mutual interests, etc. We never got around to labels, did we? But here's the thing—deliberately avoiding labels doesn't mean you have no obligations toward my feelings. You slept in my bed, you came to my derby final, met my friends, and told me I was beautiful. You bought me a dildo. There was an 'us.'

"Was," Ty said. "Was."

His chest felt like a car compactor slowly crushing inwards. He knew exactly where this was going, but made himself keep reading.

Never saying "We're in a relationship, Middleton, I care about you," isn't some magical backsies card you get to slap down whenever you need to make your escape. I know you're not planning on dumping me but I also know it's never going to be more than what it is now.
When I picture our future, I see the two of us sleeping together for months, maybe even years, me too scared to bring up commitment, you making sure I'm never really a part of your life so you can always peel me away like old Velcro if you need to. I don't want that and I think you knew it. It was like you said at the derby final; you just couldn't stay away.

I'm glad Johnno was a jerk and made me go to The Breton Club in the rain. If I hadn't heard what you said to Stormy and McPerverson, I might never have seen what was staring me in the face. When I calmed down, I realised you were probably playing up the sleaziness to get them to change the subject—I recognised your smile from all the times you pretended to be my stepdaddy— but you meant what you said about relationships. You really do have no intention of loving me.

I'm in love with you. You must know that, right? You saw it on my face, and when you did you kissed me and said something like "You're too adorable for your own good."

I'm not too adorable for my own good, I'm in love with you. I've been in love with you for a long time, maybe since we met. You know D&D headhunted me a year ago, and I decided to stay at GGS because of you. I started drinking coffee because it gave me an excuse to ask if you wanted one. I hooked up with that rugby guy in Bendigo because you were watching and I thought feeling a man's hands on me while you watched would be the closest thing to having you.

Are you scared yet? I am. I don't know why I wanted you so badly, but I did.

"Middleton," Ty said. "Don't do this."

We need to end things. Not because you're too old for me or I'm wrong for you—I think in our hearts we both know we're good together, but this is going nowhere. I don't know what your ex did to you but I don't think you want to love anyone ever again and if I stay, I will wring myself out trying to make you change your mind. I'll ruin all the best parts of myself.

I want real love, Ty—a guy who goes down on me and introduces me to his friends and tells me he loves me. When we're together, you give me just enough to imagine having those things, but it's not a real possibility. I stopped selling my panties because only having a small part of my fantasy was so painful. This is worse. You're an amazing lover, but you're not my Daddy, and I don't think you ever will be. You're a charmer. I thought you never showed me that side of yourself, the way you showed the Barbie Trolls and the guys at work, but you did, you showed it to me in bed when you were everything I wanted you to be and more.

"Middleton," Ty repeated. His hands were shaking like leaves, rendering her words almost illegible. "Middleton *don't*."

Maybe no other man will ever measure up to you and I'll be single forever, but I have to try and get what I want for myself. No all-powerful father-

figure is going to ride in and save me, I know that now. So I'm leaving. I'm
leaving you and GGS and also Australia for a little while.

"What?" Ty stared at the piece of paper, waiting for the letters to
re-arrange themselves into something that made sense, but they
remained stubbornly in the order they were, telling him Middleton
was no longer on the same continent he was.

"Is everything okay?" A voice at the door shouted.

"Yes! I'm fine!"

"Are you—"

"Yes! Fuck off!"

The person—Ty was sure it was Collins again—walked away
muttering much more audibly about how he didn't have to deal with
this bullshit. Ty ignored him and stared at the letter.

One of my Aunty Rhonda's friends is putting me up in her apartment in
Prague. I'll be pretty miserable, obviously, but it'll be nice to take a break
from everything.
I think this is the part where I say goodbye and please take care of yourself.
I'm not brave enough to mean it yet, but I hope you find someone you can
be with. You're an amazing guy and not just because you used to be a
firefighter and you're hot. You're so funny and smart and when you opened
yourself up to me, I felt like the most incredible girl in the world. It would be
such a shame if that went to waste because of the hang-ups you have about
love. Okay, I should go, sorry this letter is so long. Tam just told me to stop
apologising for things that don't need apologies, so I'll just say I'll miss
you, Ty.

Kate 'Middleton' McGrath

Ps. I know this sounds lame, but someone will call you about returning my
apartment key today or tomorrow. Goodbye again xxx

21

For three days, Ty carried Middleton's front door key. He wasn't sure what he was trying to accomplish, only that every morning he slipped it into his pocket alongside his phone and wallet. He pulled it out from time to time, rubbed a thumb along the steel, and wondered why this hurt more than having his engagement ring returned.

He had no idea. He was waist deep in post-breakup numbness and it was hard to see anything from that particular forest, especially the fucking trees. Since receiving the letter, he'd spent two nights at work in a row—a personal record. He had no idea why he preferred work to home, seeing as Middleton had never been to his place, and GGS was riddled with memories of her. Another tree he couldn't see from the forest.

Georgie had offered him her frequent flier points so he could go to Prague and try to win Middleton over but, Ty had refused. "There's no coming back from this."

"You're probably right," she'd said. "You really fucked yourself this time."

The call he'd been expecting came four days after Middleton's letter. He was in a meeting but the woman left a voicemail.

"Hi Tyler, this is Katie's friend, Maria. If you could return Katie's key and anything else you might have of hers to my place in the next couple of days, that would be great. I live at 42 Copper Street, Carlton. You can come over before ten or after four. Okay, bye."

Her tone was sunny, but Ty could hear the dislike ticking beneath it. He remembered Maria from the derby final, a tall Latina woman built along the lines of Salma Hayek. She'd glared at him at the after-party, no doubt wondering what an old bastard like him was doing with her young friend. Well, she didn't have to worry about him haunting Middleton's derby games anymore.

He replayed the message, snorting a little at the line, *"If you could return Katie's key and anything else you might have of hers."*

What else did she think he had? He'd lost Middleton's trust, admiration, and body in The Breton Club. The only thing he had left was the key, a little slip of metal that had once granted him refuge from the outside world and now served as a reminder of what a useless fuck-up he was.

All morning, he considered not giving the key back to Maria, pretending he'd lost it or given it to Middleton before she left for Europe, but that was insane. Holding onto the key was only going to make Middleton change her locks, not her mind.

That afternoon, he left work early and rode to Carlton. Maria lived in the kind of three-storey townhouse that once belonged to an Italian family of eight and would now fetch millions on the open market. He wondered what she did for a living and decided not to ask; he'd knock on the door, drop off the key, and get out. He opened the brown waist-high gate that always framed such houses and a brown kelpie bounced its way across the front yard, its face alight with doggy excitement. Instinctively, Ty dropped to one knee and started petting its ears. He'd always loved dogs.

"Caramel!—oh it's you, Tyler."

Ty looked up to see Maria standing in her doorway, a fat baby on her hip. "Hey, I'm just here to drop off Midde—Kate's key?"

"Of course." Maria gestured to her house. "Come in."

It wasn't a question so Ty couldn't think of a polite way to say 'no thanks.' The interior of the townhouse was full of plastic kid shit and big beautiful murals made up of what looked like shells.

"I'll get us coffee in a second, Tyler," Maria said, bustling up behind him. "Just let me put Emmy down."

She vanished, and in the absence of anything else to do, Ty bent down and scratched the dog's velvet ears. It had followed him inside, yipping happily and making Ty feel a fuck of a lot calmer.

Maria reappeared in front of him, sans baby. "Do you have a dog?" she said, hustling Caramel onto a nearby mat.

"Not since I was a kid."

"You should get one." There was no trace of suggestion in her voice; it was like when his sisters-in-law told him to find a new girlfriend—an order, plain and simple.

"I work late hours and I travel a lot. It wouldn't be fair to the dog."

Maria looked unimpressed. "Right. Follow me, Tyler."

She had a rich, accented voice, one he might ordinarily have found attractive, except she kept saying his name like it was a brand of toilet cleaner. *'Tyler works wonders on those stubborn hard-to-face stains. Try Tyler now and we guarantee you'll be amazed at the results!'*

Ty began to suspect this meeting had very little to do with returning Middleton's key, but he had no idea what to do with the knowledge except follow Maria into her azure coloured kitchen. She gestured toward the bench. "Tea or coffee?"

"Coffee, thanks."

His host—or was it captor?—turned on an expensive-looking espresso machine and Ty sat on a blue cushioned stool. He glanced at Maria's fridge and noticed among all the pictures of the baby and a dark-haired boy, there was one of Middleton. She was wearing a pink sundress and smiling shyly, as though she didn't think the picture was a good idea, but loved the person holding the camera too much to say no. Pain rippled through his chest, deep and dull as if someone had pressed a butter knife into it. He looked away.

"How's your day been?" Maria asked.

Ty shook his head, trying to get Middleton out of his brain. "Good thanks, yours?"

"Fine," Maria said, pulling a carton of milk from the fridge. "I work from home, so it's mostly just kids and numbers all day. What about you?"

"About the same. Only without the kids and numbers."

"I see."

Silence fell. Ty wished Caramel was there so he could pet her and have something to do with his hands.

"Here you go," Maria said placing a bright blue mug of coffee in front of him. Ty took a sip, barely tasting anything. "Thanks."

"Not a problem."

Maria came around the counter and sat beside him. Ty would have preferred she stayed on the other side. He knew what was coming next, and if she was going to take him to task, it would be better if they remained on separate sides of the counter, like true adversaries.

"So," Maria said, blowing on her coffee. "I want to apologise to you."

That was not what Ty was expecting. "Pardon?"

"I. Want. To. Apologise. To. You. Tyler. Henderson," Maria enounced as though her accent might be the problem.

"I don't understand," Ty said. "I mean, I get what you're saying, but we don't know each other, why are you apologising to me?"

Maria frowned into her coffee. "Hasn't Katie ever talked to you about me?"

"Not...not really, no."

"I see." She sucked her lips into her mouth, obviously hurt.

"We didn't really talk about each other's friends," Ty said, feeling the need to make amends, perhaps because she'd given him a coffee.

"It's fine," Maria said briskly. "I wanted to apologise to you because I was very against you two being together. I spent a lot of time telling Katie you were a selfish arsehole and I know it sounds egotistical, but I feel I contributed to how things ended between you."

"Right..." Ty, unsure of how to respond, drank some of his coffee.

"I wasn't a friend when she needed me," Maria continued, as

though he'd asked to hear more. "I distrusted you for my own selfish reasons and for that, I owe you an apology."

"Right."

"Is that all you can say?"

Ty thought about it. "No."

Maria tossed her curtain of dark hair over one shoulder. "You are such a man."

The statement reminded Ty of Georgie. "So I've been told."

At a loss for what else to do, he drank more coffee, knowing the sooner he finished, the sooner he could leave. Why hadn't he dropped the key in the mailbox when he had the chance?

Maria let out a fluttering sigh. "I'm sorry. Ever since Katie left for Prague, a lot has happened. I've been forced to...to come to terms with certain things."

He stopped himself from saying 'right' by the skin of his teeth. "Sure."

Maria rolled her eyes. "Did you get a letter from her? Written on yellow paper?"

Ty frowned. "Yeah."

"I got one also. I think they were written at the same time. I think a few of my team members got together and helped her do it. None of them are very impressed with either of us right now."

Ty recalled the boisterous derby after-party. The thought of all those funny, good-natured girls hating his guts wasn't as painful as seeing the picture of Middleton, but it wasn't pleasant, either. He'd liked them. "Why aren't they impressed with you?"

Maria traced a fingertip over the rim of her blue mug. "I...I have feelings for Katie. Feelings that made it hard for me to see her with you."

Ty raised an eyebrow. If this woman helped convince Middleton to run away and revenge-fuck a bunch of floppy-haired Europeans, he had a major axe to grind with her. But it wasn't *such* a major axe he couldn't appreciate the idea of her spanking the shit out of Middleton's backside. "What, uh, kind of feelings?"

A smile touched the corners of Maria's lips. "Not the kind you're picturing."

Bugger. Ty took another deep swallow of coffee. He was almost three-quarters done.

"Don't you want to know what I mean?" Maria enquired.

"I can appreciate you wanting to talk to someone who you think is in the same boat as you, but I don't know what to say."

"I don't want you to say anything, I want you to *listen.*"

"But, you haven't—"

"I'm a sexual dominant," she said, sharp as a dagger through a cheesecake. "I like control, and I like causing pain. When Katie first joined the Barbie Trolls, what she was struck me at once. I imagine it struck you, too?"

Ty remembered Middleton asking for directions in the GGS kitchen, how he'd wanted to pull her across his lap and lay hell on her behind. "Yeah. I noticed."

"It's fairly obvious, but you met a different Katie. The girl who joined my team was painfully shy, very uncomfortable with what she was. I decided to take her under my wing."

Again, Ty pictured Maria spanking Middleton. His expression must have shown it because Maria gave a little laugh and said, "Men."

"Sorry. It's an occupational hazard. So you and Middleton were friends?"

"Yes, and I mean it when I say it wasn't sexual; we talked, I learned about her past, and she learned about mine. But there was something not quite right about it all, she used to look at me..." Maria shot him an apologetic glance. "She used to look at me like I was a goddess, as though she couldn't believe I was real. That's an intense feeling, especially for someone like us."

Ty didn't like that she'd said 'us' but he knew what she meant. He remembered the adoring look in Middleton's eyes when he made her come all too well. "So you fell for her?"

"Yes," Maria said quietly. "It was a strange attraction, maternal and sisterly and authoritative. I didn't want to sleep with her exactly, I just wanted her close, wanted her to keep looking at me the way she did when we first met and I...I used my nature against hers to do it."

"What do you—"

"I gave her orders," Maria said. "I bossed her around and kept her from becoming close to her teammates. I told myself I was protecting her, but it was selfish."

"Did Middleton know what you were doing?"

Maria drew her full lips into her mouth then released them. "I thought not, but her letter made it clear she noticed a change in me. She started to feel obligated to me in ways she shouldn't have. By the time you two became lovers it wasn't fun for her to be around me anymore."

Maria tapped at the rim of her coffee mug and Ty noticed the thick gold band sitting on her ring finger. "How did your husband feel about your relationship with Middleton?"

"Oh, Brendan's a wonderful man," she said dismissively. "He could understand where I was coming from. He met Katie and he liked her. He was glad I was trying to help her come out of her shell."

Ty took that to mean 'he thought there might be a threesome in it for him, if he kept his mouth shut.' He picked up his mug and drained the last of his coffee into his mouth. "I should go. Thanks for—"

"Do you know much about Katie's childhood?"

"No. I should—"

"I won't go into it too much," she said a little louder than before. "But I will say the way Katie behaves toward men, the asexual la-di-dah, glitter and cupcakes stuff, is a defence mechanism. As we got closer, talked more about BDSM, she told me she wanted to meet someone. I didn't like the idea, but I knew I had to help her. She'd tried to find a daddy on her own before and..." Maria raised a dark brow. "Do you know about the selling...?"

"The selling her underwear thing?" Ty scowled. "Yes, I know about that."

Over the past week the thought that countless men owned pairs of Middleton's used panties when he didn't had caused him quite a bit of angst.

"So, you know Katie doesn't have the best judgement when it comes to getting what she wants from men. Before she started at your company, I helped her set up a Kinkworld account and took her to some play parties. It soon became apparent she wasn't interested in men *pretending* to dominate her. She wanted the real thing, which ruled out almost everyone."

"Why?" Ty said, keeping his question short so he wouldn't be interrupted.

Maria gave him a put-upon smile. "True Doms, alpha males, are four-carat diamonds. They're exceedingly rare, and no matter what they say, most women want one. They're born, not made, and they're snapped up quickly. The ones who stay single are highly unlikely to join websites like Kinkworld or fetish clubs."

"Why?" Ty repeated, feeling like a parrot.

Maria waved an impatient hand in the air. "Because it requires a kind of campy showmanship that rubs alpha males the wrong way and because there's usually no shortage of women willing to sleep with them, it's unnecessary. So, Katie spent her whole adolescence and early adulthood pining after something she had a minuscule chance of finding. I was just starting to persuade her to lower her standards when she met you."

Ty felt his face grow hot. "You're saying, what? I'm an alpha male?"

Maria gave him a withering look. "Please don't act like you don't know what you are. It's very irritating."

Ty brought his mug to his lips, tried to drink air and brought it back down again. His cheeks felt like they were on fire. Why the fuck hadn't he put the key in the goddamn mailbox?

"From the way Katie talked about you, I knew you must have been what she was looking for," Maria said quietly, as though to herself. "Still, I never thought anything would come of it. You were older, and I had no way of knowing the attraction was mutual. Then Bendigo happened."

Jesus, she knew about that? Ty cleared his throat. "I know it sounds sleazy, but I didn't mean—"

"I know you didn't mean to sleep with her that night." Maria's voice was sharp once more. "But seeing as the two of you did wind up in bed and seeing as you're sitting in my kitchen, looking like shit and trying not to stare at my picture of Katie, I'm going to go out on a limb and say the attraction was very mutual and the two of you sleeping together was only a matter of time."

"That's not—"

"Why were you even in the pub watching Katie kiss that other boy?" Maria demanded. "She told me you were the only staff member there, why were you watching her? Why carry her back to your room instead of buzzing reception and asking them to unlock her door? Why let her seduce you? Why—"

"I don't know why!" Anger that had been percolating inside Ty for days burst out in a great rush. "I don't know what you think talking about this will accomplish. Middleton's gone and it's over for me and it's over for you. We fucked up and we have to live with that. Now, are we done here?"

Maria shot him a look as though they were at an office party and he kept drunkenly demanding everyone do the Macarena. "You know, Katie called me from Prague yesterday?"

The news felt like a fist to the temple. "Good for you."

"Don't you want to know what she said about you? How much she misses you and hopes you're doing okay?"

Ty stood, pulled out Middleton's key and laid it on the kitchen counter. "This is why I came here. You've got her key, now I'm going to go."

Maria touched the key with the tip of her finger. "If that's what you want, Tyler, but I think you'll regret it."

The fact that she kept saying his full name—the way Veronica used to—did nothing to soothe his temper. "What do you want from me? Why the fuck did you invite me here?"

Maria glared at him. "Because I want my friend to be happy and I know this is a sensitive topic for you, but there's no reason to swear."

Ty thought of the baby and instantly felt lower than dirt. "Sorry. I didn't mean to be a pri—a jerk."

"That's fine," Maria said primly. "But I think it's time we got down to brass tacks. Did you ever read the blogs Katie posted on her Kinkworld profile?"

Ty scratched his head.

Maria muttered something that sounded a lot like 'ignorant idiot man' in Spanish. "Of course you didn't. Well, go look at them."

"Why?"

"You'll learn a few things about how she feels about you and perhaps it will inspire you to pull your head out of your alpha male asshole long enough to see what you're ruining."

Ty stared at her, her silky brown hair and disdainful eyes, and decided she had no idea what the fuck she was talking about. "I'm gonna go. Thanks for the coffee."

"You're welcome."

He was halfway through the kitchen door when he turned. "You never said why you saw me as a threat."

"No, I didn't." Maria had produced a phone from somewhere and was playing a bubble exploding game. "Would you like me to tell you?"

"No. We both know it's my age."

She gave a sharp, carrying laugh. "If you think that's the issue, you're even stupider than your hair colour suggests."

Ty scowled. "You said we were going to get down to brass tacks. I'm too old to be her goddamn boyfriend, and you know it."

"Mmm." Maria tapped away at her screen. "Weren't you leaving?"

Ty turned back to the door, then faced her again. "I don't know what Middleton told you about me, my scars or the firefighting or some other shit, but she doesn't know half of what's wrong with me."

"Have you killed someone?"

"What? No!"

"Then why—"

"I drink too much. I sleep on the couch at my office all the time. My fiancée left me for another man, and now she keeps calling and saying she wants us to be friends. I've got two decades of baggage on Middleton, I can't even hold her without feeling like I'm going to go out of my head or cry or something..." Ty pinched the bridge of his nose. "Look, what I'm saying to you is my life's messed up. You had the right idea when you tried to warn her off me. I'm not someone you'd want anywhere near a girl like Middleton."

"Mmm," Maria said again. "Is it easier for you to call her that than by her name?"

"No."

"I think you're lying," she said, exploding a row of purple bubbles. "I think it's much easier, just like it's easier for you to tell yourself you're too damaged to have the kind of relationship Katie wants from you."

He wanted to leave, wanted to stay, wanted to shout, but most of all, he wanted this infuriating woman to understand where he was coming from. "She wants too much."

Maria put down her phone "Is that really it? Or does she *give* too much and you're secretly convinced you don't deserve it?"

Ty decided to play his trump card. "I don't want kids. Never have. You think a girl like Middleton would be okay with that?"

Maria gave an unsatisfactory shrug. "I don't know, have you ever talked to her about it? Have you ever talked to her about anything that made you feel even the slightest bit vulnerable?"

Ty said nothing.

"You know, I trained as an art therapist. Part of art therapy is manifesting your thoughts and feelings in the physical world. Your fears are much less scary when they're on a canvas. Your goals feel much more attainable."

"What does that—"

"Katie told me you're writing a novel," she said, interrupting him for the umpteenth time. "Here's some homework for you, Alpha Male —go home and write about your relationship with Katie, write about how you wish it could be."

"Oh yeah? What's that gonna do? Make it come true like *The Secret* or some shit?"

Maria laughed. "You turn cruel when you're vulnerable, a very masculine tendency, but not one that's going to serve you very well going forward, Alpha Male. If it serves you at all now."

"Stop calling me that," Ty said through gritted teeth.

"Fine." Maria picked up her phone. "But I'm not Katie, I don't give a damn about your feelings. All I'm offering you is a chance to change the very sad road you're walking down. If you've got half a brain, you'll go home and write about how you wish it could be with Katie. You'll make it real, at least to yourself."

"I don't want to make it real."

Cartoonish music began playing from Maria's phone as she resumed zapping bubbles. "What we want and what we need are two different things. Katie might think you're a god, but I can see right through you. You won the genetic lottery, had everything handed to you on a platter. Everyone's jealous of you. They don't understand being that way brings its own problems."

"Like what?" Ty asked in spite of himself.

"Like not understanding that things don't always go your way."

"I understand that!"

"Do you? Because from where I'm sitting it looks like you've painted yourself into a misery corner. One woman broke your heart and you think you can't trust anyone with it again. You're not twenty-five, so you don't think you deserve someone as young and beautiful as Katie."

The words, as she said them, cracked something open inside him. He stared at Maria, this stranger who seemed to know everything about him and heat welled behind his nose.

How, he thought. *How do you know?*

"I'm like you in a lot of ways," Maria said, over the sound of the cartoon music. "I was born beautiful and confident, I always got everything I wanted. It was a shock to me when things went wrong, when I started getting old. I didn't understand it, I fought it. I still fight it. I loved Katie because she saw me the way I wanted to see myself. I know she makes you feel the same way, but she never loved me like she loves you. She doesn't need you to be perfect, she just needs you to be there."

Ty rubbed a hand over his eyes. "It's so goddamn hard."

"I understand, but you have to come to terms with the fact that you can't be a firefighter again, or go back in time and pick a fiancée who doesn't leave you, or be the same age as Katie. You have to accept that and move on."

Silence permeated the kitchen. Ty heard a wattle bird twittering by the window, the game music, and beneath it the faint sounds of a TV playing upstairs. Homely noises. Pleasant noises.

Ty opened his mouth to say something when a small boy in rumpled *Toy Story* pyjamas came padding up the hall behind him. He raced around Ty's legs and into the kitchen.

"Mummy?" he said in that warbling voice all kids seemed to have. "Mummy?"

Maria's face opened up like a sunbeam. She put down her phone and threw her arms wide. "Hello, my beautiful love! You're awake! Come over here!"

The boy rushed toward her and Maria took him in her arms. The boy's face as he nestled into her was radiant. Ty glanced at Middleton's picture again, thinking of all the times he'd ignored the soft look in her eyes that said she wanted him to hold her. How he'd thought he was doing her a favour, when really it had been his own fear that stopped him.

"Who's that, mummy?" the boy asked in his jangling voice.

Maria kissed his cheeks, making him giggle. "That's Katie's friend, Tyler. Say hello to him."

Ty expected the kid to ignore her, the way his nieces and nephews did when their parents made such requests. Instead, the boy turned and waved a chubby arm at him. "Hello, Tyler. Hello."

Ty felt something inside him unhinge and for a moment he was positive he was going to cry.

"Hello, mate," he managed to say.

Maria stood, hoisting her son onto her hip. "Tyler has to go, my love, say goodbye."

"Goodbye, Ty," the boy said, giggling at the rhyme.

Maria strode toward him and to his surprise, kissed him on the cheek. "Thank you for coming to see me, and good luck."

"Right."

She laughed. "I hope I see you again in better circumstances, Alpha Male, now go home and do your homework."

22

Ty shrugged off his leathers and placed his helmet on his kitchen counter. He'd rode around for an extra hour after he'd left Maria's, waiting for something to keep him from going home, and yet here he was, ready to do his homework. He'd owned his place since the 2000s, bought it cheap and renovated it himself. Every room had been perfectly designed to match his lifestyle—wine cellar, library, no backyard to maintain, no spare bedrooms left deliberately empty for the results of condomless sex, a huge pantry, and a restaurant-grade oven.

Veronica had added a few splashes to the place—the dining table and the piss-yellow breakfast nook—but nothing had really taken, the house was still his, almost every wall and surface reflecting his taste.

He could have completed Maria's task at his kitchen while he cooked dinner—he hadn't eaten since breakfast and he was starving— but instead, he climbed the stairs to his office. He shoved novels and loose pieces of paper off his desk, so the space he wanted to use was clear. He sat down, dug a fresh notepad and Bic out of the overflowing drawers and put one to the other. Instantly, his fingers began to itch.

He stood, intending to go get himself a beer and then stopped. This thing with Middleton had been born in alcohol, sustained by alcohol, and brought low by alcohol. If he was going to spill his guts tonight, he should be sober as sober could get. He walked over to the window and forced it open so that cold salty air rushed into him. It unsettled the stagnant room, rustled loose sheets and raised goose-bumps on his arms. It was uncomfortable, but it was better. He sat and picked up his pen.

Write down how you wish it could be, Maria had said. *Make it real, at least to yourself.*

It was ridiculous, a pointless exercise, but some hard part of him knew it had to be done. He took a deep breath and wrote, *When I first met Katie—*

He tore the page from the pad, balled it up, and threw it in the bin. This was agonising, like having a thousand needles jabbed into him at once. The weakness he felt, even alone writing words no one else ever had to see, was staggering. He wanted to get up, go into the lounge room, and turn on the TV. Middleton was gone, why was he even bothering?

Maria had all but told him he was entitled, incapable of handling bad times because some part of him thought he didn't deserve them. Ty didn't want to believe that, but if he turned away from this simple task just because it was hard, he'd be proving her right. He returned his Bic to the notepad.

Middleton crawled into my hotel bed because she's attracted to old men and even though I know it's a mistake, I let her have me. The sex is good. We start dating. Her family think she's insane for fucking someone twenty years older than her. All my friends think I'm having a mid-life crisis. People whisper behind our backs at parties. The age gap sounds bad and she's so baby-faced it looks worse. The fact I used to be her boss is the cherry on top of the shit sundae. Doesn't stop us from fucking one another, but the smell of it taints everything, like when there's a dead rat in your ventilation. A few years pass, I get even fucking older, my hair starts to fall out, and my dick doesn't work. Middleton meets a guy her own age. She leaves me. I die alone.

Ty threw his pen aside, swearing under his breath. Some fucking exercise this was turning out to be. He stood, but again, he found he couldn't leave the room. His gaze fell on his laptop, and he remembered what Maria had told him, the step that was supposed to have come before this one.

"Kinkworld, shit."

He fired up his laptop, opened Chrome, and logged into Kinkworld. He was briefly sidetracked by a couple of new messages from @BadBastard1995— *'You're a cunt, and I bet you have chlamydia,'* and *'Fuck you, you limp-dicked asshole'* before he returned to Middleton's profile.

She hadn't uploaded anything since the cherry nightie picture. Ty hoped that was a good sign and not an indication she was too busy making out with strangers to spare a thought for Kinkworld. He had to scan her profile a couple of times before he found the blog section, which made him feel slightly better about not reading it sooner.

Middleton's first entry was dated almost three years ago. It explained why she was attracted to the idea of daddy-daughter play. As with her profile, he both recognised and didn't recognise her voice —she sounded so confident here, so witty and unafraid. She encouraged anyone who was interested in topping her to read her next blog. Ty noticed that unlike her pictures, the blogs only had a couple of likes and no comments. Maria had been right—men, himself included—didn't seem very switched on when it came to seeking out this stuff.

Ty clicked on the next entry. It was about what she was looking for in a daddy, an almost painfully romantic musing on what it would be like to play with someone whose fantasies aligned with hers. This one had no likes and only one comment, a guy had written *Vert nice, DM me, and I will spank yuor butt.*

Despising his gender a little, Ty clicked on the next blog.

The next few entries were erotica—short stories detailing spankings, bondage scenes, and a trip to the movies in which Daddy made her blow him in the back of the cinema. Knowing she wrote down her fantasies the way he had when he was a teenager made Ty's insides ache. Some of the stories were so similar to his, it felt too significant to be a coincidence. It felt like fate. The stories got him hot but Ty was feeling too many things to jerk off, he just kept clicking through her blogs until he came to...

"Poetry?" Ty asked his office. "Middleton writes poetry?"

He winced. It was one thing to read charming sex stories, but he didn't know if he could take poetry. If she'd tried to rhyme anything with 'Tyler'...

"Man up," he told himself. "Do it."

To his relief, the nerves weren't necessary. Her poetry was good, or as good as someone who knew nothing about poetry could make out. They weren't just about sex, they were also about summer and loneliness and a woman Ty was sure was Middleton's Aunt Rhonda and a longish one called *Seaweed and Other Entanglements* that made him laugh. It sounded as though Middleton had experimented with bondage by wrapping herself up in kelp and had gotten stuck and had to be cut out by her brother. He clicked on the next blog, one dated a couple of months earlier, and found a poem called *Moonlight Baby*. His skin prickled as he began to read.

> *Even when he is there*
> *i touch nothing*
> *but bright air*
> *he had no plans to love me*
> *but i made plans of my own.*
> *i shaped myself from his sun*
> *and became a moonlight baby*

Below this, there was an even shorter poem; *Not and Never.*

> *i think it would be nice,*
> *to be loved.*

i think it would be good.
to be loved
i think it would be nice to know
someone loved me

Ty pushed back his chair. "Middleton," he growled into the silence. "Kate."

He couldn't breathe, couldn't think. Her words had done something to him, cracked him open the same way Maria's insights had done in her kitchen. He wanted to see her and tell her she was wrong, he did love her and that was the whole problem. How could he be with someone so kind? Someone so comfortable relying on him? She had so many needs and when she pressed her face against his chest he wanted to give her everything, *everything*. He'd never felt that before.

He had loved Veronica sincerely, but not like this. She hadn't needed him the way Katie did, hadn't required all of him the way Katie would. With Veronica the boundaries were well defined and impenetrable; he'd given her monogamy and a diamond ring and a piss-yellow breakfast nook, but not a baby or a house where they could start their lives fresh or even a fucking Instagram account so she could tag him in all her photos.

With Middleton it would be different, he felt like an asshole for saying it, but it would be different. Not because she was so young or pretty or good in bed, but because when she wanted something he *needed* to give it to her.

He endured days of shame when he turned down her invitation to the derby match and when he saw sense and went back to her, where had he gone? It was their dynamic, to give and take in equal but different ways. He would use her body and provide her with every single thing she desired because he was her Daddy, her lover and her protector. If she wanted a new house, he would sell his beloved beachside home and move somewhere else. If she wanted to get married in the Catholic Church, despite him being the world's biggest atheist he knew he would concede. And if she wanted a baby...

Ty's breath caught in his throat. As ugly as it sounded and as impossible as it seemed, Kate was the one for whom it would be different. It was so monumentally unfair to Veronica and any woman who'd ever wanted his child, but she was the exception and if she needed a baby, wanted one with all her heart, then he would change his mind. Find a gym with a childcare center. Go to the movies on Saturday nights. Be a father.

He started to cry then, not loud and not hard, just soft, soft as rain.

"I'm in love with Kate," he said, just to say the words aloud. "What the fuck do I do now?"

But he already knew the answer. What he and Middleton shared had gravity, it would pull her back toward him as surely as the moon pulled at the ocean tides. He could get her number in Prague from Maria, call her long distance and say "Middleton, you're everything I ever wanted in a woman. I'm your man now. Fly back to Melbourne and be with me." But that was lacking a certain romance and if he knew anything by now it was that Kate liked romance.

He'd hurt her, badly. He owed her something a little better than a bossy phone call demanding she cut her first overseas trip short. He was just starting to think of alternate ideas when his phone vibrated against his thigh. Unthinkingly, he pulled it out and answered. "Henderson."

"Tyler?"

If someone had walked up behind him and zapped him with a cattle prod, Ty could not have been more shocked. "Veronica?"

There was a short silence. "Yeah! Hi! How are you?"

His ex's tone was bright but with a quavering note of panic. Ty knew she hadn't expected him to pick up, she'd been planning on leaving another batshit voicemail. "Why the hell are you calling me?"

"I just wanted to talk to you!" She sounded so chipper Ty was surprised she didn't add *'you big silly!'*

"Great," he said, his voice a cheery imitation of hers. "What did you want to talk about?"

Veronica was silent.

"Why don't I go first? How's your husband? Heard a few people got food poisoning at your wedding. That's no good."

Veronica was breathing hard and fast down the line. Beneath it Ty could hear the sounds of cars swooshing and traffic lights ticking. He'd bet any amount of money she was calling him from her car, on her way home from running an errand or shopping.

"Okay, so you don't want to talk about Colin," he said. "That's fine. What about your son, Dominic?"

"Don't you say his name!" Veronica snapped.

"Why not? Don't you want me acknowledging you have a son?"

Faster, shallower breaths. Ty could almost smell his ex-girlfriend's lemony Hyacinth perfume, feel her hair brushing over his cheek. "I'll ask you again, why are you calling me?"

There was another short silence, and Ty became sure his ex didn't know why she was calling, she'd just had the impulse and followed it. She'd always been that way, whirlwind holidays and three thousand dollar coats, impulsivity to mask sharp bursts of fear and need. *Am I missing out? Can I have everything? Is my life as exciting as everyone else's?* Had this happened yesterday, Ty might have been angry, but in the face of his Middleton revelation, he found himself feeling profoundly sorry for his ex. "Veronica, this needs to stop."

"I miss you," she whispered. "I miss us."

"You left me for another man two years ago. I'd say that ship has not only sailed, but been boarded by pirates, stripped of all valuables, and sunk to the bottom of the Pacific Ocean."

"You're still mad at me," she said with satisfaction. "That's good, that means—"

"It doesn't mean I still care!" Ty took a deep breath. "Look, you fucked me over worse than anyone's ever fucked me over, but at the end of the day, it was for the best. We never would have worked; we weren't right for each other. Now, why the hell do you keep leaving me voicemails? And don't tell me it's because you bloody miss me."

There was no answer.

"Do you know what I think?" Ty said. "I think you've trapped yourself in a situation you can't squirm your way out of and you want my help getting free."

A small scoff. "Colin—"

"I'm not talking about your dumbfuck husband. I'm talking about your kid. He's out in the world now, no stuffing him back where he came from, no palming him off on your parents, and no matter how many times you call, I'm not coming to rescue you. You're a mum now, Veronica, there's no going back."

"Fuck you."

"It's the goddamn truth. You got what you wanted and it's time to accept it. You can't have a baby and a husband and a pining fucking ex too."

"Why not?" she said trying and failing to sound glib.

Ty thought about Maria. "Because shit doesn't always go your way. Sometimes it goes bad and you just have to accept it."

There was a short pause. "But I don't want to."

"And that used to be my problem. But then you dumped me, so now it isn't. I'm going to hang up and once I do I'm blocking your number."

"What? *Why?*"

"Because I've met someone else and I don't want to talk to you anymore. Give my best to Colin."

Ty's thumb was an inch from the red 'end call' button when she said it, "I know who she is."

He raised the phone to his ear. "What?"

"I know who your new girlfriend is, you pervert!"

The last word came out hard, like a burst of bad breath, and Ty knew Veronica was telling the truth. "How? How do you know?"

She gave a short crazy laugh. "I'm not going to tell you. Let's see how you like living with that!"

But Ty wasn't listening, he was looking at his laptop. He had a new Kinkworld message from *@BadBastard1995.* It read, *'You're an asshole, Tyler Henderson.'*

It should have scared him that some anonymous internet troll knew his full name but it didn't, because it wasn't an anonymous internet troll. The answer was so clear, so neat and tidy, he felt stupid for not seeing it sooner. Veronica had always been a chronic snooper. Throughout their relationship he'd busted her going through his laptop and phone looking for evidence he was cheating. He tuned back in to the voice in his ear and listened to Veronica tell him they needed to have dinner and talk about everything.

"You're still reading my emails, aren't you?" he said dully. "You didn't stop doing it when we broke up. You've been stalking me and when you saw the confirmation email for me to create an account on—"

"Kinkworld?" she shrieked into the phone, all semblance of self-control gone.

"Yeah, Kinkworld," Ty said, cringing a little at the silly word. "You logged into my profile, didn't you? You guessed my password and—"

"It was the same one as your email password!" she shouted as though it was his fault she'd gone through his private information. "I can't believe you, Tyler! That Kate girl is your employee and she's twenty-five and she's a retard!"

"*What?*"

"She has ADHD. She's a spastic and you've been sleeping with her."

For the first time since this conversation began, Ty found himself getting angry. No, not angry, *furious.*

"How," he said, through gritted teeth. "Do you know Kate has ADHD?"

"I had Becky do a search on her at work," Veronica said triumphantly. "What she has is severe as fuck. She'll be on brain pills for the rest of her life. I can't believe you would ever—"

"That's enough!" Ty got to his feet, so mad he could barely think or breathe. "I don't know who the hell you think you are, but ADHD isn't a disability and even if it was, what you did is a crime. I could get you and Becky thrown in jail."

Veronica gave a high hysterical laugh. "Oh, really?"

"Maybe not jail. But I could make sure neither of you had a job that wasn't folding t-shirts ever again."

That shut her up, for about ten seconds. "You've got some nerve threatening me when you're taking advantage of a girl who's mentally ill."

"ADHD isn't a—"

"I'm not talking about her fucking ADHD!" Veronica screamed. "I'm talking about the twisted fucking games you've been playing with her, I've read your messages, I know everything, *Daddy*."

Ty cringed but was determined not to let his ex get the upper hand. "She's an adult, we're not hurting anyone, and this is none of your business."

"Oh, isn't it? If I'd known that's what you wanted when you made me call you that disgusting word, I would have cut your dick off. That's pedophilia, Ty. Pedophilia and incest. You made me a part of that."

These were the accusations that had terrified him since puberty. They'd dominated his nightmares and his daydreams, kept him from pursuing the sex he wanted in any way, shape or form. He'd lived in fear of those words 'pedophilia' and 'incest,' convinced they applied to him even though they made him feel sick. And yet now that they were being levelled at him, all he could think was, *what a waste of time. I was so fucking scared and it was all a waste of time.*

He closed his eyes. "I don't know if you looked around Kinkworld while you were stalking me, Veronica, if you took a moment to admire the view, but if I'm a depraved pervert then I'm one of millions. What I do to a consenting adult woman is not wrong. Comparing calling me 'daddy' to the most disgusting crimes in human existence, on the other hand, is the shittiest thing you've ever done to me, and that includes stalking, cheating, and leaving my ass. That you think you have a right to judge my sex life after what you've done is a fucking joke."

He moved his thumb to the red 'end call' button but again Veronica spoke before he could tap it. "I'm sorry. I didn't mean it. I *liked* calling you Daddy, you never made me say that—"

"That's enough," Ty said, his jaw was so stiff every syllable was an effort. "I'm not listening to another word that comes out of your mouth. We're done. If you ever come near me or Kate again I'll go to the police and tell them you had a friend abuse her role as psychiatrist to stalk me and we'll see where that takes us. Goodbye."

He hung up and knowing she would call back, knowing she wouldn't be able to help herself, he blocked her number. Then he sat down at his laptop and changed all the passwords on his email, work, and social media accounts. When he was done and his breathing was slightly more even, he picked up his pen and began to write.

A girl showed up at my work; the prettiest thing I've ever seen. She's so sweet it hurts your teeth, and I hate her for it because I've lost my taste for sweet. Still, I want her more than I've ever wanted anything. I kept my distance for a while but the pull we felt toward each other was too strong. I rescue her on a work trip. I hope she never knows what I rescued her from, I hope she never feels any kind of pain again. She climbs into my bed that night and puts her hands on me. When she does, I can feel every plan I had being smoothed away, replaced by thick fat arrows pointing in her direction. It's the start of something big and I'm so fucking scared I back away.
She's braver than me, though, she refuses to take no for an answer. She comes to me and when we kiss I lose myself in her. We start dating and after I pull my head out of my ass we make it official.
People talk but it doesn't matter, we're in love. We fuck a lot and drink a lot of wine. We travel the world together and get a dog. By the time she's thirty no one will give a damn about the age gap. When people ask when we're getting married, I'll smile and say, "What do you think Katie, do you want to be Mrs Henderson?" and she'll laugh. One day she'll say yes.

He hesitated, then added a final line.

Maybe we have kids, maybe we don't, either way, we'll be happy.

The minute Ty was done, he put down his pen and headed downstairs. The paint he could do tonight, he thought, grabbing his keys. Veronica's books and clothes he could give to the Salvation Army tomorrow. The new kitchen table would be a pain in the arse, but maybe Georgie would want to go to IKEA on the weekend. She fucking loved that stupid place.

"Where are you going?" His neighbour asked as Ty climbed into his Hilux. "Out for dinner?"

"Gotta get some stuff for the house," he said.

"Bit late, isn't it?"

Ty couldn't help laughing at that. "Yeah, but it's better late than never."

———————

23

The woman's stamp hovered over Kate's form. "You're sure about this?"

"Definitely. One hundred percent."

"You'll have to get all new identity documents. We're talking a new driver's license, passport, bank accounts, electoral enrolment, and insurance."

"I can't wait to do that stuff," Kate said honestly. "Please stamp it?"

The woman eyed her once more, gave her a look that said if there was any way she could get out of doing this she would, then she thumped her stamp down on the form.

"It's done?" Kate asked.

"It's done." The woman's lips twitched upward. "Congratulations. Just lemme go get the documents you need to apply for new identification."

As she stood up, Kate gripped the marble counter, dizzy with the truth of what she'd just done. She had a new name. Well, an old name, but it was officially new. "Set fire to the princess," she whispered.

"Pardon?" The woman was back with a fat sheaf of papers.

"I said erm, 'thank you?'"

"Right." The woman gave her another suspicious look. "I'll just talk you through how these forms work and then you can leave."

Kate listened, took the forms and headed outside. Only when she was breathing in the fresh spring air did she allow herself to say it out loud. "Kate Rhonda McGrath. Kate. Rhonda. McGrath. Finally."

She pulled out her phone and updated the list she kept in the notes app, a digital version of the one Casey, Tam, and Rapunzel had helped her write all those weeks ago. She added 'change name to Kate' to the completed section and basked in the satisfying glow of crossing something big off her to-do list.

It was a little addictive—in the two weeks she'd been back in Melbourne she'd cut her hair to her shoulders, told her family to stop sniping at her or she wouldn't come home for Christmas, and thrown her first party. It had been eighties themed, and she and Rapunzel had spent the next week picking glitter out of their hair, clothes, and rugs. Rapunzel and her cat Pebbles had moved in while Kate was still in Prague, helping to water the plants and check her mail and throw out her expired dairy products and whatnot.

When Kate arrived home, Rapunzel helped her tackle a few of the larger items on her list—organizing the party and selling Aunt Rhonda's creepier naked lady statues on Greys.com so Kate could afford to re-decorate the apartment.

It had been hard, packing away her aunt's beloved things, but one of the items on her list had been to finally accept the Elizabeth Street apartment was hers and make it a home rather than a shrine to her incredible but definitely deceased Aunt. As of now, there were only three things left on Kate's list: *buy new, non-princess clothes, delete Kinkworld account,* and *throw away dildo.*

The last two items on her list were, in theory, the simplest, but Kate would have preferred to spend all day trying on ill-fitting cream blouses and bad skirts than tackle them. While she no longer felt comfortable on Kinkworld, she couldn't escape the feeling that Ty might try to contact her there and for weeks the glass dildo he'd given her had been the only thing that could get her off. It was almost certainly a psychosomatic affliction, but still. Getting rid of both of them would feel like shutting a door on hope *and* pleasure. Her phone rang, and she answered it. "Hello?"

"Certified?" Rapunzel asked.

"Hell yeah, it's certified."

Rapunzel hooted so loudly Kate had to take the phone away from her ear. "Well done, Peach! Or should I say Just-Kate? Are you home to delete your perv account and chuck out the dildo, then?"

Kate grimaced. "I know I should, but—"

"Get your arse home right now." Rapunzel's voice was stony. "You made a promise, today's the day."

"But—"

"Do it, Middleton." Rapunzel had developed the habit of calling her that whenever Kate was dragging her feet. She'd noticed that, probably because of all of Ty's spankings, the word had a galvanising effect.

"I will, but—"

"You'd do it if Dexter asked you to do it. You'd be sprinting home to chuck out your dildo. *Yes sir, no sir, I'll have it in a landfill by midnight, sir.*"

"Shh." Kate glanced around as though Ty might be standing nearby, smiling his sardonic smile, his hands shoved into the pockets of his beautiful coat. "You know it's redundant to invoke Ty's name to make me do things designed to help me get over Ty, right?"

"Not sure what that means, Peach, don't really give a shit either way. Catch the tram home and throw out your magic dildo."

Kate groaned. "Okay, god, I will."

"Excellent. I'll expect you within the hour. If you're any later than that I'll start setting your books on fire." She hung up.

For a weed-dealing dropout and Uber Eats driver, Kate suspected Rapunzel would make an excellent Fortune 500 corporate dictator.

She put in her ear buds and caught the tram home, listening to happy music and trying to brace herself for what was about to happen. Her broken heart had scabbed over a little on her trip to Prague, but she still missed Ty like fire. Part of her longed for her early days at GGS when he was her unobtainable crush and their future was way out in front of them. Back then, she'd thought just getting to sleep with him once would make her the happiest girl in the world. The truth was both lovelier and more painful than that. There was a glossiness to loving someone from afar that loving someone up close couldn't match.

Part of her still hoped Ty would reach out to her and say that he changed his mind and was ready for a real relationship, but seeing as he hadn't, she'd set herself a deadline—a month of pining, and then no more.

And hell, Kate thought as she strode into her building, *if I miss the dildo that much, I can always buy the same one again then take a leaf out of Casey's book and sage it.*

"Katie?"

She looked up to see Stephen the security guy smiling at her from the front desk. "What's up?"

"Can you please empty your post box? It's reached bursting point again."

"Shoot."

Kate always forgot to check her mail because why the hell were people sending her mail, anyway? She headed back outside toward the metal rack of post-boxes. Stephen was right, several corners of brightly coloured paper were protruding from her slot. She unlocked it and despite her best efforts to contain the explosion, brochures burst out like bad confetti.

Sighing, Kate picked up all the Domino's fliers and ads for two-for-one mud facials before spotting something unusual—a thick white envelope gleaming with pearlescent lustre in the afternoon sun.

She groaned. One of her lesser known cousins had to be getting married. Kate was on slightly better terms with her family now that she'd confronted them about being buttholes, but that didn't mean she wanted to spend nine hours with them at a wedding. She picked up the envelope and turned it over, expecting to see a little heart sticker and a 'save the date' and instead saw something that made her jaw drop.

"Are you okay?" Stephen said, sticking his head through the front door. "Need a hand?"

"I'm okay, I'm okay. Really." Kate scooped all of her mail into a big messy pile. "Thanks for letting me know about the mail, I won't let it happen again. I'll see you later!"

Stephen barely had time to agree before Kate sprinted toward the elevator. The thirty-second journey up was agony and as soon as she reached her floor she ran toward her apartment with the fervour of someone being chased by Predator. She flung the door open, dumped all her junk mail on the floor and tore into the white envelope.

"Whoa!" Rapunzel called from the couch. "The fuck's happening, Peach?"

Kate was too wound up to answer. From the moment she'd seen Ty's return address on the back of the envelope, she only had room for one thought—*why?*

Why would Ty have written to her? Was he mad? Happy? Sad? Dead and his funeral invites were really flipping fancy? Re-engaged to his old fiancée and inviting her to his wedding as a final cuss-you?

She pulled out a card, the same shining white colour as the envelope, and read it so quickly she only took in half the words. Safe in the knowledge he wasn't dead or getting married, she took a deep breath and read it again.

Middleton,
I'm in love with you. I'm sorry for what you overheard at The Breton Club,
I was an idiot and I didn't mean a fucking word. You were never my dirty
secret, I was ashamed of what I felt, I couldn't believe a girl like you could
ever really love me. I was wrong, and for that I'm sorry. If you can find it in
your heart to forgive me, come over to my house this Saturday at 7 pm.
Wear a nice dress.
—Ty

A smile like warm butter spread itself across her face. "Oh my gosh."

"Language!" Rapunzel bellowed from the couch.

"Oh my god!" Kate said obligingly. "Fucking hell!"

"Better." Rapunzel sat up, her braid flopping over the couch like a lethargic snake. "So, old mate's come crawling back, has he?"

"It would seem so."

"Thought he would. What did he say?"

Kate stared down at the envelope in a daze. "He says he loves me."

Rapunzel grinned. "Well, it's a good thing you didn't throw out that dildo, hey?"

24

"Are you okay?" the cab driver asked.

Kate immediately stopped slapping herself in the face. "Sorry, I was just...trying to wake up."

The driver, a handsome Pakistani man, shrugged. "Fair enough, lady."

Kate tried not to laugh. She was so freaking nervous she was a danger to herself and others. All afternoon she'd been driving Rapunzel and Pebbles up the wall trying on a million different dresses and asking a million 'what-if' questions.

"I have no idea what's going to happen, Peach," Rapunzel bellowed. "But Dexter already said he was in love with you, so calm the fuck down!"

Kate tried, but it didn't last very long. She was going on a date with the guy she was in love with. A guy she hadn't seen for weeks. A guy who'd sent her a card and then flowers and then champagne and then a book of Rilke poems and then a book of Rumi poems and then had stopped sending her stuff because Rapunzel found him on Facebook and told him he was trying too hard and she was sick of all the delighted screaming.

Ty's place was big and narrow, almost like a lighthouse. It seemed familiar to her, but maybe that was just the smell of salt on the wind and the rhythmic sound of the sea rolling in and out. Sensory experiences that were both intrinsic to her childhood and a hell of a lot more pleasant to recall than the scent of perpetually damp laundry and boiling mince.

She stood on Ty's doorstep, inhaling and exhaling with the ocean before hitting the doorbell.

A minute passed, and her brain started telling her she'd gotten the wrong time, the wrong place, that Ty had meant to send the envelope to another Middleton—he called all his girls Middleton. Thankfully, common sense made her press the doorbell again *before* bursting into tears and she heard the pounding of heavy footsteps coming toward her.

"Sorry," Ty called out. "I was getting dressed."

Just the sound of his voice made her mouth go dry.

"It's all good," she told the door.

The wood swung open to reveal Tyler Henderson in all his glory. The sight of him was a shock, like being shoved into a pool in your best shoes. He looked different. Gorgeous, but different. He'd gotten a haircut, and stubble grew across his jaw like gold sand, but it was more than that. Something had changed, something Kate couldn't quite put her finger on...

"Hey," he said, grinning broadly. "You cut your hair. It looks beautiful. You look beautiful."

"Thanks," Kate said, running her hand through her shorter locks. "I...thanks. It's a lot easier to wash."

"Added benefits, huh?" Ty stepped back and held the door open for her. "Want to come inside?"

"Are we not going out for dinner?"

He ducked his head. "Well, actually, I'm, uh, making us dinner."

"Oh." Her brain whirred frantically, trying to make sense of this unexpected development. She should have brought something, she realised—flowers, wine, Pictionary, *something*. After all the things he'd sent her, why hadn't she brought him *something*? "Sorry, I didn't bring anything."

"It's fine." Ty held out a hand. "Please, come inside?"

Kate stared at his hand, so big and hard and freely offered. She took it and let him lead her into his home.

It was a lovely place, polished floorboards and big windows Kate was sure framed fantastic beach views during the day. The colour scheme was blokey—blue, burgundy and black—but it wasn't too overpowering. The art on the walls was nice, landscapes and bold oils that reminded her of Aunt Rhonda's place. *Her place*, Kate corrected herself.

Ty brought her into his kitchen. It was a cosy, handsome room with an exposed brick oven and cream walls. A few candles were burning on the wooden counter, tall white pillars that would have reminded Kate of church, if church had ever been warm, romantic and scented with roasting meat.

"We're having lamb for dinner," Ty said, gesturing to one of the burgundy bar stools. "Hope you're hungry."

"I am," Kate said, then she had to ask. "You can cook? Like actually cook?"

"Uh, yeah."

"Wow." *Wait till Casey hears about this, she'll kill me then wear my face as a mask and try to get Ty to fall in love with her.*

Ty walked over to a side cupboard and pulled out a crystal champagne glass. "Is me knowing how to cook that surprising?"

"No, I guess I just never heard any of the guys at work talking about it."

That made him laugh. "Good to know I have some secrets left. I worked in a couple of restaurants after I graduated uni. Thought about being a chef."

"Seriously?" Kate imagined Ty in a white jacket barking orders from behind a gleaming kitchen counter. "I think I can see that. Why didn't you?"

Ty produced a dark green champagne bottle from his fridge and began peeling away the foil. "Lifestyle didn't agree with me. Long hours, shit pay, lots of drugs. I still like cooking, though. It's creative and practical at the same time."

He popped the champagne cork and caught the sparkling fluid in the glass, where it shone like captured starlight. He placed it in front of her.

"Thank you," she said, reaching for it.

"Hang on a sec."

To Kate's surprise, he grabbed a second smaller bottle and shook a few purple drops into the champagne.

"Are you poisoning me?" Kate asked, as the purple liquid billowed through the bubbles. "Is that what all this has come to? You luring me here under false pretences and murdering me?"

He laughed, the skin around his eyelids crinkling. "It's blackcurrant liquor, not poison."

"Sure," Kate said, like she knew blackcurrant liquor was a thing. "So, why aren't you having any?"

"Because it's for you."

Kate understood what he was doing, just like she understood why she'd never come to his house before. Some people didn't give a damn about their homes, considered them no more than a place to store stuff and sleep. Ty clearly didn't feel that way. His house was like the brother of Aunt Rhonda's apartment, an externalisation of himself. Just looking around she could tell everything there had been chosen because he loved it, everything that was on display was because he wanted to see it. Bringing her into his home would have been like showing her his insides and before now, neither of them had been ready.

Kate sipped her drink; it tasted like her feelings—sweet excitement. "Thank you."

"Anytime." Ty busied himself slicing potatoes into thin layers and fanning them across a baking tray. Kate immediately felt guilty for sitting on her ass. "Can I help you with anything?"

Ty smiled. He was doing that a lot tonight—she'd never seen his denim-blue eyes so warm. "Not a chance. Tell me about your new job. You're back at work now, yeah?"

Kate told him about D&D, her new desk, her nice colleagues, and the fact that there was a morning tea roster so her brag-worthy baking talents wouldn't go to waste. As they talked, she made a concentrated effort to focus. It was all too easy to fall silent watching him move about his kitchen, sprinkling olive oil and crushing lemons. It was so attractive to see his precise, talented movements but more than that, she could perv on him without looking like she was perving and think about all the sex they might have once their meal was over.

Before she slept with Ty, Kate had gone years between lovers, but now, after mere weeks, her need was monumental. There had been nights in Prague where she'd felt like she was going crazy from wanting him. She'd lay arching back into her bed like a cat, touching herself as she re-imagined every scene, spanking and blow job. She'd have traded anything she owned for another five minutes of sex. Not *even* sex. Five minutes of Ty's hand in her underwear. Now she was in his home, a monumental experience she should be appreciating for all it was worth, and she couldn't stop thinking about screwing.

"Middleton," Ty told her, when she licked her lips for the hundredth time. "Are you having trouble focusing?"

"No," she lied.

Ty flipped a checkered tea-towel over his shoulder. "Then please stop staring at the front of my pants and tell me about your party."

"Okay," she squeaked. "Sorry."

"Don't be sorry," Ty said, refilling her champagne glass. "I just want to talk to you."

As Kate drank and relaxed into her surroundings, she caught another familiar smell beneath the slowly roasting meat. "Have you been painting?"

"Yeah." Ty wiped his hands on a tea-towel and then used it to lift the rack of lamb from the oven. "I did it a few weeks ago, but the smell sticks around. See that area over there?"

Kate turned and saw the cream-coloured alcove. "It's nice."

"It used to be lemon-coloured."

"Gross."

Ty laughed long and loud and Kate decided she'd ask him about it some other time.

He served their food the way they did in restaurants, pinkish slices of meat arranged beside stacks of vegetables and shiny swells of gravy. They ate in the dining room, at a huge table lit with candles and when they first sat down Ty raised his glass of red to hers. "To first dates."

"To first dates," she agreed, because though she'd eaten with him many times, on her couch and then in restaurants, she knew as well as he did that this was their first date. She thought of the card that said he loved her and her heart squeezed tight as a fisherman's knot. They talked about Prague, about how she, Rapunzel and Casey had been recruited to skate for Victoria in a country-wide derby scrimmage next month. He told her the first draft of his novel was finished and in the hands of his friend Georgie.

"Is she an editor?" Kate asked.

"A heart surgeon. She has good taste, though. If it's shit, she'll let me know."

"And if it isn't?"

"I'll do another draft and then you can read it if you like."

Kate excused herself to go to the bathroom and ensure she didn't cry into the best lamb she'd ever eaten.

"I like your poems," Ty said when she got back.

"I *literally* just stopped myself from crying."

He laughed. "Sorry, I just thought I should tell you they're good."

"I...I'm not a professional. That is, if anyone's a professional poet these days. I just like it."

"I liked it, too." Ty leaned closer. "Do you want to talk about it?"

Kate knew he meant everything that had happened from the moment they'd met up until now, all the misunderstandings and complications. She wanted to talk, she really did, but not now. "Can't we just leave it for tonight? Not forever or anything, just tonight?"

Ty's smile was soft. "Okay, just let me say one thing?"

"Sure."

"In your letter you said I never charmed you except in bed."

Kate's stomach twisted up with guilt. "I'm sorry."

"Don't be, you were pretty much right. I never tried to win you over that way because I didn't know what the hell to do with you. From the start you made me feel things I didn't understand and I resented it. I resented you."

Kate looked down at her hands, remembering all the times he'd ignored her at work, glared at her as though she was the most irritating girl in the world.

"I was an asshole," Ty said quietly. "I was an asshole and a coward, but I was never pretending. When we were together the attraction I felt...it scared the shit out of me. I didn't understand it and when we started having sex and I realised I liked you as much as I wanted to fuck you..."

"It got worse?"

Ty nodded. "It's hard to charm someone when you don't think they deserve you. I know that sounds like a line and you don't have to believe me, but it's true. I was sure I didn't have a right to someone as sweet as you. I wasn't using you for sex, I was letting you use me and hoping that was all you ever wanted so I wouldn't disappoint you."

Kate swallowed, her sinuses were hot and tight. "Ty..."

He rapped on the table with his knuckles. "So, that's all I wanted to say. That and I love you. But you, uh, might already know that from the card. And the poem books. I'd have tried to write one for you, a poem I mean, but, uh, I'm no good at that kind of thing."

Kate couldn't help herself, she giggled. "That's okay. I don't expect a poem."

"I wish I *could* write you one, but it would probably be shit."

"It's totally fine."

"Jesus." Ty ran a hand through his hair, looking mortified. "I'm forty-six next week, I should be a lot smoother than this."

"I like what you've done so far," Kate said. "Although, I am in love with you, so I like pretty much everything you do."

Ty smiled. "Come over here."

When she walked over to his side of the table, he pulled her onto his lap. "I've missed kissing you more than I've ever missed anything," he said, sliding his palm across her cheek. "I had dreams about kissing you."

"Same," Kate whispered. "But I had more about spankings."

"First things first..."

Ty took his time, running his fingers through her hair, pressing his lips along the line of her jaw and stroking her skin, so that when their mouths finally met, Kate felt like her whole body was shaking apart. It was a long kiss, a perfect kiss. It felt like coming home. Ty didn't try to take things further. He led her to his lounge room where a fire was crackling in the grate. There was a smell Kate loved and had forgotten she loved—sea-salted wood burning on an open fire. As soon as the scent of it entered her nostrils, she started to cry. Not cute, little tears—big old sobs.

"Is everything okay?" Ty asked, looking panicky. "Is something wrong?"

"No, it's all too much. It's too good. I don't...I have no idea what to do with all this goodness." She pressed a hand to her heart. "It's too much, you know?"

"I'm sorry," Ty said, taking her other hand. "I know I did that. Made you feel like pleasure always came with a price."

"You didn't. I had messed up—fucked up—ideas about love ages before you came along."

Ty's hand tightened around her own. "One day we'll talk about everything. What happened when you were growing up, why things turned out the way they did. We'll lay it all out until everything that's rotten dries up and all that's left is the memories."

"But not tonight, right?"

"Not tonight," Ty agreed. "Do you want dessert?"

She instantly perked up. "Maybe? Yes. Yes, please."

Dessert turned out to be a honey-chocolate torte that could have been used to negotiate world peace. They talked—about what, Kate didn't know. After so much concentration she was starting to fixate on sex again. Her new underwear grew damp between her legs and she contained herself by remembering she didn't have long to wait.

When Ty was done scraping up the last remnants of his torte, Kate all but snatched his plate away and launched herself at him.

"Easy, Middleton," Ty said, holding her at arm's length. "Do you want to watch something? A movie? A documentary? I bought a box set, hundreds of hours of nature at its finest."

Kate frowned.

"We don't have to watch anything about lobsters," he added. "Although they might come up, I'm not sure what's on the DVDs."

"It's not about lobsters," Kate said. "I thought we'd...you know..."

Ty kissed her hand. "I don't want to rush this. I don't want to pressure you or make you doubt what I wrote on that card."

"The card was great," Kate agreed. "But, like, sex?"

He gave her a considering look. As though assessing if she was sober enough to drive. "I can kiss you again if you like?"

"What the...no!" Kate ducked under his arms and relaunched herself at his face. Ty put up a token resistance, but within seconds they were making out like teenagers. Kate slung a leg over his hips, determined to get him so wound up he wouldn't think about saying no. She'd barely straddled him before Ty's hands were buried in her hair, pulling it taut in his fist. "You're a bad fucking girl, aren't you?"

Kate smiled. Hearing him call her that alongside a sting of pain was like a chorus of angels serenading her right in the ear. Loving, respectful Ty was great, but filthy, punishing Ty was the one she wanted right now.

"I am a bad girl," she told him. "I need you to put me right, Daddy."

Ty's gaze grew hotter, his hands releasing her hair to close over her breasts. "You've been hurting without me, haven't you, sweetheart?"

Kate nodded, whimpering as his thumbs stroked over her nipples.

"I think I can help you with that." He closed his arms around her and stood, carrying her out of the room and toward the front of the house.

"Where are we going?" Kate asked, slightly worried he was going to deposit her in his Hilux and drive her home.

"Bedroom."

She beamed. "Oh. Cool! I can walk, by the way?"

"Not after this, you won't be able to."

Kate groaned theatrically.

Tyler Henderson's bedroom was as austere and manly as the rest of his house. He had a black bed frame and dark blue sheets. He laid her down on top of them, flicked on the bedside lamp and started taking off his clothes. Kate watched as he removed his pants, then his shirt, exposing the thick ripple of scar tissue on his back. She wanted to cry again, not because she was sad, but because she knew stripping off right where she could see him was another way of showing her things would be different. Of course, when he pulled off his briefs, she wanted to cry for another reason.

Ty spotted her looking and grinned, gripping himself in one hand. "Want this, do you?"

"So much. Come to bed?"

His brows drew together. "Ask me nice."

"Please, Daddy, come to bed?"

"Better." Ty lay down beside her, passing his fingertips over her arms and collarbones.

"Don't," he said when she reached to touch him. "Not just yet. I want to play with you."

And so he did, kissing her neck, caressing her skin. He slowly removed her dress, then her bra, and finally her underwear. Such prolonged, intimate touching would have been welcome any other time, but right then it was torture.

"Can we please go faster?" Kate begged.

Ty shook his head. "Not yet. I've thought about you being in my bed for a long, long time. I've gotta make it last."

He began kissing his way down her body, taking generous detours to both breasts.

"Spread your legs," he said as he kissed down her midriff and when she did, he knelt between her thighs and began kissing them, passing his lips over her hips and then down to her pubic mound. Kate shivered. This was a compromise and she loved Ty for kissing her there even if he wouldn't ever—

"Oh my God!"

Ty's head jerked up. "Are you okay?"

"Yes, but you just *licked my pussy.*"

"Is that a problem?"

"No, I just thought..."

"Shh," he said. "I want to take care of you."

Before she could say anything, he returned his mouth to her cunt and within seconds she could do nothing but scream.

When he was done, Kate was so woozy it was like she was drunk. "You just...and you made me...I thought you didn't do that."

Ty sat back on his heels and wiped his mouth. "I thought I told you it wasn't about a lack of skill. I can do it. I like doing it."

"Then why...?"

For the first time since she'd come to his door, she saw hesitation in his eyes. A cold drop of fear slithered into her stomach. "It's okay, you don't have to tell me."

Ty took her hand. "It's the intimacy. You're so close to everything a woman is when you're down there, putting your mouth between her legs—it's too much sometimes. When it came to you I already felt so many things, I didn't want to feel any more by tasting you."

Kate smiled. "Well, it was amazing. Almost worth the wait."

"Almost?"

"Yeah, I mean, it was good, but it's been *months,* man. You're so far behind on the oral sex ratio it's not even funny."

"Is that right?" Ty dropped back onto his elbows between her legs. "Guess I should get to work on that."

When they were done, he pulled her into his arms, and they lay there for a few moments. Eventually Kate roused enough to ask. "Sex?"

Ty shook his head. "Tonight is for you."

"But I want sex, so shouldn't you give me sex?"

He hesitated. "I think we should take things—"

She launched herself at him and again, it wasn't a very hard sell. He took her missionary-style, just like in her fantasies. Kate watched as his body bore down on hers, in all its beautiful, scarred perfection and when she came it was like a pebble bouncing down a stone staircase. It started shallow and went deeper, deeper,

deeper until she was screaming the word 'daddy.' It affected Ty the same way it always did, made him grunt and snarl and buck into her so that she felt like she was splitting in two. When he came, he sank his teeth into her collarbone and she'd never felt so happy to be hurt. Afterward, they lay side by side and stared up at the ceiling.

"Do you think we're weird?" Kate asked, because that was the thing she'd always been afraid to ask.

Ty pulled her into his arms. "We're weird in the best possible way."

"So...yes?"

He laughed. "Everyone's weird, Kate, we're the perfect kind of weird for each other."

It was a good answer. They lay entwined in each other's arms, silent and content.

"Would you like to come to Patagonia with me in December?" Ty asked.

"Oh my god, yeah!" she paused. "I just got back from Prague."

"You're young, you can take some more leave."

Kate poked him. "Changed your tune, haven't you?"

"Yep." Ty yawned. "Plenty of time to work on your career when you get older. Come to South America with me. I'll write you a permission slip, if you like. 'Katie May needs six weeks off to explore South America because I said so, signed her daddy.'"

Kate slapped him. "That's not my name anymore, I told you."

"You'll always be Katie May to me, Katie May."

She leapt on him again, this time with intent to maim.

Once they were done play fighting, Ty gave her a nervous sort of smile. "You can meet my friend Georgie next weekend, if you like. She's dying to meet you. We could have drinks."

"Sure," Kate said, trying to sound casual, even though everything inside her was sparkling like fireworks. "That would be great."

"Give it another month and I'll tell the guys at GGS we're dating. They'll be petty as shit and probably guess we were fucking while we worked together, but who cares? They can't do anything about it."

Kate smiled. "Sounds good. I'll tell the people at D&D I'm dating a charismatic, older gentleman then, too."

"That makes me sound like Dracula. Just say you've got a boyfriend."

Kate turned away so he couldn't see that her eyes were welling up. "Okay."

Ty stretched his arms above his head and yawned. "I'll tell my parents about you next time I call 'em, but it might be a while before they meet you, they live in the middle of butt-fuck nowhere Queensland."

"Oh, are you from Queensland?"

Ty glared at her. "Think you're funny, don't you, Middleton?"

"Yes."

"Well we'll see how fucking funny you are when your ass is on fire."

Ty's impromptu punishment set off a chain of events that kept them busy for the next hour and a half. When they were done, they crawled under the covers, which were every bit as warm and Ty-smelling as Kate had dreamed.

"I mean it," Ty told her, pulling her body into his. "You can meet my family, and I'll meet yours, but you need to give them a heads up about how old I am. I don't want any of your brothers trying to take me on. And don't gloss over it, give an exact age and make sure your parents know we probably went to the same fucking gigs in the nineties."

Kate laughed, the sound full of the very specific joy that comes from giving someone good news. "Ty, my parents had me when they were in their forties. They're seventy-three now."

There was a moment's silence, then Ty slowly, victoriously, raised his fist into the air.

The End

ACKNOWLEDGMENTS

Thanks go to cousin Matty who taught me many things about engineering, equal thanks go to Jem who taught me many things about firefighting, ooh and Jess C who taught me many things about flat-track roller derby, including that Victoria has the best women's team in the world (fuckin' A).

As always the heart of every novel can be divided equally between my boy, my sister, and my best friend. They listen to me ramble about the plot, they offer gentle advice, they hug me when I need hugs (all the time). I *might* be able to write without these people forming a holy trinity of support around me, but it is very likely I would have cut off my own ear by now. So thank you guys.

More acknowledgements go to the illustrious Skye Warren who offered some very helpful advice as I was writing this book and has been an amazing supporter of my work.

And finally to Jess R who edited this book like no one has ever edited it before—you are such a talented and gracious woman and I thank you with all my heart. And Kole who could proofread god's emails on the celestial MacBook and wouldn't miss a single (fucking) comma.

Okay, cool is that everyone? Can I get drunk now?

ABOUT THE AUTHOR

Eve Dangerfield's novels have been described as 'genre-defying,' 'insanely hot' and 'the defibrillator contemporary romance needs right now' and not just by those who might need bone marrow one day... OTHER PEOPLE! She lives in Melbourne with her beautiful family and can generally be found making a mess.

ALSO BY EVE DANGERFIELD

Daddy Dearest series

Act Your Age

Not Your Shoe Size

Playing For Love series

Begin Again Again

Return All

First and Forever

Back Into It

Snow White Series

Velvet Cruelty

Silk Malice

Lace Vengeance

Bound to Sin (3x1)

Beyond Bondage Series

Degrees of Control

James and the Giant Dilemma

Taunt (A Why Choose Romance)

Captivated (with NYT Bestseller Tessa Bailey)

Bennett Sisters series

Locked Box

Open Hearts

Paying For It

Baby Talk

Silver Daughters Ink Series

So Wild

So Steady

So Hectic

She's on Top Series

Something Borrowed

Something Else

Dysfunctional

Sweeter

Made in the USA
Las Vegas, NV
26 December 2023

83513650R00213